A Window over the Sink

Other books by Peg Bracken

The I Hate to Cook Book

The I Hate to Housekeep Book

I Try to Behave Myself

Appendix to The I Hate to Cook Book

I Didn't Come Here to Argue

But I Wouldn't Have Missed It for the World!

The I Hate to Cook Almanack

A Window over the Sink

A Mainly Affectionate Memoir

by

Peg Bracken

Drawings by Paul Bacon

Harcourt Brace Jovanovich, Publishers
New York and London

Library of Congress Cataloging in Publication Data
Bracken, Peg.
A Window over the sink.
1. Bracken, Peg.
2. Home economists—United States—Biography.
I. Title.
TX140.B7A38   640′.92′4 [B]   80-8739
ISBN 0-15-196986-8

Printed in the United States of America

B C D E

Contents

Once upon a time I was dining with an English writer. More accurately, he was dining with me, for though he wrote mainly minor verse, he was quite as hard up as any major poet. But I had admired his work, which was charming, and invited him to dinner.

Midway between the soup and the espresso, he mentioned a book he had written, called *Bones and Aspidistras*.

"What is it about?" I asked him.

"Well . . . bones and aspidistras," he said.

This book is about a window over the sink—how it got there and some of the things I saw out of it. It is dedicated with love to my brother, Jack Bracken, who remembers McKinleyville and Ganister, too.

AN EXPLANATION

Some names have been changed to protect the
author, who feels it necessary to stress, as well,
that McKinleyville is not Filer, Idaho, the pleasant little town where she had the good sense to be
born. But being a drifter and ne'er-do-well at the
age of one, she left there, only decades later to
head west again to her eventual and present home
in Hawaii.

What memories do we bring with us out of childhood? The significant ones? I think we do, even though they often seem unimportant, unrelated to one another. Sooner or later we all discover that the important moments in life are not the advertised ones, not the birthdays, the graduations, the weddings, not the great goals achieved. The real milestones are less prepossessing. They come to the door of memory unannounced, stray dogs that amble in, sniff around a bit, and simply never leave. Our lives are measured by these.

—SUSAN B. ANTHONY
(grandniece of Susan B.)

A Window over the Sink

1

What Happened Was . . .

You may have noticed, as I have, that if ever you find yourself declaring emphatically and unequivocally that you will never do some one particular thing, chances are good that this is precisely what you will one day find yourself doing.

I don't mean that declaring you will never win a Nobel Prize or the Crosby Open is a sure ticket to Stockholm or Pebble Beach. No, I refer to those negative-positive pronouncements that usually begin "They'll never catch *me* buying [or going or doing or signing or driving or marrying or wearing or pretending] . . ." That is the sort of statement to be wary of; for as sure as the Lord made little green artichokes, you will find yourself doing exactly what you said you'd never be doing, one fine day, and like as not on the City Hall steps at high noon.

I have become increasingly cautious about this since I first became aware of what generally happens as a result. And I can't say that I've found tapering off to be too difficult. There seem to be fewer and fewer things these days that I feel positive enough about to say No to. Name it, I might do it. For as the years romp by I seem to be growing increasingly broad- or feeble-minded, one or the other; in some areas it's hard to tell the difference.

However, once upon a good while ago, I did overhear myself saying, "They'll never catch *me* designing my own kitchen."

Now, there were two good reasons for this.

For one, I already had a kitchen. Economics enters in here. In spite of a long though fretful affiliation with cooking, as a food writer of sorts, it is my habit to drag my feet when it comes to buying kitchen equipment—even little things. As for building a kitchen from scratch, at present rates you could have your meals air-ferried from Maxim's for the foreseeable future and still be money ahead.

The other reason, equally cogent, was that I had recently watched a friend design and hatch a kitchen. Triplets would have been easier.

Her labor pains were atrocious and they went on for months. Should the sink and the oven be here? Or here? In her head was some sort of a mystic Work Triangle—at first I thought she meant Pyramid Power—that had to be prayerfully, carefully followed, some arcane geometry of sink, oven, and reefer. That is what her builder called the refrigerator, and so now I do too.

And what of the sink? Did she want the one-holer, big enough to soak the family wash? Or the three-holer with the cute little basin for the garbage? And if the sink went *here*, what of the built-in butcher block?

And so it went, with my friend choreographing virtually everything she'd ever find herself doing in the kitchen except cry. Baking a cake. Boning a chicken. Making a quiche. Cooking a breakfast. How many more steps would it take if the pot lids lived here instead of there?

It wasn't that my friend didn't have an architect for the job.

She did. And every evening my friend, who is a forceful little thing, made tissue overlays of his blueprints, so that each morning he found fresh surprises. Finally, with resignation, he said, "All right, if that's the way you want it," instead of the hell with it, which might have been better all around.

The result was predictable. When the kitchen was done, it was beautiful but full of bugs, and my friend's hindsight spoke louder than all her foresight had. The pantry door should have been sliding or accordion-pleated or programed to self-destruct—anything except what it actually was: hinged to swing the wrong way, so it bumped her in the nose. Work space was too skimpy near the reefer (which was in the wrong place, after all) and too ample near the range top. The wall oven should have been where the glass cupboard was, and vice versa. Et cetera. And misery of miseries, she had no one to blame but herself.

It was at about this time that you could have heard me declaring with the same childlike certainty that was very likely Eve's on another occasion ("Apples? Who, me?") that they'd never catch *me* doing a kitchen.

And, accordingly, a year ago . . .

What happened was a house we bought, my husband and I —a house we liked, with reservations, chief among which was the kitchen.

Had this kitchen been a restaurant, it might have been called *intime,* but as a kitchen you could only call it terrible. The place had been built and more or less inhabited by a lively bachelor with better things to do than cook. In its miserable claustrophobically compact kitchen cubicle, you had to decide whether it was Blender Day or Toaster Day; you certainly couldn't have both appliances out and working at once.

Worst of all, there was no window over the sink, or any possibility of one unless we wanted a good straight shot into the guest room. In fact, there was no window at all.

This, for me, was a first. Looking back at all the kitchens in my somewhat kitchen-freckled past, I realized that not one of them had been wholly windowless. They all looked somewhere—across a lawn into a forest of Douglas firs or onto a fire escape, into somebody's garage or over a beach to the water, across the street to a row of frame houses or onto a picket-fenced yard frequently brightened by the presence of a small red curly-haired child who is now grown up, with a kitchen window all her own. But *some*where!

And this is important. As everyone knows—at least everyone who's ever had a kitchen—the official stance for thinking long thoughts is at the kitchen sink, looking out the window. But I found, staring at the spice rack in this windowless cell, that I was thinking only extremely short thoughts, like how dusty the cinnamon was getting, and making no distance at all.

It was on a Saturday last August, sweating lightly and doing the usual boomps-a-daisy with my husband, rear to rear, as he opened the reefer door while I opened a can of cream-style corn, that I experienced what used to be known as a moment of truth, though I believe epiphany is the in word now.

This was one resounding little epiphany. It went, if memory serves: "What are we doing in this hole?" And the second line went: "Let's tear out this mess and build a new kitchen on the other side of the house." With an architect to help, I amended prudently, remembering my strong-minded friend.

Our architect turned out to be a handsome young German, born in West Berlin a shockingly short time ago, but a full-fledged and talented architect for all that. A golden-mustachioed, broad-shouldered, sun-bronzed Siegfried, you'd think he'd just schussed a neighboring slope, except for his understated faded tapa sports shirt (he has a nice taste in sports shirts). It was easier to picture him building a Bauhaus-type marvel on a mountaintop, all glass, steel, and tube lights, than a kitchen in Hawaii. But he was interested in kitchens, it developed, and in food, too.

His name was Uwe (pronounced Oova) Schulz. I liked that. I couldn't help but feel that a kitchen designed by someone named Uwe would have more panache than a kitchen designed by, say, Joe Fenslinger down the road. And certainly more than one designed by me.

An Uwe would think Spacious, whereas I inevitably think

Snug, would think Tomorrow, where I tend to think Yesterday. And an Uwe could be counted on (I felt) for classy touches—some ceramic tile here, some stained glass there. I can always count on myself for touches like a soup bowl full of paper clips and dry cleaners' receipts and rubber bands.

"So! Now tell me what you have in mind for your kitchen," he said, at our first meeting in his office. He was seated behind a big desk in front of a handsome framed print from Leonardo's Notebooks, an elegant gold pencil poised over a note pad. "What do you want?"

"Space," we said, in unison.

Uwe nodded and made a note. "And?" he said.

"And a window. A window over the sink," I said.

He nodded again and made another note. "And?"

I paused. My mental picture of this new kitchen was, I suddenly realized, fuzzy to the point of being surrealistic. "And . . . well, lots of room to store things in," I said. "You know, like pots?"

Uwe made another note.

"And . . . um . . . running water," I added.

"That would be nice," he agreed.

And we thought some more. But I didn't come up with anything and neither did my husband. Presently Uwe put his pencil down.

"I believe you have not thought this thing out," he said, pleasantly but firmly. "You must do this. You must ask yourself: How do I live? How do I cook? Ask yourself: What kind of a kitchen do I like? Then you come back."

Clearly, Uwe wasn't about to do our thinking for us. His, all right, but not ours. It was a shame.

All right, I asked myself later in the privacy of my own sun deck, how do we live? And the answer bounced off the ridgepole of a neighboring grass shack: Casually. On our small Hawaiian island, even though it is one of the travel agents' favorite Resort Paradises of the Pacific, where proud luxury hotels are displacing palm trees to a rather alarming extent, it is still barefoot living, and cooking, too, at home; and now that both daughters are married and coping with their own kitchens, I cook only for two, except for guests.

As for the kind of a cook I am . . .

I would like to say Competent, but I know that Absent-minded is closer to the mark. My brain is practical but lint-prone. Though I try hard to be competent when the chips are down, I am generally thinking about something else.

Awkward is another adjective I'll own to, when it comes to certain basic procedures, like garnishing a salmon or a turkey, or arranging a festive platter of canapés. I am as clumsy as the next one, if the next one happens to have two left hands.

And Reluctant. My nearest and dearest will agree that I am no overachiever. And I admit to being pro-choice. I could initial many a meal I've cooked the way Cardinal Mindszenty did his confession, with a c.f. for *coactus feci*—"I did this under pressure"—for the times when cooking seems necessary are so often the times I feel least like doing it. And although I agree that the discovery of a new dish does more for human happiness than the discovery of a new star, it is my own feeling that, over the years, the invention of the Chinese back scratcher has probably provided more pleasure than either.

Well, I returned to Uwe's office and told him all this. He was wearing a smashing pale-blue chambray safari shirt with a lot of pockets. And he nodded and made some more notes.

"I think you make progress," he said, finally. His English is excellent, with only a faintly sibilant *th*, sometimes, that turns *think* into *sink,* as in kitchen. "And so now we get to work. Now I think you must consider the convected oven. . . ."

"Why?" I asked, not caring to admit that I hadn't heard of it.

And so, listening to Uwe explain the convected oven, as well as catalytic continuous-action cleaning, machinable cultured marbles, and a number of other complexities, I perceived that much had been happening to kitchens while my back was turned. Science doesn't sleep nights the way the rest of us do. And, clearly, I would have to outreach for some updated input to get any relevant feedback on viable options for top-level new-kitchen decisions in order to achieve any meaningful relationship with Uwe at all.

What finally happened was that he gave me a large four-color book full of kitchens to take home, with instructions to call him if anything puzzled me, and, as it developed, they all did, these kitchens, one way or another.

I mean, what has happened to kitchens?

For instance, there was Kitchen #1, which had a country mile of natural-wood counters under a cathedral ceiling festooned with Manila's entire annual output of rattan baskets, full of green-growing things all growing greenly. It made me uncomfortable just to think about that many high baskets all dripping on me, not to mention all gathering that special kind of thick, greasy, dusty sludge that can make kitchen-cleaning such an endless delight.

That is what they would gather in our house, anyway, because our house backs up against a sugar-cane field. The cane grows in red dirt, which, when dry, becomes red dust. And red dust, when it can't think of anything else to do, comes right into our house through walls, doors, and closed windows. One good stiff breeze and you can plant your own cane crop in the kitchen sink.

(I mean Clean-up Area. While I wasn't looking, the kitchen sink had become the Clean-up Area, just as the kitchen table had turned into the Food Preparation Center. "Officer, I was standing right here in the Food Preparation Center when I heard this funny noise that seemed to come from the Clean-up Area. . . .")

Well, and then there was Kitchen #2. Kitchen #2 was a salad-cool study, to quote the caption, in Celery, Avocado, and Snow, apparently lit for surgery, with clinical fluorescent tubes. This kind of light seems unnecessary to me unless you plan to clone a pork chop, and it is about as becoming to people as running sores.

The next one, Kitchen #3, was done in a solid hot sunflower yellow, needing only a smiling uniformed attendant and a gas pump. Its Cooking Area resembled a little stage, so your friends could all sit around and watch you try to fish your contact lens out of the spaghetti.

Kitchen #4 was a cozy concoction of calico and geraniums, a welter of old wooden butter molds and churn paddles, with a microwave oven snuggling into the hand-rubbed pine wall, and a quilted cozy discreetly covering the Cuisinart. Not really an honest kitchen, I thought, nor was Kitchen #5, a Normandy-type place with a tiled hutch and a fireplace. This one was unrealistic as well, because though you tend to visualize Grandma in a rocker beside the fire, shucking peas, Grandma these days is more likely to be relaxing in the bean-bag chair in her Vegas condo, if she isn't working out with the ball machine on Court #5 to get more torque into her forehand. And the peas are probably in the reefer, preshucked and frozen.

Finally, there was Kitchen #6, and that was where I quit. Number 6 must have been poured out of a pitcher—all futuristic curvy wavy black-and-white plastic flowing like heavy cream, the counter oozing into the oven, the oven melting into the cupboard. Perfect for a family of large amoebas, I thought, but not for most people.

Now, it is true that we could have moved into any one of those kitchens without actual pain. We couldn't go anywhere but up. Besides, experience has taught me that kitchens, like deck chairs, tend to take on your own contours, and fairly soon.

But not one of them really spoke to us. Nor were we speaking to them. At least we weren't hollering Eureka!

I was guiltily aware that I hadn't done quite all the homework Uwe wanted. I knew I should analyze my work system or lack of it; I should watch myself, and discover whether I customarily work clockwise or counterclockwise, whether I am a left-handed lunch-packer or a right-handed cake-baker or a left-footed sink-kicker. But I didn't have it in me. Technological time studies are not my style, and as for choreographing a meat loaf, I'd sooner be pecked to death by baby ducks.

So I knew it was time to grab the bull by the tail and look the facts in the face, because—here was the clincher—I was getting good and bored thinking about it. We all have our built-in limits.

Thus it was, a day or two later, that I took the book back to Uwe.

"Uwe!" I cried. He was wearing a white crinkly madras sports shirt, sensational against his tan. "I know what I want!"

He beamed. *"Wunderbar!"* he said.

"What I want," I said, "is a comfortable, realistic kitchen. With some bookshelves and room to stow things. And a good big corner sink. With a window over it. A window over the sink."

He looked at me oddly. "And?" he said.

"That about wraps it up," I said.

"Forgive me for mentioning it," said Uwe. "But . . . perhaps . . . something to cook with?"

Of course he was right.

"I'm glad you thought of it," I said.

And so, as it turned out, you see, I didn't design my own kitchen after all, which was just as well; I'd probably have forgotten the stove. Moreover, I was, in the last analysis, true to myself, which is always a good feeling. They'll never catch *me* . . . I'd said. They didn't, either.

And so it began.

I mean, the kitchen construction did and, in a way, this book did, more or less together. They both ended, too, and I've thought a good deal since then about beginnings and endings. Are beginnings always neater than endings are?

I suppose that depends: the beginning or ending of what? Jelly and jam start sloppy, with a leaky basket of fruit, but they end up neat, in a dozen dazzling jars. An operation starts bloody but usually ends up neat, with a tailored scar. And lives begin more neatly and easily than they generally end, and love affairs, too, as well as other journeys, which start in high spirits with a neatly packed suitcase but finish in a tired tangle of dirty laundry.

But books and kitchens have their similarities, I've found. A book starts neat, with a neat glimmer, gets horrendously messy en route, and ends up neat again, with luck, in crisply printed pages, neatly bound. And the kitchen Uwe built started neatly, all lovely straight lines on drafting paper, got horrendously messy along the way, and ended up neat again, too.

It was an exhilarating experience, I can tell you, watching three thousand cubic feet of back-yard air being transformed into a functional part of the house; to see the outdoors become the indoors. And of course this effected enough changes in the immediate ecological picture that it's a wonder no one asked for an environmental-impact statement.

The changes were all to the good, though, so far as we were concerned. A straggly ginger hedge gave way for the reefer-and-freezer wall, which was all right. The ginger hadn't seemed entirely happy there anyway. Some myna birds lost their bathroom; a favorite perch of theirs had been one of the jutting timbers over the deck. That was all right, too. Then some wicked red centipedes lost their cozy quarters under an old rotten log—good riddance—and two banana trees got marching orders, to go march elsewhere.

Small loss. Uwe came up with a good realistic kitchen. Not a hi-tech kitchen, and a good thing; for I am a lo-tech person. But a comfortable, workable kitchen, some Formica and some tile, some wood and some wallpaper, room to cook things in and hide things, a good place for cooking, ruminating, standing, and staring, for remembering, gossiping, laughing, and moping, and doing all the other things one customarily does in a kitchen. He even provided us with a small, but workable, pantry; and I am relearning that a pantry can be a comfort, even though it does leave me with no good excuses for running out of catsup.

Best of all—certainly most surprising in its effect—is the window, the window over the sink.

At long last, the construction was done and the painters gone, the screens up and the window open, with me looking out. And that morning I was astonished at the way my mind took off in seven-league boots—I suppose I should put that in kilometers now, but no matter—took off across the rolling sea of glossy cane that billows from the edge of our small back yard, up and away, beyond the Mountains of the Moon and the far horizon. I was traveling farther still—eastward ho, across the ocean, past the Rockies and the small Idaho town where I was born, to the small Missouri town where I grew up, and to some other places where I may have grown up some more, though I'm not entirely sure about that.

This is where I have been for the past good while, at the kitchen-sink window, occasionally lifting my eyes to the hills and simultaneously walking around in the far corners of my mind, as one would in a familiar but half-forgotten room, fingering this object, gently blowing the dust off that one. . . .

Yes, and doing the same thing quite literally as I move dishes and utensils and pots and books into their new quarters. Pondering where to hang Grandpa's silver tea ball this time. Wondering if my mother's old cookery manual, *A Thousand Ways to Please a Husband,* belongs with Thurber and the other funny books in the living room, or here in the kitchen. Trying yet one more time to find an intelligent place for the big electric skillet where it will be entirely convenient and entirely out of the way. Deciding where to put Aunt Liz Noah's cracked soup tureen that I can't quite bring myself to throw away. . . . And learning what a murmurous room a kitchen can be, how alive with insistent faces and places, even when it is quite, quite still.

And so this book, which was to have been all about food, and about my kitchen, seems to concern itself with a number of other matters, too. But, as I have observed before, that's the way it is with kitchens. You never can tell what is going to come out of them. So much depends upon the cook.

2

A Consideration of the Egg

*or How They Broke up the Gangs
at Public School #1 in McKinleyville, Missouri*

It was a great day in the morning, the day the kitchen appliances arrived. Though I've never exactly enjoyed spending money on kitchen things, still there is always something exhilarating to me about getting something new, no matter how small. To acquire a brand-new sink, oven, and reefer all at once was truly breathtaking.

And I like them all, especially the reefer. Obviously, it had been designed by someone who had purchased—just once too often—a carton of sour cream when she already had two of them, only they'd been hidden for weeks behind a big shortening can. The shelves in this reefer are shallower though a trifle wider than average, so that it is harder to lose things. That is a blessing.

But I confess to being a bit baffled by the title of the accompanying glossy pamphlet, *How to Get the Most Out of Your New Refrigerator*. It has been my experience that you get out of your refrigerator about what you put into it. Or what someone else puts into it. I once had a landlady who would deposit dishes of rice pudding in my refrigerator periodically when I was away at work, but she meant well, and the rent was low.

Still, this pamphlet was jam-packed with helpful pointers, one of which especially caught my attention. "'You will note," it began, "that there is no egg compartment on the inside of the refrigerator door."

I had, indeed, noted that. Curious, I'd thought. And I had wondered why. Nearly all my grown-up life, I have enjoyed transferring my newly bought eggs from their molded cardboard container into the handy, round-bottomed, perfectly fitting plastic concavities on the inside of the reefer door—a minor enjoyment, to be sure, but some days you can't be too choosy.

The pamphlet went on to explain that when eggs are kept on the inside of the door, its frequent openings and closings jostle the eggs, which ages them prematurely. This reefer company recommended, therefore, that the eggs be allowed to repose quietly on one of the shelves, in a compartmented plastic tray thoughtfully provided for the purpose.

This seemed to me to be another good example of the way Science keeps resolutely solving problems I didn't know I had, like blah hair and ice-cube odor and waxy yellow build-up. If my eggs had been aging prematurely, I wasn't aware of it, though this may be one of the things your friends won't tell you. But if you can keep anything from aging before its time, I am, God knows, in favor of it, and so my eggs now sit in chilled serenity on a stationary shelf in my new refrigerator.

However, this reminded me of something—something I'd read recently, something about how eggs were cooked by shepherds in the olden days. I had made a note of it, which I eventually found, filed under F, for Fancy that!

The shepherds had a singular manner of cook-
ing eggs without the aid of a fire: they placed
them in a sling, which they turned so rapidly

that the friction of the air heated them to the
exact point required for use.

—ALEXIS SOYER

Now, this Alexis Soyer was one of the very first English cookbook writers, and a popular one, too. These lines are from his big best seller, published in 1854 and called, forthrightly enough, *Soyer's Shilling Cookery for the Poor.* (Today this would probably read *Soyer's Gourmet Bargain Cuisine for the Economically Disadvantaged,* and I consider the 1854 title much the better of the two. Like the good clear prose on Manhattan's trash bins, LITTERING IS FILTHY AND SELFISH SO DON'T DO IT, and a sign I saw recently in a gift shop, SHOPLIFTERS WILL BE HAPPILY BEATEN TO A PULP, it says what it means—a type of statement that has become an increasingly endangered species.)

Soyer's news about the shepherds interested me greatly. *There,* I thought, is egg-jostling with a purpose, for, if true, all that air friction could effect some worthwhile savings in power. Look at the way we waste it now. Picture, for one fevered instant, approximately 120 million top-of-stove burners burning busily every morning from coast to coast, each one using up five minutes' gas or electricity to cook our nation's soft-boiled eggs. That is a lot of gas or electricity.

There might even be some esthetic fallout with the shepherds' system, I thought. All that whirling might result in handsome homogenized eggs, a pleasant custard color throughout instead of the tacky old two-tone kind we've been stuck with for so long. At the very least it might scroddle them. "Scroddle" is a ceramic term that means mottled with different colors, applied so they don't blend, and scroddled eggs are a good substitute for scrambled if you're out of milk, yet tired of the classic fried-egg look.

In fact—now my mind was whirling, too—all that muscular effort could even mean some worthwhile firming-up of the upper arms. I couldn't wait to go out in the back yard and try it out.

My first sling was a simple cheesecloth sack, the egg dropped into it and the sack then thumbtacked to the end of a yardstick. But the shepherds must have used a different kind, or else they had better thumbtacks. On the third whirl, the sack fetched loose and pinked a neighboring Labrador, who then retrieved it and made quite a mess of it on the lawn. It was necessary to get another egg.

This one stayed on the stick, in its pocket, but after ten minutes' whirling nothing had happened except for incipient bursitis in my right shoulder. The egg was still new-laid raw.

Then I came to my senses. "If it's whirling you want," I said to myself, "why not put it in the salad-greens whirler?" (We have one of those centrifugal-action basket affairs that does a fast job of drying wet lettuce.)

So I started whirling the egg in it, and the racket brought my husband into the kitchen at a high lope.

"What the hell are you doing?" he asked.

"Whirling an egg in my lettuce basket," I replied.

He watched me for a little while in silence.

"Well, whatever turns you on . . ." he said finally, and went away again.

So I whirled and whirled, and then . . . but I don't think I'll go into what happened. Perhaps you would like to try it for yourself. It was a learning experience and really not too hard to clean up.

Speaking of the two-tone egg, as I believe we were, I have often reflected that there are mainly two kinds of people in this world, the kind who customarily have more egg whites than yolks left over, and the kind with more yolks than whites. The first kind use yolks for painting tempera pictures or making hollandaise sauce, and the second kind make numerous egg-white meringues while the yolks go begging.

The hollandaise people and artists are lucky, because egg whites keep so well. They are easy to freeze in ice-cube trays or old peanut-butter jars, and they thaw obligingly, too. You can thaw a bit occasionally to whip up and add to an omelet or a scrambled egg or whatever you think needs more ebullience. Or use three of them—about half a cupful—as a base for good simple meringue cookies.

The leftover-egg-yolk people don't have it that easy, as I

happen to know, being one of them. Egg yolks don't keep as well. If they are immersed in water and kept covered in the refrigerator, they'll be all right for a few days, but they presently start looking like rheumy old eyes and you still have to think of something to do about them.

Of course, you could hard-cook them and goldenrod them over vegetables. But people don't goldenrod things so much any more. Like making rosebuds out of radishes and corrugating carrots, it was always more trouble than it was worth, and I think it went out with sun porches and razor strops and isinglass vaccination bubbles and one-speed bikes.

There is, by the way, a nice hand lotion you can make out of egg yolks. Egg yolks and some other things. I ran across it in an old-time South Carolina cookbook—Eliza Pinckney's, which was published in 1756.

FOR THE HANDS

Boil 4 Eggs hard take out the yolks and beat them, blanch a quarter of a pd. of bitter almonds and beat them in brandy put to them a half penny loaf grated, as much honey as you like. It will keep seven years together.

It seems rather a shame to put all those good ingredients on you instead of in you, and with all that honey on your hands you'd be a real attraction for the ants. Still, Eliza Pinckney was highly regarded back in 1756.

As a general thing, I tend to regard the egg yolk as an evil blob of cholesterol and drop it down the drain. That is about the only time I ever think about cholesterol, but it just goes to show that it's good for something, if only to let you dispose of your yolks with a clear conscience.

On mature reflection, I suppose it is just as well that our eggs are classically two-toned, for if they weren't, you couldn't devil them, and then what would you do about picnics?

My Kansas grandmother Em deviled a mighty nice egg, I always thought, and still think, although since encountering the Calabrian Dozen I have realized that hers were not the very last word.

Good, all right, smooth as chocolate creams, and exceptionally savory, perhaps because she always added, to the usual smidgen of mustard, salt, pepper, sugar, and mayonnaise, some horseradish. Just a whisker of horseradish, Grandma said, a whisker being somewhere between a smidgen and a dab. And she would be beating and beating and *beating* it, long after any sensible person would have packed it up and headed for the park, while my grandpa Ben chafed at the bit because he wanted to get the picnic over. He always said that if the Lord had intended people to go on picnics He'd have had the hens lay their eggs deviled to begin with, and He'd also have done something definitive about mosquitoes.

But this Calabrian Dozen, now! I first ran into it, not in Calabria, which is in the toe of the Italian boot, but in a Scottish newspaper in Edinburgh, on the Home & Food page. The idea intrigued me so much that I looked up the country that presumably invented it. "Mountainous, arid, and economically backward," my *World Book* says of Calabria, and I could see what they meant.

 1 Anchovy paste, French dressing, cream
 2 Foie gras
 3 Tomato pulp
 4 French dressing
 5 Minced ham, mayonnaise
 6 Chopped olives, olive oil
 7 Chopped chicken, mayonnaise
 8 Butter, sliced sauteed mushrooms
 9 Chopped prawns, lemon juice
10 Butter, chopped watercress
11 Butter, grated cheddar
12 Crumbled bacon, mayonnaise

Imagine! All those ingredients! Any country that devils a dozen eggs like that has much to learn about economy.

The vulgar boil, the learned roast an egg.
—ALEXANDER POPE
(*The Second Book of Horace*)

Now, some time ago, a Viennese doctor named Heinz Humplik made a stirring pronouncement about hard-boiled eggs and diets. It is true that people tend to pay close attention to Viennese doctors, even if they only say gesundheit. But these particular findings would have made waves if they'd come from anywhere, including Kansas City.

Dr. Humplik discovered, or thought he had, that digesting a hard-boiled egg requires more calories than the egg itself contains: 92 calories, compared with the egg's 80.

Logically, then, if you ate nothing but hard-boiled eggs and kept right on eating them, the skinnier you'd get, till you eventually faded entirely away like the Cheshire cat, leaving only a smile hanging in midair behind you, or, more probably, a gentle burp.

I don't believe anyone ever tried it though, and presently the world's attention was distracted by something else—skateboards, possibly, or frozen yogurt.

> *Eskimos believed that eating any eggshell was to "cut your mother-in-law." One banty-rooster-type Eskimo I knew devoured eggshells by the mouthful. Crunching, eyes glittering, he chewed shells even as he was dying of tuberculosis. His fat mother-in-law would come to visit him in the sanatorium and she would sit like a sleepy frog with a gloating grin on her face. She didn't like him, either.*
>
> —GRACE FIRTH

Howdayuh wuntcher eggs? Sunny side up? Over easy? Perhaps your habitual answer to the standard question is a clue to your personality. People are so different. My mother liked hers gently scrambled, using butter and coffee cream. My father wanted his hard-boiled and hot, in a small saucer. Then he'd chop them up with butter, salt, and pepper. My brother liked his egg any way at all so long as it was drowned in catsup. I usually prefer mine raw in a cup to swallow like an oyster, because that's quickest.

Scrambled Eggs to Go

My aunt Liz Noah always said to make sure the grocery clerk puts your eggs in the sack first, so if they break they won't run all over the rest of the stuff.

I believe she also said, Don't count your chickens till you see the whites of their eggs—though I may not have been paying close attention at the time.

All in all, a great many eggs
It has been calculated that the number of eggs laid by the salmon is roughly about 1000 to every pound weight of the fish, a 15-lb. salmon laying 15,000 eggs . . . the turbot, 14,311,000. . . ."
—ENCYCLOPAEDIA BRITANNICA

In view of nature's lavishness in the matter of fish eggs, it seems odd as well as a great waste of the hen's potential that the hen can lay hers only one at a time. Clearly Mother Nature prefers fish to chicken.

But it is regrettable that many a hen who would be a good mother never gets a chance to prove it, she is so busy laying eggs for the Egg Co-op people—eggs that they never let her hatch. Equally, many a hen who would be a good companion to some rooster will never know the simple joys of knocking around the barnyard on a May morning, taking a random dip in a rain puddle, and fluffing out her feathers in the sunshine. If only she could get her quota over with once and for all—lay fifteen thousand eggs simultaneously the way the salmon does, instead of this perpetual one-a-day forever and ever till hell freezes, then she might be able to make some kind of a life for herself. It isn't easy to lay one egg a day. I used to write a daily column, and I know.

Whatever you do with it, though, the egg is a marvel: the yang and the yin of it, the elegant shape of it, the taste of it. And the smell of it, if it has been hard-boiled—a smell that will nearly always regress me back to my early school days at Public School #1 in McKinleyville, Missouri. (When I say hard-boiled, by the way, that is what I mean. It was years before refinements like "hard-cooked" came along.)

A square two-story arrangement in red brick, floored throughout with linoleum the color of tobacco spit, with walls like pale caramel custard, this wasn't a very big school. But then, McKinleyville wasn't a very big town.

It was a real town, though—not merely a shopping center off a six-lane highway with a spatter of tract houses around it, like so many places today. McKinleyville had a courthouse and five churches and a drugstore and a two-story brick hotel where Babe Ruth had once talked to the Rotary Club and a Post Office that called itself a Post Office, not a Postal Facility. It also had a barbershop with a sign over it that didn't say HAIR STYLIST; it said BARBER SHOP. But despite all these amenities, it was a small town, bounded on all sides by my father and mother and brother, with my grandparents and Aunt Liz Noah across the state on the far Kansas periphery, and school right smack in the middle.

As I say, thinking of eggs brings back to me the smell of a bunch of hard-boiled ones being opened all at once in a snugly closed chamber, which in turn triggers the memory of the gang warfare that generally followed the witching hour of twelve noon in Miss Edlefson's stuffy third-grade classroom. Most especially it brings back the brannigan between Florence Ashenbrenner and me.

Twelve noon was when we all opened our lunch boxes or our brown paper bags (the crummy school didn't have a cafeteria)—opened our lunches and our eggs, so that their dark-brown sulfur-dioxide smell rose and spread like an old-fashioned London pea-souper to settle eventually with all the gentle effluvium of a backed-up sewer over everything from the chalk-dusty blackboards to the—I believe—shores of Tripoli.

You could smell it everywhere for hours. A former elementary schoolteacher once confided to me that the smell was the principal reason she was now a former elementary schoolteacher: that inimitable public-school amalgam of chalk dust and urine, sweat and wet galoshes, steam heat and newly opened hard-boiled eggs. If she ever wrote the story of those years, she said, she was going to call it *Barfing All the Way*.

Then, after we had eaten our eggs and sandwiches, we would go outside so Miss Edlefson could open all the windows and fan vigorously—she had a perpetually runny nose, and I think that's how she kept it going—though another reason was that it was also outdoor playtime or recess.

But none of us girls ever played—I mean swung on the swings or bounced on the teeter-totter or played softball or tag the way the boys did. I don't know whether or not the eggs had anything to do with it, but we didn't play; we wrangled.

I don't mean physical combat. No fisticuffs, no hair-pulling, except for Florence and me. I mean twitting, taunting, making fun of. Or—here it is—snirtling. That is a fine old English word I ran across only the other day, and I think it is nicely descriptive of what we did.

Snirtle. We'd snirtle anybody for anything; and that is mainly what I remember about being eight or nine years old and in the third grade.

If somebody was short, she'd catch it. Or tall, or fat, or skinny, she'd catch it. Or light or dark. Or rich or poor, though poor was better than rich because we had more of them. In fact, we had one boy from the County Orphans' Home, who was especially fun to make fun of—I suppose because he'd been dumb enough to lose his parents altogether and get slapped into an orphanage. His name was Daniel, and was *he* ever in the lions' den. Not only parentless but pediculous, he had had his head shaved. (We snirtled boys, too, from a safe distance.)

Oh, we'd make fun of anybody for anything. For instance, Opal Henking. She had recently moved with her family to McKinleyville from the southernmost section of the Ozarks, the spit-whittle-and-breed part, and she pronounced now *naow*, like *meow*, and so we meowed at her a lot, here kitty-kitty-kitty. Or Hazel Imes. (Our roll call was composed of good sound names like Hazel and Ellen and Opal and Florence, not a Cindy or a Jill or a Karen in the lot. The same with the boys: no Kevins or Christophers or corny-chic Jeds and Zekes, just good basic Jameses and Charleses and Roberts and so on. Nor were we ethnically exotic: second- and third-generation Irish, German, French, plus a Bjorklund and a couple of identical tow-headed Knudsens.)

And so at recess, if some mysterious movement of the tides or the planets informed us that it was Hazel's turn, somebody would lead off with a "Nyaaaah, your mother can't put her hat on straight!"

No matter that Hazel's mother was strictly a class act, the jazziest dresser in the whole P.-T.A., the only mother, in fact, to own a silver-fox chubby. No matter at all. The gauntlet had been imperiously thrown. And was as grandly picked up by Hazel, with a rapier thrust, "Nyaaah, your mother wears dirty underwear."

Then we would choose up sides, and once we were back in the classroom, tiny folded notes would zip around, proselytizing. (Years later, my mother showed me one she'd found in my pocket: LUCILE IS A DOP.) And at the next play break, we'd go at it with renewed vigor.

Perhaps it would be Alice's turn. Alice's father worked for the Department of Sanitation, and Lucille (or some one of us) would give her the old "Stick outcher can, here comes the garbage man!" And Alice—no flies on *her*—would say, "Nyaaah, your father *eats* garbage." Then Lucille's riposte would probably be, "Your father eats double garbage!" which might remind Alice of a favorite ploy we all used, on occasion: "Anything you say about me goes double for you." Then Lucille—no flies on Lucille either—would say, "Nyaaah, you're beautiful, so I'm twice as beautiful, nyaaah, nyaaah, nyaaah!"

This could well interrupt the momentum momentarily, allowing us to gather matériel for a major offensive next play period, or else enjoy some well-earned R & R—probably stand around snickering over what Lucille (who had an older married sister) had told us about how babies start. In truth, it turned out that Lucille was dead right, but whoever in her right mind would of believed a thing like that?

With Florence Ashenbrenner and me, on this particular early March day, things got a trifle out of hand. It was a shame, too, for it was no kind of a day for fighting, but a soft, primrose-air sort of a day, balm to the spirit after a long harsh winter. We were outdoors in sweaters instead of overcoats for the first time in months, and Opal, a demon skip-rope jumper, was teaching us a new one she'd learned.

> *Charlie Chaplin went to France*
> *To teach the girls the hula dance,*
> *First on the heels and then on the toes,*
> *Round and round and round she goes.*

It was my turn, I remember, and I was just about to jump in when—sudden as thunder—Florence picked a fight.

Well, Florence was a feisty little girl, anybody'll tell you that. Besides, she was nearly as good a speller as I was, though not quite. This always riled her, and in that morning's spelling quiz I'd scored 100 to her 95.

Now, spelling isn't a fuzzy thing like writing or drawing. On the contrary, it is a clear-cut thing, like two times two. Right's right and wrong's wrong—at least it was then—and so there really wasn't much sense to Florence's "Nyaaaah, no wonder you got a hundred. Your father's the superintendent." Besides, my father *was* superintendent of the McKinleyville school system, and any implied nepotism always graveled me considerably.

So I moved away from the arcing jump rope, gave her a meaningful look, and said, "Nyaaah, you couldn't get a hundred in anything even if your father *was* superintendent instead of a dumb old printer in a dirty old apron." (Her father ran a linotype machine at the McKinleyville *Advocate*.)

And she said, "Shut up."

And I said, "I don't shut up, I *grow* up. But when I see you, I *throw* up." (This was popular with our third grade then, and not an original number with me, I'm glad to say.)

And she said, "Violets are blue, bluebells are bluer, if I was your sweetheart I'd jump in the sewer"—there was a lot of this going around, too—and it was about here that my wild Irish, as it were, rose.

I jumped her, jumped her hard and got her down in the

playground gravel, where we rolled over and over, kneeing, kicking, pulling hair, scratching, doing whatever it is you do in that situation—it's been a good while since that afternoon, and I forget. But I know she got a handful of my pink-checked gingham dress at the neck, ripping it right down the middle, so I was stripped to my underwear, right there in front of practically the whole third grade.

And I remember with painful clarity the interview later in the principal's office and being sent home with a note from the principal, too. So was Florence, of course, but her father wasn't the superintendent. *She* should worry. . . .

And when I got home, it was a heavy scene, all right. Very heavy.

All the same, our whole bunch was pretty sorry when the war games came to an end, as all good things must.

And they did. I don't know if it was cause and effect or co-incidence, but a new gym teacher appeared the very next week, a hearty, wholesome, athletic type replacing little old Miss Dabney, who had previously been in charge, more or less, and never cared a hang what we did so long as it didn't scare the horses.

The first day on the job, this hearty athletic type chewed us out like a top sergeant—gave us what-for till who laid the rails —and, worse than that, gave every one of us an F in Physical Education and Good Sportsmanship.

This brought the parents in, an outraged swarm that included Hazel's mother in her fur chubby and Alice's father right off the truck. But the new teacher explained to them what thoroughgoing little rotters we all were, and unfortunately the principal backed her up.

So everything went to pot. From then on we had to do all kinds of hearty, wholesome, athletic things—jogging and jumping, basketball and Junglegym, softball and hopscotch— and it was a shame. Fighting was a lot more fun.

As to whether Miss Edlefson fanned herself into an early decline and a terminal sniffle trying to get rid of the hard-boiled-egg smell, I don't know. It was a losing battle, I think.

Anyhow, not too many years later they tore the school down, and the new one that replaced it contained a cafeteria—macaroni salad and hot dogs and baked beans by the tubful, and not a hard-boiled egg in sight.

3

A Word about Punkin Soup

and My Brother, the Masked Gunman

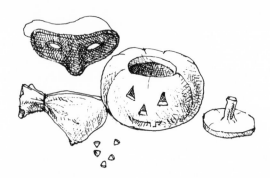

On a rainy October afternoon not long after we had more or less settled into our new kitchen, I was making pumpkin soup for the first time, from a recipe given to me by a new friend in California; and, as I stirred and measured, I was regretting all the lost foolish years I'd thought of pumpkins only in connection with jack-o'-lanterns and pies. And this had me wondering why pumpkin soup is so infrequently found on menus, compared with clam chowder or cream of tomato, till I heard myself answer.

"Because most people like pie better than soup, that's why," I explained. "And since pumpkin has always been a gorilla in the Pie Department, it had to take second place or so in Soups. It can't have it both ways."

"Oh, so that's the reason for it?" I said.

"At least it's a reasonable hypothesis," I replied.

"Well, thank you for giving the matter your attention," I said.

"Don't mention it," I answered. A while in the kitchen can have you talking to yourself, even in a nice new kitchen like ours.

I had tasted this pumpkin soup on a recent occasion of unexpected warmth in a strange and lovely California house that seemed to overlook the entire universe, though it may have been only the western half of it. The circumstances undoubtedly affected my judgment, and still do. I've noticed that bits of emotion often become permanently commingled with the tastes of things, the way a tatter of egg yolk, once in the egg white, is almost impossible to get out. So far as I'm concerned, cinnamon will always say home-and-mother, and red grapes taste like Christmas, and oyster stew is merry and loving, and chocolate mousse is nearly always pugnacious if not downright bad-tempered.

And so pumpkin soup, besides being a fine lunch with a green salad and a glass of wine, will doubtless remain faintly exotic to me—a surprising transformation, really, for the pumpkin used to be anything but a sophisticated vegetable. Back in McKinleyville, when someone did something unusually gauche, it was customary to ask him which wagonload of punkins he rode into town.

Still, it has filled various needs for various people. Thoreau considered it something to sit on, if need be. At least, he would rather sit on one all by himself, he said, than be crowded on a velvet cushion. And it served as a document file, if you remember, in the historic case of the Pumpkin Papers. It was also a coach-and-four to Cinderella, at least till 12:00 P.M.

Not long ago in the mysterious southland, I found an interesting pumpkin recipe as well as an interesting way to spell it, in the old Eliza Pinckney recipe book I mentioned earlier.

To Preserve Pumkin for Tarts
Slice your pumkin thin and cutt it in slips about the width of your little finger put shreds of lemon peel among it. Wet your sugar with orange juice (don't toutch it with water) and

*boil it into a sirrup then put your pumkin and
lemon peel in and boil them in the sirrup.*

A good, tangy, sticky filling, I should think, but probably
not so good as pumkin soup. Anyway, pumkin to me generally means pumpkin out of a can.

When someone once asked my brother, as a little boy, what
was his favorite vegetable, he said punkins, and when his in-
terrogator asked why, he said because they smile a lot.

It is clear that he was thinking of Halloween, as I couldn't
help doing, too, in putting together the punkin soup. I don't
believe any food is quite so inextricably tied up with one particular holiday and season as the punkin is. You can love
strawberries in December as you did in May, and turkey is
about as good in July as it is in November, and oysters have
been tamed and trained to perform in many a month without
an *R* in it. But punkins belong inalterably to Halloween.
They belong to it and I am sure they will outlast it.

My own feeling is that Halloween is on its way out. Now
that we've unhappily learned we have even more frightening
things to contend with than witches and warlocks, the holiday
seems to have lost its point. For years, it has only given the
amalgamated dentists and confectioners a good boost in their
continuing efforts to rot the tots' teeth out as fast as possible,
with all those trick-or-treat sani-wrapped candy bars.

When my brother, Jack, and I were growing up in McKinleyville, Halloween was just easing into the transition from
the old-fashioned graveyard-and-mischief Halloween to the
newer-fashioned trick-or-treat Halloween. How you cele-
brated it depended mainly on which sex you belonged to.

My brother and his group felt impelled to tip over out-
houses and put scarecrows on rooftops, because they had
heard their fathers reminisce about such deeds of derring-do.
However, since McKinleyville had outgrown (though just
barely) its Chic Sale days, and had no scarecrows to relocate
either, they had to make do with what they had, which, in
retrospect, wasn't much. (They showed more creativity on

April Fool's Day, scattering instant pulverized-dirt molehills around before sunup on the town banker's green velvet lawn.)

But, as I say, Halloween was in a transitional phase; and the boys couldn't think of much to do about it. If a house looked empty, they might soap a window or tip over a garbage can. Otherwise they'd only beg, along with the girls.

Because that's all we did do: dress up and beg. They hadn't yet invented the phrase "trick or treat." We just begged. And generally we did well. At evening's end we'd have quite a sackful: some fruit (unexciting, because apples and oranges always ended up as lunch box fodder), and considerable candy—not the homemade variety, if we could help it, but grocery-store or drugstore candy. That's the kind we wanted, for back in the Halloween time of which I write, anything natural, home-grown, or homemade was purely ho-hum, with the single, splendid exception of Mrs. Pruitt's individual pumpkin pies.

I can see them still: each one about the size of a salad plate, flaky pastry abrim with a richly spiced velvety custard and loaded with pecans. We'd all have crawled a mile over broken glass to get one. And she'd made them in quantity and handed them out for two years in a row, so there was no reason for her to quit now, was there?

It did seem odd, at that, for Mrs. Pruitt to go to the bother and expense of making what must have been at least three dozen individual punkin pies to give away. But we never analyzed it, never thought, as I think now, that it could have been a forlorn popularity bid for Marcie and Josie, her two little girls—an attempt to win over their friends so they'd come over in days to come and play. But if that's what it was, it didn't work. All we wanted was the pies.

Marcie and Josie Pruitt were a grade behind me. Marcie, the elder, must have been dumb or something, because she was in the same class as her younger sister. Theirs was the small square brown house at the end of our block, and summer evenings when we all played Kick the Can or Tap the Icebox or One Foot Off the Gutter till well after dark, we'd play in any yard but theirs.

It wasn't that we didn't like Marcie and Josie all right. The problem was their mother, the punkin pie lady. Not only was Nell Pruitt quick-tempered, with a tongue that would clip a hedge, but she really liked to whip kids.

Now, it is true that any one of our parents enjoyed giving us a good belt when we had it coming, which was—as my aunt Liz Noah would have put it—almost periodically. But Mrs. Pruitt had a buggy whip that she kept for the express purpose of whipping Marcie and Josie on their bare legs. She did it so often and so hard that their legs were habitually covered with pink welts, but Mrs. Pruitt didn't even look mad when she did it. On the other hand, she was very kind to animals, birds, bugs—a real bleeding heart, forever trying to collect funds for the animal shelter and the antivivisectionist league. I once saw her standing over a well-salted garden slug that was melting away in the sunshine, crying her eyes out.

Years later, when I was grown and married, my mother told me that it was guilt that drove Nell Pruitt, and in curious directions.

As I remember her, she was a tall, darkly good-looking woman, though old, of course, anyway thirty. And the trouble was that before she married Henry, they had had—and here I hesitate; I am not quite sure how to put this in McKinleyville's terms—they had had carnal knowledge of each other? No. Intercourse? No, they would never have said that. They had, well, gone to bed? No. Or—I've got it—they had had relations. That's it. And she had marched down the aisle of the Presbyterian church with—wait a minute—a bun in the oven. Which turned out to be Marcie.

And so Nell Pruitt later considered it a judgment upon her, and condign punishment, when Henry was killed in a railroad accident before their fifth anniversary, and also much later, when Marcie was mangled by a rabid dog and died in a few days at the age of seventeen.

I don't think the entire town knew, at the ceremony, that Nell was pregnant, though of course it did later. Women have always been adept at counting on their fingers, at least up to nine, and when Marcie was born she had hair enough to braid. But Nell herself knew it at the time, and her mother-in-law undoubtedly did, too, and if you think her mother-in-law ever let her forget it, you've got another think coming.

Her mother-in-law, known as Old Lady Pruitt, happened to be our landlady. She lived just above us in a big shabby frame house that was divided into three flats. Ours was the ground floor.

She was of the Pentecostal faith, known locally as the Holy Rollers. Some Sunday nights the place would shake till its old bones rattled, with all that rootin-tootin religion going on upstairs. Old Lady Pruitt was not, needless to say, in favor of relations except for procreative purposes—she got her own jollies on the Glory Trail—nor, most specifically, was she in favor of them till the preacher gave permission.

And so she never quit giving her daughter-in-law hell (never mind that her son, Henry, had had something to do with Marcie's untimely appearance, too), and Nell never quit passing it along to Marcie and Josie, and Josie has presumably passed it along to her daughters by now, and that's the way it goes, everyone a victim of a victim, one way or another, and no wonder it takes so long for us to get anywhere.

There was no psychiatrist around, either, not around our town, and anyway you'd have been crazy to go to one. In McKinleyville either you were okay or you were in the insane asylum, no in-betweens, though the sorry fact is that a number of in-betweens like Mrs. Pruitt were running around loose. Today, I suppose a neighbor would report her to the authorities, and the local court would issue a cordial invitation, and they'd presently cool her off. But not then, and many a family had a picturesque live-in relative: a wafty old man who wandered or dribbled, or a mongoloid child, or a big strapping idiot who could nevertheless shovel snow—just part of the McKinleyville scenery, they were, and their families put up with them or took care of them as best they could.

> . . . *Remember how tranquil the hours, and*
>   *good,*
> *When over the river and through the wood*
> *To Grandmother's house we'd ride?*
> *They kept her tied . . .*

So there she was, Nell Pruitt, whipping her kids and crying over kittens, and my father, who had a neat way with a phrase, called her the Grim Weeper. The name stuck, though I doubt if she ever heard it. At least, she was always polite to my father and she never took out after me—never did, that is, till this particular Halloween night I am thinking of. Which was, all in all, quite a night.

Now, as I believe I have indicated, certain sex differences were readily apparent in the girls' and the boys' respective approaches to Halloween.

One of them was the clothes they wore. Girls would put a great deal of time and effort into their costumes, while boys seldom changed from their customary schoolgoing shirt-sweater-and-dirty-knickers combo, one leg of the knickers buttoned, the other generally at half-mast. They'd just add a ten-cent black eye mask and possibly a charcoal mustache.

For example, on the Halloween night under discussion, I planned to go as Cinderella and Florence Ashenbrenner was going to be the Wicked Witch of the West; and I can see that I had better explain right here how come I knew what Florence was going to be, or even cared.

The fact is, almost immediately after our fight in the schoolyard, Florence and I had made up, to become bosom companions. On that lively afternoon, we had tested each other's metal, you might say, and found it sterling. As a result, we were friends forever and ever till death do us part, at least for six months. Indeed, the previous summer when we were both experiencing a serious cash flow problem, we had even developed a lucrative small business. As you may or may not know (either way is perfectly all right), muddling white sand with pastel chalks colors the sand beautifully, and if you layer it in jelly glasses you can sell it as bath salts. For a short while there—very short—our part of the town could well have been renamed Sandy Bottoms.

And so, on this Halloween night, Florence and I were going to go begging together. While she was pasting cut-out skulls and crossbones on somebody's old black raincoat, I had been styling up the orange cheesecloth number I'd worn as Second Nasturtium in the school play, gluing hanks of Christmas-tree tinsel here and there to achieve that ravishing Cinderella-ball-gown look, though the effect was somewhat modified by the warm brown sweater my mother said I had to wear over it.

However, my glass slippers twinkled satisfactorily. They were my mother's old black shoes painted with aluminum paint—closest thing I could get to glass. Mama had big feet and, hence, big shoes, though I thought I could probably clump along in them all right, once I tied them on with stout twine. (Any Prince I happened to meet that evening had better be stone-blind.)

As for my brother, Jack, all he had bothered with was the black eye mask and . . . But perhaps I had better explain about my brother, Jack.

Well, he was, in a word, loathsome. Or, to put it another way, unbearable. Not only was he a boy, he was three years older, having been a knee-baby when I was a lap-baby, a situation that makes for all sorts of traumas, the way being born apparently always does. Furthermore, when I was very little, he gave me a nickname it took me thirty years to live down.

And not only was he three years older, he was five years faster and ten years stronger, and when our family went for automobile rides on summer nights, as people used to do, he always got to the car first and sat down on the best side of the back seat. Whichever side he picked was the best side, and through some remarkable but unfailing coincidence, it was always the side I wanted, myself.

So I would slap him when he wasn't looking, and then he'd hit me, and I'd pull his hair, and then he'd hit me a good one, and I'd cry, and Mama would say *Now*-what's-the-matter, and Jack would explain, and I'd scream, and Daddy would say SHUT-UP-BOTH-OF-YOU, and we wouldn't, and once back home again he'd get out the razor strop and blister our behinds with it, and it was all Jack's fault.

Or Jack would be allowed to play outside an hour later than I could, so I'd kick his bicycle, and he'd smack me, and I'd butt my head into his stomach, and then he'd smack me a good one, and I'd cry, and Mama would say *Now*-what's-the-matter, and Jack would explain, and I'd scream, and Daddy would say SHUT-UP-BOTH-OF-YOU, and we wouldn't, and so he'd get out the razor strop and blister our behinds with it, and it was all Jack's fault.

Or he was allowed to go to the Airdome Movie all by himself and I wasn't. So I would hide his fielder's glove. . . . And so on, as stylized as a minuet.

Furthermore, whenever we pulled a chicken wishbone, he always got the big part. Jack had a very tricky pull.

So, as I say, I loathed him. Obviously he was rotten to the core.

And yet, if pinned down, I suppose I'd have had to admit that Jack was a lad of parts. He was capable, I had to hand him that. He could do everything. He could ride his bike no hands or standing up, whereas I had to concentrate hard just to keep my own seat in reasonable proximity to the bicycle's. He could play baseball, football, basketball—even the trombone. And he could run—oh, how he could run! It was family legend how I was forever chugging along in the rear—I was short-legged—hollering, *"Wait for Poofsie!"* But Jack had long legs, great legs for running.

Moreover, Jack was a keen observer of natural phenomena. It was he who pointed out to me my first (and now I think of it, only) personally observed instance of transmogrification. Playing in Grandpa's back yard one day, we saw a large black dog run under the porch and a large black cat run out, and we never saw the dog again. Clearly, as Jack explained, the dog had turned into a cat.

And—conclusively to show the kind of material we're dealing with here—consider the matter of my brother and the hominy.

You must understand that at our house we were expected to eat whatever was set before us, and generally we did. For the most part, it was good plain simple Midwestern food. Salmon came in cans, catfish was for cats, chicken was for Sunday, and some weeks ran fairly heavily to meat loaf. Because my father was averse to what he called spare parts, we were never faced with (*ulp*) sweetbreads or (*yuck*) brains or (*ble-e-ch-h*) liver. Indeed, if we shied at the parsnips or the turnips or the sauerkraut, my mother had only to threaten us with a curried-rice-and-kidney dish she'd been faced with once at her uncle Sid's in Philadelphia. A mere mention of Sidney's Kidneys and we would eat anything.

Except, in my brother's case, hominy. There it was on the supper table one evening, accompanying the pork chops—a large bowl of canned hominy, hot, buttered, salted and peppered—and my brother said he couldn't eat it.

"Yes, you can," Mama said.

"No, I can't," Jack said.

"Yes, you can," said Mama.

"No, I can't," said Jack, and he explained that he'd eaten it once before and it had made him sick.

"Nonsense," Mama said briskly. "Eat it," and she put a generous helping of hominy on his plate, a shapely white cone.

Now, I would never have mentioned this matter at all if it were going to get disgusting. I have my standards. But the sensational feature of Jack's performance was that it wasn't disgusting in the slightest. He ate all the hominy, every single kernel, and in approximately seven seconds it came back up looking exactly the way it looked before it went down, after one of the fastest round trips since they invented the esophagus. There it was, the same hominy Fuji, except that this time it was neatly deposited on the dining-room rug instead of on the plate.

He never had to eat hominy again.

It is plain that we have here a lad to reckon with.

Well, Halloween. I mean, this particular Halloween, a few centuries ago in McKinleyville, Missouri.

My problem was (as it developed) that the Wicked Witch of the West had all unexpectedly come up, or down, with a fat case of chicken pox. Right after dinner that night, Florence telephoned me, crying her little black heart out as she explained why she couldn't go begging.

I regret to say that I don't remember feeling sorry about her. But I certainly did feel sorry about me. There I was, high, dry, and up the crick—nobody to go with.

My brother was, of course, primed and ready for an evening with his peers, masked bandits all, equipped with water pistols, a water canteen, and laundry soap. But, unluckily for him, he hadn't yet left the house when Florence telephoned. Too late, he perceived that he was about to get royally stuck with his little sister, for as he tried to slide out the back door, Mama headed him off at the pass pantry.

"Jack, you've got to take your sister with you," she said. Understandably, Mama could do without the pleasure of my company, too, sulking around all evening as I was bound to be doing.

I can still see Jack's anguished look and hear his "Do I hafta?"

"You heard your mother," Daddy said from behind his newspaper. It was one of his favorite lines, and he delivered it well.

Of course none of this surprised me. When you are somebody's kid sister with a Buster Brown haircut and short fat legs, you grow accustomed to feeling like the polecat at the picnic; it goes with the territory. As Cinderella, I'd have no magical coach-and-four, only four boys pretending I wasn't there—I knew that—and if it had been any night but Halloween, I probably wouldn't have tagged along. But Halloween was, after all, Halloween.

So there we presently were, out in the crisp October night, the sidewalks acrackle with oak leaves and candy wrappers, a classic Allhallows Eve weather-wise, the gibbous moon sailing high behind scudding clouds, dark but not so dark you couldn't see other short shadowy weird shapes scuttling onto and off porches, up and down the street.

I plodded behind Jack and the other three masked gunmen, stopping periodically to fix my big loose shoes, which wouldn't stay tied on. Inasmuch as the boys stopped once in a while, too, to unhinge a gate or soap a window, I managed to keep up, though of course they were pretending they didn't know me. And I really missed Florence to giggle with, though I couldn't blame the boys. (I wish people three years older than I am still seemed that much smarter to me; I wouldn't worry half so much about the state of the nation.)

As it worked out, I was mouthpiece and bag lady both—we had one great big grocery sack for the five of us—because we learned fast that we got more loot that way. I would knock, and when the door opened, say the ritual

> *Gimme cold*
> *Gimme hot*
> *Gimme gimme*
> *What you got*

while I held the bag invitingly open. When the woman, usually a mother we knew, brought out the whatever-it-was, my masked escorts (to use the word loosely) appeared as if by magic, and she would likely toss in a casual half dozen more. Usually we got more when they didn't count.

And so we conscientiously covered the familiar streets, up Central and down Maryland, up Bemiston and over to Meramec. Business was good. Luminous toothy punkins grinned from some of the front windows, and we knew we could expect handouts there, but we didn't by-pass the other places either. Just because they weren't quite up to carving a punkin didn't necessarily mean there wouldn't be a plate of doughnuts handy, maybe. Or some candy corn. Or *something,* even it it was just some old fruit. And so we missed few houses, and the bag grew heavy as the evening grew late. There wasn't another roving band in sight by the time we hit the Pruitt house.

Well, the first thing we noticed was how foul the place smelled. You couldn't help but notice, and from a fair distance. Earlier visitors, it seemed, had gone to considerable effort, dragging a great full garbage can around from the back stoop and through the side yard, to dump it all over the front lawn. You'd think, smelling the garbage and possibly trouble, that we would have had brains enough to walk on by. And we might have done so if it hadn't been for those agonizingly delicious memories of Mrs. Pruitt's last-year's punkin pies, which were uppermost in our minds.

"You go in first; you've got the sack," said one of the gunmen. (And did they ever leave me holding it.)

Proud of my responsible position, I rang the doorbell and, as the door opened, unfortunately proffered the sack with a "Gimme gimme" before I got a good look at Mrs. Pruitt's face.

It was grotesque: twisted with black rage as she unleashed a torrent of invective that wouldn't stop, a spate of language that would have curled a jackhandle—stuff I'd never heard the likes of before and seldom have since (while beneath the awful ongoing shriek of it I could also hear the clatter of masked gunmen racketing back down the porch steps and off into the middle distance).

The thrust of Mrs. Pruitt's harangue seemed to be that *I'd* made the mess in the front yard. And of course she should have known better. I couldn't have budged that heavy garbage can one linear inch. Even if I had, would I have shown my face later?

But she was probably drunk. Tumblers and a bottle were visible on the living-room table behind her, and so was a man, back there, too, in the shadows. I believe now that we had interrupted a congenial evening with one of her out-of-town friends. (Marcie and Josie seemed to have a good many visiting uncles.)

So there I stood, mouth agape, I'm sure, wishing I were anywhere else in the world, scared to death, trying to ease out the door backward, but I couldn't, on account of my big flapping shoes. Trapped, I was, trapped like a fart in a mitten—boys gone, porch empty. I'd looked around.

And *that's* when Nell Pruitt nailed me in a steely grip so suddenly that I dropped my big bag while her other hand grabbed the buggy whip from the corner behind the door. And it was at this precise moment that I was grabbed from the other side of the doorway by—now, you may not believe this, and I found it hard to believe, myself—by my brother, Jack.

Yes, there was apparently one redeeming shred of decency in the boy, one tiny sliver of human feeling amid all the rottenness. He hadn't deserted me with the others; he'd only hidden behind the porch pillar.

It was my brother who, out of the dark, grabbed me with a suddenness that loosed Mrs. Pruitt's grip. It was my brother who got me out of the doorway and down off the porch, and if one of my big shoes fell off and stayed behind, who cared? Not me. As I see us now, at the telescope's far small end, we blur like adagio dancers, Jack pulling me so fast I'm parallel to the sidewalk, feet off the ground, hair streaming—though I suppose it couldn't have been quite that way; he wasn't that much bigger, and anyway my hair was short.

But it seemed that way. He got me out of there and back home, and a good thing, too, or I'd have ended up—well, how? Flayed alive? More likely right in the gravy, along with the eye of newt, toe of frog, and whatever other terrible things Mrs. P. was undoubtedly stewing up in some big pot in the back yard. That's what I thought. Talk about your witches. Talk about scared. Whew.

So I always felt that Jack saved my life; and after that, we didn't fight quite so much.

I was grateful, of course. But I was also puzzled. Here was the thing: he hadn't grabbed that handout bag I'd dropped, that big luscious sackful; he'd grabbed *me*. Instead of saving —as he could have saved—7 Nut Hersheys, 8 Baby Ruths, 5 Clark Bars, 6 Peanuttos, 12 doughnuts, a hatful of penny jawbreakers, Bananamels, Mary Janes, and chocolate-covered marshmallow punkins (not to mention as many apples and tangerines as Job had boils), he'd saved me.

An inexplicable choice. But there it was. I couldn't have guaranteed that *I'd* have done it, in his place. You had to admire a person like that. I felt I could trust him.

And so, as I say, we didn't wrangle quite so much after that, and when we did, he didn't hit me quite so hard. I am not sure of his reasoning. But it may be so that when you save someone's life, you feel in some measure responsible for it. Or you may feel, with some kind of inverse logic, that they can't be all bad or you wouldn't have done it. Something like that.

Whatever the reason, things improved—improved with the speed of glaciers approaching, to be sure, but nonetheless improved, to the point where we are now downright fond of each other.

Still, a regard for candor compels me to add that considerably later, when I went away to college three years behind my brother, and he felt it necessary to lay wise counsel upon me from his superior vantage point of three years' seniority, he strongly advised me—should I ever fall among evil companions and spirituous liquors—to stick to sloe gin. It simply goes to show that you can never trust anyone quite all the way.

As for the pumpkin soup I made in my comfortable new kitchen, it turned out fine, just fine. Or, well, almost fine: pulled a nine, say, on a scale of one to ten. It is only that a few intangibles were missing: the surprise element, the Cloud-Cuckoo-Land feel of that earlier California place where I'd tasted it first, and the particular company.

Which didn't surprise me. Indeed, if I might be allowed to formulate one law, like Parkinson, who discovered that any job will expand to fill the time allotted, and Murphy, with his "If something can go wrong, it will," I will sponsor as my own personal statute, "It will never taste quite as good as hers did."

4

Many Ways with Ambrosia

or Sex in the Fourth Grade

Counter space is a lovely thing in a kitchen, as I had learned while living without any, and I had mentioned to Uwe that it would be nice to be able to roll out biscuits without first putting the toaster-oven on the floor. Obligingly, he gave us several yards of counter, along one side of the room and around the corner.

That is the reason we have a fruit-ripener now—simply because we have room for it. I suppose this is merely another extension of the Parkinson's Law we just passed: objects will, in time, appear and metastasize to cover all available kitchen counter space, no matter how many clear, clean square acres of it one might have had to begin with. A wooden bowl here, a copper pot there, a cookbook holder here, a fruit-ripener there . . . And like barnacles on a boat bottom, these objects tend to remain.

"Wouldn't you like a fruit-ripener?"

It was my sister-in-law who had asked me the question, before my birthday not long ago, and with that swift grasp of basics that has long distinguished my every move, I replied, "Well . . . uh . . . I don't know. Don't you think . . . uh . . . I mean, do you suppose we'd really . . . uh . . . What is a fruit-ripener?"

So she gave us one, and I found out. A fruit-ripener is a round, shallow bowl about fifteen inches in diameter, with a domed lid that is about fifteen inches high, the whole thing resembling a large translucent pear. It is made of clear hard acrylic, pierced at strategic intervals with small round holes that cause, I gather, something of a hothouse reaction. Put a hard green tomato in there, or an adamant avocado, and things will start to steam up so your fruit is ready to eat by the time you've found the lime juice. Or, well, not quite that fast, perhaps. But it still beats a sunny window sill by a considerable distance.

And so we put those things under the big lid, as well as papayas and bananas and mangoes, when we pick them early to get ahead of the birds. (We have birds that look like flowers here and also flowers that look like birds, but the careful observer can easily tell them apart by remembering that the flowers don't eat your fruit.) Oranges seem to thrive under the lid, too; they sometimes roll in from the mainland pretty hard. But whatever there is in the fruit-ripener is usually a good base for ambrosia—probably not the classic ambrosia, but a variation, of which there are many.

Indeed, you might be mildly surprised, as I was, to learn just how many. The constant seems to be fruit plus coconut. It might be said with some truth that the fruit bowl is to ambrosia as the refrigerator is to meat loaf. If it's in there, add it.

And so there is Age of Aquarius Ambrosia, from an old Marin County Flower Child cookbook, involving plain yogurt, dates, coconut, and granola. Oddly enough, it didn't call for mung beans. And there is a rich California Ambrosia —walnuts, pineapple, brown sugar, coconut macaroons, vanilla ice cream, and Chartreuse liqueur—as well as a Texas

Ambrosia, which calls for all six of those things plus bananas and pecans, and that's Texas for you.

Then, as if that weren't enough, Craig Claiborne makes an Ambrosia Cake, an arrangement of cake layers, coconut, oranges, pastry cream, frosting, and kirsch—rather a damp cake, it seems to me, but people who prefer their cake wet (as in Tipsy Cake or English Trifle) would probably like Ambrosia Cake, too.

And then there is Miss Williams's ambrosia. Miss Williams was my teacher in the fourth grade. Her ambrosia contained chopped marshmallows, which I considered an interesting and perhaps even elegant touch, though not quite valid. No one is more conservative than a fourth-grader.

Still, I'm sure I gave her the benefit of the doubt. Had she grown up in McKinleyville she'd have known better— that is, grown up in it when I did, when it was a small Midwestern county seat instead of the expensive West End of a grown-up city that it is today. For, while my back was turned —an interval of some twenty-five years—its neighboring large city was pushing out, oozing and flowing into and around the little town the way a big pond might overflow and incorporate a puddle.

The real McKinleyville is gone now, one with ancient Rome. *More* gone than ancient Rome, which still has its Colosseum and catacombs and some nice old arches. When I last saw McKinleyville, the only familiar landmarks were a wing of the old courthouse, and the Catholic church.

But, as I say, had Miss Williams grown up there, she, too, would have known that the real, the true, the classic ambrosia consists of chopped-up oranges and bananas, slightly sweetened with confectioners' sugar and mixed with shredded coconut out of a box. The coconut people hadn't thought of canning it yet, or, if they had, the news hadn't reached McKinleyville. Ours came shredded, boxed, and rather dry. Once opened, it became quickly drier, dry as excelsior, so you picked ambrosia out of your teeth for days, though partly it was orange membranes. My mother never bothered to remove them, which was sensible of her. People are supposed to eat more fiber. This probably wasn't why she left it on, but it was still a good thing to do.

I would have been mystified then, I am sure, had someone told me the actual meaning of ambrosia—the heavenly nectar-of-the-gods meaning, that is—because so far as heavenly went, they had to be kidding. Not that it wasn't okay. But *heavenly?* A double chocolate soda now—*that* was more like it. Or, better still, a Brown Cow—a Brown Cow being root beer poured over vanilla ice cream in a tall glass, then swoozled around till it sipped like thick custard, taffy-colored and immoderately delicious. *There* was heavenly for you. *There* was ambrosia.

Besides, I knew Ambrosia was a girl's name. A man named Ambrose cut the grass for some people down the block, and Ambrosia was the name of his little daughter. So I supposed that some other Ambrosia had invented the orange-banana-coconut combination, and they'd named it after her. (The same way Brown Betty was probably a real person, too, maybe a cousin of smiley old black Aunt Jemima, who invented the pancake.)

Now, you probably don't consider Ambrosia a particularly voluptuous or—if I may use the sorry word—sexy dessert. And yet to me it is inextricably bound up with matters of the flesh—very mysterious matters—for some good sound reasons that I am determined to relate. These reasons have greatly to do with the Miss Williams I mentioned earlier. I seldom make ambrosia without thinking of her.

Miss Williams wore her bright auburn hair in a lovely soft bun at the nape of her neck. She was just a bit plump, with a little round almost potbelly, and plump freckle-spattered hands with beautiful almond-shaped nails that were my private envy and despair. (I chewed mine when there wasn't anything else around to eat, which was enough of the time that I seldom had any fingernails worth mentioning, or chewing, either one.)

Miss Williams also had large candid blue eyes, and in my autograph book—this was the year we all had autograph books—she had written:

Always be fair,
Always be true,
And always paddle
Your own canoe.

But that was all right. Every grownup who wrote in your autograph book somehow felt impelled to preach a little. My father had written:

Think straight, do right, vote Republican.

He apparently found no contradictions there. And my mother had inscribed a nice stanza from *The Prophet.* (The children of the sixties think they invented the Prophet, but they actually didn't at all.)

Anyway, you expected teachers to preach, too, and she had inscribed her verse in a rounded, eminently legible hand that was a pleasure in itself.

She also had a smile like a sunset that leaves a nice rosy afterglow, not one of those rubber-band smiles. Best of all, one noontime, when I had been sent to deliver a telephone message to the teachers' lounge, where she was eating her lunch, she'd given me the two chocolate cookies she'd brought along to eat with her ambrosia.

"I'd give you the ambrosia, too," she said, with that warming smile, "only it's nearly gone." As indeed it was—only a few marshmallow bits left in some orange juice at the bottom of the Dixie cup, which is how I happened to learn about her variation on the ambrosia theme.

Approachable, that's what Miss Williams was. And that —besides the fact that she was, after all, our teacher at the time—is why Florence Ashenbrenner and I selected her to enlighten us about sex.

As I have said, since Fight Day, some time back, Florence and I had been an inseparable giggling twosome. In her autograph book I had written:

Whate'er dark clouds may gather o'er
Life's dark and stormy sea,

We'll sail the good ship Friendship
Through all eternity

which I considered a beautiful sentiment, beautifully put.
And in my autograph book, Florence had written:

Ikka bakka soda cracker
Ikka bakka boo
If your father chews tobacco
Shame on you!

As an avowal of friendship, this left, I felt, something to
be desired. Furthermore, it was a rhyme you jumped rope to,
not something you'd write in somebody's autograph book.
But I was charitable about it, realizing that I came from a
wordier family than she did, and had better sources to crib
from.

And of course we told each other all our secrets, even
though between us we didn't have one worth telling. And
the reason we didn't was . . . Well, I suppose I should take
a minute to explain that situation.

In a recent issue of our local paper, the "Ask Shirley"
column for teen-agers published a letter that I am reprinting
here:

Dear Shirley,
   I would like to have your advice. I am almost
fourteen years old and there is this boy I like a
lot and I am about to start my sex life. But I
would like to know first which contraceptive do
you think is the best.

                              [Signed] Hot to Trot

And Shirley congratulated her on her sound good sense in
asking, then gave her a brisk rundown on the diaphragm,
the Pill, and the whole picture, concluding with a cheery
"Good luck!"

Shirley, where were you when we needed you? Not that
Florence and I were fourteen years old yet, of course. More
like ten. And not that we would conceivably have gone that

frolicsome route even had we been fourteen. The distance between the present teen generation's head set and that one so long ago can be measured only in light-years.

But there were some things Florence and I wanted badly to find out. And I well remember what had triggered our latent, smoldering curiosity: a book I'd borrowed from the drugstore lending library, a novel called *Village Virgin*. This girl went away with this older man. Then she came back home with a baby but no marriage license, and everyone was mean to her—all of which left Florence and me abristle with questions. What had happened? And why? And how?

Mainly, how. To repeat, we had no grandiose notions of stepping out and living life to its fullest. We only wanted an update on the stork.

Well, we tried books, the first one being, logically enough, the *Britannica*. Which was no help at all, couldn't make head or tail of it. Nor were there any clues in *Growing Into Womanhood*, which Florence snitched out of the school library. It was all about eggs; didn't tell us a thing we wanted to know. As for fiction, still nothing. This was before D. H. Lawrence and Henry Miller happened, you understand—happened to me, that is—and before numerous other things did, too.

Oh, not that there wasn't some titillating stuff available for the eager, prurient little mind to play with. There was, for instance, *The Hunchback of Notre Dame*.

Fortunately, the book isn't on my shelf here or I would feel obliged to look it up. But as I remember, Quasimodo spent an immoderate amount of time chasing Esmeralda around the Notre Dame choir loft, Esmeralda clad (and here comes the good part) *only in her shift*.

I didn't know what a shift looked like, only that it was underwear. The dictionary told me that much. But I knew, deep in my bones, that it couldn't possibly resemble the button-up drop-seat union suits I was stuck with, or in.

"An undergarment; a chemise," the dictionary said. I hadn't heard of a chemise either, and it's a good thing I didn't have to pronounce it, for it would have rhymed with *revise,* but, boy oh boy, could I ever see one in my mind's eye. Short, pink, filmy; sheer, wildly scanty, *French.* Though I couldn't in any way visualize what the sight of it would do to Quasimodo, or what he as a result might do to Esmeralda, the mere idea of it all had me halfway up the bulkhead.

I will assert here, too, that Victor Hugo had it all over Louisa May Alcott where the broader education was concerned. Though I was a devout Alcott groupie, I had to admit that she was zilch on sex. Very big at drawing discreet curtains, very big at leaving discreet intervals, she was forever dropping a row of asterisks exactly where you didn't want them, so you never did find out what happened. Presto, and Meg shows up with twins.

To repeat: how come?

Now, I can understand that right here one might inquire, reasonably enough, why didn't we ask our mothers?

Well, I *had* asked my mother about the Village Virgin, and a fat lot of good it did me. Suddenly there was that tight white look across the bridge of her nose, the look that scared the liver and lights out of me, as she told me crisply that I was too young to read books like that, and forget it.

Florence's mother? "She'd whale me," Florence said glumly, and I saw no reason to doubt it. Mrs. Ashenbrenner, a well-muscled woman, worked at the Kum-As-U-R Kafeteria in town, where she schlepped eighty-pound cook-pots around as if they were teacups. She also operated on a notably short fuse.

And of course those aren't the only reasons we felt so hamstrung where our mothers were concerned. There are all sorts of things you conceal from your mother, not because you don't respect or love her, but simply because she is your mother, and you'd sooner tell anyone else, from the lady at the dry cleaner's to the cop on the beat.

Finally, there were our fathers. And asking them, as Florence and I agreed, was unthinkable.

Thus we had, as we saw it, two choices. One was to ask some older girl, like Margie Haddon in the seventh grade, who wore lipstick. On the school bus, once, I'd overheard her giggling with one of her peers about the girl who asked the doctor how not to have a baby and he said, Drink buttermilk, and she said, Before or after? and he said, Instead of.

There it was, the first naughty story I ever heard, and it might as well have been "Little Red Riding-Hood." Impatiently I wanted to butt in and ask, Instead of *what?* But of course I didn't. It would have meant admitting my ignorance and probably not having it explained anyway, and getting laughed at into the bargain.

Our second choice, as we saw it, was to ask a teacher. And of the teachers we knew, Miss Williams was the likeliest choice—likeliest if not ideal. There were, indeed, drawbacks that had Florence and me pondering for weeks before we took any action.

For one thing—a distinct possibility we had to face— maybe Miss Williams didn't know either. After all, she wasn't married. But then, not one of our teachers *was* married. Though matrimony was allegedly a holy state, it apparently wasn't considered so in McKinleyville, where married women weren't allowed to teach. I've wondered since about the School Board's oddly ambivalent attitude. While motherhood itself was okay, there seemed to be something vaguely soiled about mothers themselves.

Come to that, though, McKinleyville wouldn't hire a Catholic either. Or a Jew, a Mormon, a Buddhist, a Christian Scientist, a Hindu, a black, a Moslem, an American Indian, a saint, or a Hottentot, and as for a homosexual, gracious to goodness and mercy me. For no one is as snooty as a rich WASP, except a poor WASP, who is snootiest of all, and I give you the McKinleyville School Board as living proof. No, I can't exactly do that; they're all dead. But believe me.

At any rate, for teachers, marriage was out. You had to be a spinster, and a prudent one, too, for the tiniest peccadillo could make a great big wave. The school buzzed with it for days, after word got out that Miss Williams had been spotted in a downtown restaurant smoking a cigarette.

However, for Florence and me, that cigarette was a definite plus. It struck a worldly note we had been listening for, and it also helped counteract the fact that Miss Williams blushed.

For blush she did, frequently and gloriously. The deep-raspberry glow was visible first at her modest neckline—goodness only knows where it began—then traveled steadily north to suffuse her plump throat and her face, clear up to the roots of her pretty dark-red hair.

I remember clearly the hygiene class she devoted to the body's elimination system, when she picked up the big dark-green classroom wastepaper basket for illustrative purposes. That is when the blush started. She had worked out this neat simile. Just as we drop our unwanted trash into the wastebasket, she said, so must the body dispose of its unwanted—she blushed harder here—waste material.

"In the can?" suggested Art Hoadley from the back row. Art was one of those insolent outsize slobs every teacher would like to kill. He was tall as Miss Williams already, and he came to school on alternate Thursdays or something, or whenever they closed the poolroom.

"Arthur!" said Miss Williams, warningly.

"Excuse me, the terlet," he said.

"Arthur, leave the room at once and report to the principal," Miss Williams said.

He shambled out.

In retrospect, I think Florence and I could have acquired all the information we wanted from Art Hoadley, including lab projects and field work. But it would never in all this world have occurred to us to ask him. He wasn't a nice boy. He was, in fact, an Awful Boy.

Anyway, Florence and I figured that if Miss Williams knew about stuff like elimination, it was possible she knew about the other stuff, too. If she didn't, it could be terribly embarrassing all around, of course, but this was a calculated risk.

Carefully, then, we laid our plans. Nearly every Friday it was Miss Williams's habit, we knew, to stay after school correcting papers, usually till around five o'clock. Therefore, we decided, we would play at Florence's house after school on the following Friday and return around four-thirty, when there would be no one around to butt in except the janitor,

Mr. Hawkenspit (so named by some smart-aleck eighth-grader because of an obscure sinus condition you could hear all over the building). But he would doubtless have his hands full cleaning the Boys' and Girls' Toilet Rooms, where there was always plenty to do by the end of the week. We would then knock on the door of Room #4 and go in when invited, as surely we would be. And we would then ask Miss Williams, woman to woman, "How do babies start?"

And so it was, the next Friday afternoon, that we went back to school. I can see us now, Florence and me, creeping up the broad central stair in the gloom of the fading autumn afternoon, to the quiet, dusty, darkling upstairs hall. But lights on in Room #4 indicated that Miss Williams was there.

Well, things didn't work out quite according to game plan (and we were too young then, of course, to know how seldom they do).

For one thing—a minor point, to be sure—Room #4's door was open. This in itself wasn't disturbing, and Miss Williams was there all right, in the room. But something was apparently the matter with her. She had her head on her arms, on the desk. There was no sound at all, as we crept to the doorway, but her shoulders were trembling, ever so little. She was crying—we could tell that. Crying.

And this was a stunner. It was the first time it had ever crossed my mind—Florence's either, probably—that teachers ever cried or could possibly have any need to cry. Because teachers weren't like anyone else. Teachers might have strange teeth (the principal's stuck out in all directions) or halitosis (the art teacher had a breath you could chin yourself on) or headaches or backaches or bad colds (like Miss Edlefson's perpetual sniffle) or any number of minor afflictions. All the same, teachers were omnipotent and certainly invulnerable to any of the real problems that beset us lesser mortals. And to think that they just might possibly not be so invulnerable after all! I believe we both felt the world shake a trifle beneath our feet.

And so we stood there, Florence and I, barely breathing.

Just stood, in the dusty dusk of the hall outside Room #4, afraid to move lest she hear and look up, afraid not to move lest she look up anyway and find us where we didn't belong. For we were witnessing something we shouldn't be. We at least had sense enough to know that.

But what now? Indecision had me paralyzed. I didn't know *what* to do—fish or cut bait, pee or go out to lunch— and Florence apparently didn't either. But she recovered first. At long last, she pinched me, pointed to our shoes and pantomimed to remove them and beat it.

Which we did.

As it turned out, Miss Williams could probably have answered our questions after all. Because what happened was, she resigned almost immediately after that to get married and/or have a baby: I never did find out which happened first. However, it seemed that that round little stomach of hers wasn't merely the result of too many marsh-mallows in the ambrosia. I overheard my father telling my mother about it, and I, of course, passed along the word.

"Shucks, now we never *will* know," Florence said, totally discouraged.

It was a shame, all right, a real shame.

Still, I was glad for Miss Williams. I really liked her, and besides I was gung ho for romance, any which way. His name was Luigi Antonolli and he was in the produce business, as she put it in her letter of resignation to my father. And he was indeed, had his own fruit-stand downtown—ambrosia on the hoof, as it were—which I considered another nice break for Miss Williams. We heard later, too, that the baby was just darling, and, so far as I know, they all lived happily together ever after.

I wish I could say the same thing about the relationship between Florence and me. But it wasn't to be. I consider it fairly ironic, too, that after all we'd gone through, sexwise, it was Sex that proved to be our undoing. Sex was, indeed, the reef in Life's dark and stormy sea upon which our good ship Friendship foundered—foundered, released a lot of bilge, and sank without a trace.

Briefly, what happened was that I finally got hold of a secret worth telling, a fat juicy secret concerning Barry O'Donnell. And told it.

I haven't yet mentioned Barry O'Donnell, I think. But his name was bound to appear sooner or later in any chronicle of our class, for Barry was the Cutest Boy in it. And a terrible boy, too.

There is a big difference between Terrible and Awful. Art Hoadley was just plain Awful, a walking argument for retroactive abortion. But Barry was Terrible, which is what we called him, with giggling delight, when he tripped us (it was a pleasure and a privilege to be tripped by Barry O'Donnell) or when, at lunchtime, he talked about disgusting things like mashed gopher guts and French-fried eyeballs as we ate our potted-ham sandwiches and hard-boiled eggs.

Oh, Barry was terrible, all right! In fact, he had the dubious distinction of being the only eighth-grader, a few years later, to be suspended from school for a solid week for writing his Shakespeare theme entirely in Pig Latin. Not your common garden variety of igpay atinlay either, but his own distinctive brand. *Shalefakespeare the Immorlfortal Barlfard,* his title ran, which totally convulsed the class when he started to read it aloud, though it didn't convulse the teacher any, and he didn't get far—she saw to that. And at about the same time, in chorus, he discovered the hilarious effects to be achieved with songs like "Santa Lucia" by dropping into the pauses a just barely audible "between the sheets."

So we were always squealing, "Barry, you're just terrible!" and not meaning a word of it. Because he was, as I say, the Cutest Boy. A bit short (but who cared?), with lots of Irish in him—coal-black hair, gray-blue eyes set in with a sooty finger, to use the good old Irish idiom, and thick curly lashes you wouldn't believe.

(I must say here that I am impressed, looking back, by our healthy acceptance of ourselves and each other. It's a shame it didn't last, but then, I suppose it seldom does. Once you're grown, you're forever trying to improve on the status quo—trying to play better tennis or read faster or develop ESP or relieve minor arthritis pains or shed unwanted ugly pounds or become a better person. But way back then we were reasonably content with ourselves and with each other, generous about our good points and at least philosophical about our failings. It was as though we sensed some roughly compensatory principle at work in the universe, or at least in our part of it, which had proved valid thus far: nobody had everything, but everybody had something.)

Thus, it was accepted fact, like the weather, that Charlie Mason was the richest—Charlie, a conspicuous little consumer, brought a five-cent Hershey bar in his lunch every day—as well as the fattest. And no wonder. This was back in the days when a five-cent chocolate bar was a comforting fistful (as well as instant acne a bit later, when our hormonal juices started to flow) and always wrapped in collectible tin foil under its outer paper jacket. Charlie's enormous solid ball of it was the envy of the group.

And Art Hoadley was the strongest, but his mother and father were divorced.

And Ernie Olinger was the best-natured but the dumbest; any dumber and he'd have been a begonia. Nobody seemed to know just what was the matter with Ernie. Today he would be in a special class for the developmentally disabled or something. But then he was just dumb.

And Carl Krepps was an arithmetic shark but couldn't read for sour apples.

And Freem Fuller was Best Orator—everyone admitted he could talk the birds right out of the trees—but his father was a Democrat.

And Opal Henking was Best Skip-rope Jumper—nobody could double-Dutch like Opal—but she talked funny and had warts.

And Lucille Brueggeman could certainly play the tuba but she wore teeth braces.

And Augie Barnes was the Best Athlete but the Worst Speller. (With my mind's eye I can still read his entry in my autograph book: "I hope you will rember me as an athelic boy with many mucles and power.")

And I was Best Speller, but hand me a baseball bat and I couldn't hit my own behind with it, let alone a baseball. . . .

So it went. And I have a morbid suspicion that if this particular McKinleyville fourth-grade class should ever, God forbid, reconvene, no matter what our adventures have been in the intervening years, we would automatically slip into our same old roles and find them comfortable as well-worn shoes. Barry would still be the Cutest Boy, Freem would still be Best Orator, Charlie would still be the richest and the fattest. . . . Thus it was written and thus it shall ever be.

But I digress. I wanted to introduce Ellen Bishop, who was by all odds and beyond the shadow of a doubt the Cutest Girl: a luscious-but-slender, rosy-faced, brown-eyed blonde who had the rest of us looking like cakes in the rain. (According to the principle of compensation we just passed, there must have been something wrong with her, too, though I certainly couldn't have told you what. Unless it was her missing front tooth. She'd barely had time to get acquainted with her second teeth before a front one was somehow knocked out, so that she wore a little one-tooth bridge that she could remove and then spit through the hole any time she felt like it. But we all considered that a real plus.)

At any rate, Ellen being Cutest Girl and Barry being Cutest Boy, it was unarguable that they belonged together, Princess and Prince.

That is why it threw me a wide fast curve when Barry, one day, waited for me after school (it was the week I was blackboard monitor) and walked me home. I was well aware that he was basically Ellen's. It was Ellen he accidentally bumped and jostled and tripped the most, Ellen he always accidentally stood or sat next to, Ellen he gave the chocolate heart to last Valentine's Day.

So I wasn't kidding myself. But I wasn't about to argue either, and I was flattered right out of my ankle sox as he walked me *past* home, actually, to his house, which was just a hoot and a spitball up the block from ours. And he said they had some new kittens in their garage and would I like to see them?

Sure, I said. I loved kittens, though if it had been woolly worms or black widow spiders I'd have said yes, too. And I walked as slow as I dared, to give more people a chance to see us.

And so we went into his garage, which was empty, not a cat box or a kitten in sight. And the next thing you know, I was hearing the classic old time-mellowed-if-not-hallowed proposition, "I'll show you mine if you'll show me yours," as Barry fiddled with the front of his green corduroy knickers.

Well, it really blew me out of the water, or, more accurately, out of the garage. Because I didn't *want* to see his. For one thing, I knew more or less what it would look like. There were the Greek statues in the mythology book that had had Florence and me snickering and poking each other. Also, my brother and I were laundered together in the same tub when we were smaller.

Barry's wouldn't be much different. No big deal.

But the situation was different; I knew that. It was a different ball game. And no way was I going to show him mine, not in a hundred million years.

And so I ran—ran all the way home, checked in, then ran straight to Florence's house, for what good is a secret if you can't lay it on somebody? She was eating a jelly sandwich in the kitchen and made me one, too, as I pledged her to eternal silence as to what I was about to divulge.

"Promise?"

"I promise," she said.

"Double promise?" I said.

"Kiss a pig and hope to die," she said.

So I divulged. And she listened, satisfactorily goggle-eyed, and we had a fine old afternoon, or what was left of it.

Next day at school, I tried not to look at Barry. But when our glances just happened to cross, he grinned, and I couldn't help but feel disconcerted. He wasn't acting a bit different— was flying paper airplanes during geography and poking

Ellen Bishop in recess line just as always. You'd have thought nothing had happened.

Well, nothing much had. And yet I *felt* as though something had. We had shared—if not exactly a tender moment, no, you could hardly call it that, but—something.

And of course, when Florence's eyes met mine, we had to muffle our giggles, although (as it turned out) they were the last mutual giggles we'd be enjoying for a good long time.

That afternoon was a cold rainy one, typically Missouri in November. Because it seemed such a long wet way home on foot to my house, I went over to my father's office in the adjacent high-school building, to curl up with a book in the outer office and eventually catch a ride home. And it was because my father happened to drive straight up Maryland Avenue instead of taking his customary roundabout route down Forsyth to Central that I happened to see them through the rain-sloshed car window. *Florence. And Barry. Together. Hurrying up the driveway. Barry's driveway. And right into Barry's garage.*

Well, I didn't know what to think.

I'll take that back. I did too know what to think, but I didn't want to think it. Also, I didn't want to judge Florence on insufficient evidence, however damning it looked. She was, after all, my friend. . . .

And it seemed a long old time before I could get the straight of it, too. Once home, I couldn't telephone and ask her, for I well knew that the Ashenbrenner telephone was centrally located, right between the kitchen and the dining room. And the next day—wouldn't you know?—it was still raining.

This sort of raw weather was one of the larger lumps in the tapioca of life, back in the fourth grade, because it meant that play and recess periods were held indoors, and *that* meant the basement gym, a dark oblong hole designed by trolls to grow mushrooms in. Its air circulation was minimal. After fifteen minutes of ghastly team games and horrible folk dances, it smelled like the bottom of the hired girl's trunk, and thirty-five minutes still to go. Never was a minute hand more ardently watched than the one on the basement-gym clock—watched by me, anyway—as it crept like a sore-footed snail toward the magic moment of Ten Till, when the blessed harsh clang of the electric bell would send us back to the classroom.

And so I hadn't a chance of catching Florence alone till after school.

Then I walked her home. And stopped her in her cold, sodden front yard, the leaves squishing underfoot, and a cold wind blowing. And said, without preamble, "I saw you and Barry yesterday going into his garage."

And she said, "Oh, yeah?"

And I said, "Oh, yeah."

And she said, "No, you didn't."

And I said, "I did *so.*"

"Sew!" she said. "Buttons on your underwear!" (Oh, she had a fast mouth.)

"All right, what'd you do in there?" I said.

And she said, cool as ice cream, "Snoopy poopy, ashcan-oopy, nosey posey . . ."

"Did you show him yours?" I said.

And she said, "Mine to know, yours to find out."

And I said, "Did you?"

And she said, "None of your beeswax."

I moved in on her, and she backed off a little. "What'd you go into that garage for?"

"To see the new kit . . ." she began, the lie dying in her mouth as she remembered I knew jolly well there weren't any kittens.

"Ha ha ha," I said coldly. "I'm going to tell."

"Tattletale, tattletale, soak your head in ginger ale," she said.

Well (and that's a hole in the ground, as Florence would have been the first to point out), why did I give a hoot? Florence had merely been pursuing our mutual line of research, hadn't she? Yes. And I had no hold at all on Barry O'Donnell, did I? No.

But I wasn't an impartial observer, and I was hotting up fast, from a low simmer to a full rolling boil. Because I felt—well, how? Betrayed? Double-crossed? Gypped? Well, chewed up and spit out—that's how I felt. Not to mention good and mad. All I knew was, she was a dirty little stinker and I'd have to jump her again.

So there we were, the next minute, thrashing about in the mud of her front yard, kicking, biting, scratching, and this time, I'm happy to say, I ripped *her* dress right down the middle. If Barry had been around, he'd have got another eyeful, mainly underwear this time. . . .

And of course Florence got in some good licks. My lip was bleeding and both scabs were off my knees (I always sported a matched pair, two round brown medallions), and by the time we finally quit we were both in considerably less than mint condition.

We glared at each other. Then she stalked up the porch steps and into her house, and I stalked—mud, blood and all —down the street to mine.

Oddly enough, my mother and father didn't give me much of a going-over this time. Sometimes parents show more sense than we give them credit for. Anyway, this time it wasn't on school property.

But I'm afraid we've come a long way from ambrosia, and I did want to get back to it, however briefly. Our local variety here in Hawaii is worth a mention, and some part of it is usually busy ripening in our fruit-ripener. If you mix chopped mangoes or papayas and bananas (or pineapple and bananas) with sour cream, a little brown sugar, and some fresh grated coconut, you can call it Island Ambrosia and eat it with pleasure nearly any time.

5

My Mother Was a Good Plain Cook

or Genevieve's Shining Hour

Now, book room, to me, is an important feature of a kitchen, and I had reminded Uwe of this several times. Accordingly, he provided some. Over the pass-through to the dining room, on the kitchen side, we have a broad shelf now that accomodates a fair number of books—all kinds, but mainly cookbooks. Somehow their number gently but inexorably increases.

One reason is that I have my mother's cookbooks now. Not many—she didn't have or want many—but some; and I have kept the ones she used the most. Among them are a venerable brown-bound *Boston Cooking School Cookbook*, a *Ladies' Guild Cookbook* (printed in 1889 under the auspices of the Presbyterian Church in Ganister, Kansas), and a first-edition *Joy of Cooking* that is nicely counterbalanced, I'm glad to say, by a first-edition *I Hate to Cook Book*.

These are all somewhat blistered and spattered and occasionally scribbled in: "better with brown sugar," "needs more lemon," "John liked" . . . That was my father, a mainly uncommunicative man—a loving man but an uncommunicative one; and I am sure the word *love* never sullied his mouth. He was noncommittal about food, too. He didn't comment; he simply ate. A "that was all right" from him was the equivalent of another man's tossing his hat in the air and yelling "Wheeee!"

One other book of hers that I kept is entitled *A Thousand Ways to Please a Husband*. This is, oddly enough, a cookbook, too. Published in 1917, only a few years after my mother was married, *A Thousand Ways* takes a newly married couple week by happy week through their first year of culinary adventures. Bettina does the cooking, with Bob invariably applauding the results, and sometimes you wonder why. Bettina didn't hesitate to serve her chicken à la king on hot biscuits accompanied by date-bread sandwiches, a hearty steamed pudding, and hot cocoa. Or she would organize some cream-of-mushroom soup, macaroni and cheese, hot corn muffins, and a rich banana pudding. . . .

No matter. Her husband was always delighted, and though they certainly must have waddled into their sunset years, I am sure it was hand in hand.

They apparently did very cute things with food back in 1917, or at least Bettina did. For instance, Sunbonnet Baby Salad. To achieve this, you establish canned pear halves round side up on lettuce leaves (which curl closely about the pear to make the sunbonnet, you see). Then you plant cloves for eyes, blanched almonds for ears, and you push thin slices of canned pimiento into slits you've made for the nose and mouth. And for Valentine's Day, Bettina would major in—you'll never guess—hearts: heart-shaped baking-powder biscuits, heart-shaped date-bread sandwiches (this girl was very big on date-bread sandwiches), heart-shaped ice cream with individual heart-shaped cakes. . . .

My mother didn't cook this way though. I think she kept *A Thousand Ways* more as a literary curiosity than a working cookbook. About the only thing she used it for was the Brown Betty recipe. That page is well freckled with something—cinnamon or age spots—for Mama made it a lot. The recipe is annotated: "better with some chopped nuts."

Basically, my mother was what they call a "good plain cook," a phrase that always gives me a mental picture of some homely aproned woman singing hymns. But that wasn't my mother. My mother was a tall, quick-moving, capable, warm, and often funny lady who cooked for as long as she had to—as long as there was someone to cook for, that is—and then stopped cold.

Like that. There are ways to get along in this world without cooking, and I'm sure Mama knew them all. (Even in her cooking days, her heart wasn't truly in it. Her heart was at Innisfree, for the most part, before it moved to Lambaréné. She had positioned William Butler Yeats at one side of the heavenly throne, with Albert Schweitzer holding down the other, and Escoffier nowhere in sight.)

I have always loved my mother and admired her many outstanding qualities, not least among which was a certain bulldog determination when doing something she considered worth doing. At age seventy-nine, in San Francisco's most decorous music store, where the other customers were probably hunting some esoteric little thing of Vivaldi's, my mother had the nerve to ask if they could find for her a recording of "Too Pooped to Pop." This was Arthur Godfrey's song about the little popcorn kernel who was so tired he could only sit there, and Mama wanted it as a warning for me, because she thought I was working too hard. (Mothers always think you are working either too hard or not hard enough.) They managed to find it for her, too.

But, as I was about to explain, my mother cooked good plain food, as nearly everyone else did in McKinleyville, for this was during Prohibition, before the inland colonies had discovered Europe and vice versa: before the quiche and the crêpe, the fondue and the pizza, the *sabayon* and the coq au vin.

Kitchens were different then, too—not only what came out of them, but their smells and sounds. A hot pie cooling smells different from a frozen pie thawing. Oilcloth and

linoleum and apples in an open bowl and ruffled rubber
aprons make a different aromatic mix from Formica and
ceramic tile and mangoes in an acrylic fruit-ripener and
plasticoated aprons printed with "Who invited all these
tacky people?" Yes, and tea towels that say "I'd rather play
tennis" and potholders that say "Kiss the cook." (Indeed,
future archeologists, sifting artifacts, may well ponder the
fierce urge to sound off, today, not only in the kitchen, but
everywhere else. I don't remember any bumper stickers when
I was growing up. Mail Pouch Tobacco on barns, maybe,
and politicians on telephone poles, but no inspirational or
proselytizing signs on cars. No one felt impelled to affirm
publicly that he loved Jesus or whales or redwood trees, perhaps because of the unquestioned assumption that there was
enough of each to go around and would continue to be for
the foreseeable future.)

And the kitchen sounds. I am not sure that today's kitchen
is noisier. But the noises are different. Today you get the
song of the food processor and the blender, the intermittent
hum of the reefer and the freezer, the buzz-slosh-and-grunt
of the dishwasher, the violently audible digestive processes
of the waste disposer in the sink. Then it was the whir and
clatter of the hand-powered eggbeater, the thunk-thunk-
thunk of somebody mashing potatoes, or, in green-pea season,
the crisp pop of a pea pod and the rattle-rattle-rattle of peas
into the pan. Outdoor noises are a part of the difference, too.
This was back when lawn mowers made a sociable clattery
chirrrr instead of the loud nerve-grinding growl you get with
the power kind.

As to food, while I was growing up I think Mama cooked
mainly what her mother had cooked: creamed chipped beef
on toast, corn chowder, pork chops, baked beans. Roast beef
(well done) and roast-beef hash. Chicken, chicken croquettes,
meat loaf, salmon loaf, ham and ham loaf; and if it happened to be the third time around for something, Mama
would generally cover it up with cheese sauce. "That good
meat loaf in a nice cheese sauce," she would say hopefully,

when queried as to what's for dinner; and I've heard myself using the same con about last night's green beans, say, if I plan on re-serving them this evening.

Salads weren't tossed and green, either. They were grated-carrot-on-cream-cheese-on-pineapple-on-iceberg-lettuce, or pecans-on-mayonnaise-on-banana-half-on-iceberg-lettuce (see Sunbonnet Baby, earlier), or possibly an apple-celery-nut-mayonnaise Waldorf, or—once in a very blue moon—a square of tomato aspic full of chopped celery and sliced stuffed olives.

What we eat these days is different—there isn't a doubt of it—thanks to time and travel, wars and technology, viticulture and television. A great many of us are more knowledgeable about food than our parents were.

And yet, looking at the glossy and expert food magazines that adorn our coffee tables, I can't help feeling that groups of culinary overachievers are happily editing them for each other. Normal people wouldn't make that much of a to-do over green peppercorns and grated raw vegetables and whether *carpaccio* is in or out. And they do beautiful things with pork throat and tabbouleh, and they serve their mignonettes of veal lapped round with crayfish sauce. . . .

Meanwhile, back at the ranch, business seems to go on about as usual, in less rarefied air. The rest of us cook fairly simply, with the exception of a few special things we've developed or mastered—dishes that take a bit more trouble than they're worth to cook for people we want to confuse into thinking we are more expert than we are. And should a guest marvel at the production and the time it surely took, one is supposed to say with a silvery laugh, "Oh, heavens, no, I just whipped it up. After all, I didn't leave the operating theater (courtroom, board room) till after five. . . ." This is known as Women's Rites.

And frozen items continue to sell the way hot cakes never did, and so do refrigerated biscuits, ready-mixed piecrust, ready-grated Parmesan, prepared salad dressings, and other heinous products.

The other day I was grocery shopping with a good friend who is also a good cook and a well-equipped one, with everything from barquette pans to a well-seasoned wok. I asked idly what she planned to serve the family that night.

"Pork chops," she said.

"How will you cook them?" I asked.

"Oh . . . pan-fried, I think," she said. "Maybe with some apples, and that good frozen spinach soufflé, and custard for dessert. . . ."

Well, custard. That's something else Mama cooked. Indeed, her desserts were as basic as the other things: fruit pie, mince pie, pumpkin pie; sponge cake, gingerbread, hermits, rocks, fudge cake; baked apples, prune whip, floating island, tapioca, ambrosia, rice pudding, and, as I have said, Bettina's Brown Betty, which naturally became known in our family as Brown Bettina.

Brown Bettina with hard sauce. To me, that's soul food. These days, I put Triple Sec in the hard sauce instead of vanilla, if I have some Triple Sec, but it is still soul food, and evocative soul food, too. It is almost inextricably bound up with my fifth-grade classmate Lucille Brueggeman, because it is the dessert we usually had, at my earnest request, on those rare occasions when Lucille's mother would let her come to dinner and stay all night. I say rare, because Lucille's home responsibilities were so many and so demanding that we generally had to play at her house instead of mine.

Brown Bettina in the rainbow-glass dishes. I can see it now, plain as plain, the warm pudding topped with a generous dollop of hard sauce beginning to melt and run down, like snow on a mountain on a warm June day. Possibly two dollops of hard sauce if you happened to be on good terms with the cook. (Mama was nice about that.)

I can see Lucille Brueggeman, too, with her taffy-colored braids and her small triangular freckled face and the gray gummy-looking braces on her teeth. Hers was the first tin grin in the whole fifth-grade class.

In fact, I saw Lucille Brueggeman yesterday—thought I did, anyway, in one of those aberrational split seconds that can erase five decades like a damp sponge down a blackboard. There she was in our little Hawaiian county library, same face, braces, braids, skinny sloping shoulders, but wearing khaki cutoffs, Adidas, and a T-shirt that said "I Got Lei'd Today," which I suppose is what jolted me back into the 1980s. Then I realized they've probably just run out of patterns for people now, and are beginning to repeat them over and over.

But, as I was saying, Brown Bettina, and lamb chops. These are the delicacies I insisted that Mama cook when Lucille came, since nothing was too good for Lucille, and since this, in my estimation, was one classy menu, a dinner fit for a gourmet (or so I'd have said if I'd ever heard of a gourmet, which I had not), though unfortunately there always had to be an accompanying vegetable, probably carrots-and-peas.

In McKinleyville, when you said carrots, you had to say peas right after or you'd have bad luck all day. Peas went with carrots as infallibly as ham went with eggs. For years I thought carrots and peas grew on the same vine. Usually they came creamed, as did most vegetables. Apparently the rule was, if you can cook it, you can cream it, so do it. Cream your potatoes, your turnips, your celery, your string beans, your cabbage, your cauliflower, your carrots-and-peas.

I learned much later, incidentally, that Lucille would probably have considered macaroni and cheese a real treat instead of the lamb chops, because her father had the meat-market concession at Piggly Wiggly. The family often had to eat up what hadn't sold, and I think Lucille went vegetarian at about age sixteen.

She was very polite, though, never said boo about the chops, was stoic about the carrots-and-peas, as we all were, and I know she liked the Brown Bettina. And the reason this mattered so much—the reason I wanted her to be happy—was that she was my best friend. Ever since Florence and I had gone finally and irreversibly *Phffft,* Lucille and I had been inseparable every chance we got; and I think this may be as good a place as any to recount briefly an episode we shared, which was at least a step forward in our continuing education.

I don't mean to imply that Lucille and I were pursuing with any degree of vigor the sex research that Florence and

I had begun. In fact, it was undergoing a definite phase-down. So far as sex research went, I had shot my wad, at least for the time being. That day of nerving myself for the confrontation with Miss Williams that never happened had taken something out of me, and I was discouraged.

So was Lucille, as I learned early in our acquaintance, the afternoon we were pooling our ignorance about these things. It was, after all, her own older married sister, as I believe I mentioned earlier, who had told her this preposterous stuff about how babies start (though it actually did turn out to be the straight dope).

But we didn't believe it, and as Lucille said that afternoon, if you can't trust your own sister on a thing like that, who can you trust? And even though Lucille's father was knowledgeable about animals—a point I'm coming to in a minute—he was a fair-haired Nordic type who blushed easily and rosily about all sorts of things. Somehow I just didn't think we could expect much hard news sexwise out of Mr. Brueggeman.

No, I am referring to an occasion in the small hours of a cold morning at Lucille's house, when Genevieve the Gerbil gave birth and we were there to watch. It was, as they put it now, a learning experience.

But let me say this about learning experiences: they're weird. Or put it this way: what you learn from a learning experience is generally something else. And the animal situation at the Brueggeman place was a case in point.

The thing is, Mr. Brueggeman just loved animals, and he had a houseful.

As I look back on it now, this seems rather odd—I mean, for a butcher and all—though I don't think I wondered about it then. It may have been that he kept and pampered all these pets as reparation of a sort for all the chops and cutlets he had authored in his time (and would presumably continue to author into the foreseeable future). Too, he probably put dogs and cats and birds in another, quite different, category, painwise or miserywise, from cows and chickens and pigs, as indeed most of us do. (I was recently faced with a Chinese menu featuring Steamed Cat Dumplings and Dog-meat Curry, which gave me rather a turn, though the boiled beef tongue I had had for dinner the previous evening hadn't bothered me at all.)

Or perhaps he actually believed what he so often said, that pets are very good for children and teach them all kinds of valuable things.

I suppose that's one way to look at it. Maybe they do. I know they taught Lucille something, all right—namely, the wisdom of staying after school in the band room nearly every day to practice the tuba. It was a Brueggeman house rule that whoever got home first had to clean up after the animals, and, accordingly, no one ever got home first. Except Mrs. Brueggeman, that is. The children saw to it that they had something to practice at school, music and sports being the only excuses allowed for not coming straight home. (Lucille's brother became an excellent all-around athlete, too.)

I've thought, since then, that the Brueggemans may have stumbled quite by accident upon one of the great, basic child-rearing principles: even wholesome, community-approved activities can look good to the child if the chores the child would otherwise have to be doing are sufficiently cruddy.

Lucille's mother was a small graying woman with a hunted look. I remember her as forever scuttling around with mops and wet rags to wipe something up with, or else burning a length of twine tied to a dangling light bulb. This was before the world went all dainty and deodorant-minded, but you still had to do something when you had a basement full of dogs—Agnes the Airedale was remarkably prolific—plus seven or eight cats, three large and well-populated birdcages, and a gerbil box, jocularly named by Mr. Brueggeman "the Gerbilarium."

So it is no wonder Lucille became proficient on the tuba. When I went home with her, there was always a small smelly mountain of newspapers to be changed, and numerous containers to be cleaned out before we could buckle down to our own various pursuits.

All in all, though, I enjoyed visiting the Brueggemans and staying the night there, because Lucille and I always had a good time. The only minus factor besides the cleanup work was the grapefruit we would usually have the next morning. Mrs. Brueggeman didn't know how to cut a grapefruit—apparently didn't know it was supposed to be cut, into sections, I mean. Or perhaps I just didn't know how to eat one; there was always that disturbing possibility. It's true that I seemed to be the only one getting an eyeful and frontful every time I stuck the spoon in (because all Mrs. B. did was cut the grapefruit in half, and from then on you were on your own). I always headed for school with my dress-front sticky. But this was a minor matter. . . .

Lucille's and my special projects at this time were pasting up a World Scrapbook and cooking. This scrapbook was to contain everything important in the whole world and be buried in the back yard, so that when the world ended, we would still have left our mark. (Some crazy prophet was always getting newspaper space for predicting the end of the world day after tomorrow, and we always believed him, though in a comfortable sort of way.)

As for the cooking we did, it was, every once in a while, dinner. Looking back now, I am amazed that Mrs. Brueggeman would occasionally let us (we considered it a great privilege), and I am even more amazed that the family ate what we cooked. But cooking there was always interesting because, as I have said, Mr. Brueggeman generally brought home whatever hadn't sold, if it looked about to go west, and he could always tell.

So you never knew in advance what you'd have to work with. We would make strange meat loaves, odds and ends of anything, often involving peanut butter, for we thought a touch of peanut butter improved anything, the way some people feel about a touch of curry. We, too, creamed whatever was creamable, in order to serve it in patty shells, once we learned how to make patty shells. And we were inventive with casseroles. I especially remember one improbable production, a beef-liver-and-cauliflower medley that was about as appetizing as a train wreck. But the Brueggemans were staunch folk.

And we invariably made fudge. Making fudge was stand-ard operating procedure, then, when you stayed overnight with anyone. We would personally hand one small token piece to each parent, before taking the rest up to polish off in bed.

So that's what we were doing at about eight o'clock on what I always remembered thereafter as Gerbil Night—mak-ing fudge, or, more accurately, arguing about whether to pour the fudge we'd just made into a square buttered brownie pan or onto a round buttered plate. And that's when Mr. Brueggeman came rushing into the kitchen with the big news. Genevieve the Gerbil, their first, one and only, female gerbil at this point, would undoubtedly be producing her first litter before morning. There were signs, he said mysteri-ously. Signs.

Well, it's no wonder Mr. Brueggeman was excited. I had noticed before that he seemed to be really freaked out on motherhood. He was forever telling us about various kinds of animal mothers and their cute tricks. Mr. Brueggeman was an extremely enthusiastic man anyway, always bubbling. He walked with an extraordinary coiled-spring bounce, and he talked so explosively he spattered, which is why my mother didn't buy her meat there—said she didn't want him spitting all over her chops.

But I can see him now, all aglow, clean and jolly, pink and white, his scalp blushing rosily through his white-blond hair as he described all these mothers: mother whales balanc-ing their new babies on their noses to start them breathing, mother honkers shedding their flight feathers so they can't even fly for weeks, mother hens turning their eggs over every day so they'll hatch right, mother kangaroos letting their little joeys live in the old family pouch for months and months, mother rabbits gnawing the fur right off their own fuzzy chests to line a nest with . . . all this and much, much more.

It was mildly interesting. At least I thought so at the time, though Lucille had heard it frequently before. Her father did repeat himself a lot.

Anyway, on this particular evening, Lucille had no trouble restraining her enthusiasm at the prospect of more gerbils to clean up after, and I wasn't too excited about seeing them get born either. I didn't care how gerbils produced gerbils, I just wanted to know how people produced people; and people had little to do with gerbils that I could see, except in a custodial or janitorial capacity. Genevieve could have her babies hanging by her tail and whistling "Dixie," for all I cared, though I was too polite to say so. In fact, I lied with a promptness and credibility that I'm sure was a credit to my parents. Be sure you wake us up if she starts having her babies, I said, dutiful little apple polisher that I was. No matter *what* time. Yes, *sir!*

Well. He did, all right. You just better believe it. At half past three in the morning—I could see the clock's luminous dial—Mr. Brueggeman rapped on our door, then opened it, stuck his head in, and bounced on tippy-toe into the bedroom.

"Hurry up!" he whispered. "Genevieve's a mother! Two already and more on the way!"

"We'll be right there," I whispered back as he hustled out. Then I nudged and poked Lucille, who was a good sound sleeper.

Eventually and blurrily we found robes and slippers, for it was a cold night, and descended to the dazzling-bright kitchen. The big ceiling light was on, and Mr. Brueggeman was over by the Gerbilarium, looking into its depths. Just as we came in, he looked up, his astonished face brick red.

"Jesus!" he said. "She's eating 'em!"

Well, I was shocked. He shouldn't have said Jesus like that. But, fascinated, Lucille and I tiptoed over to the big box and stared, following the flashlight beam into the darkest corner. And, sure enough, there was Genevieve, sedately breakfasting on her babies, a tiny last bit of one disappearing into her mouth as we watched, and three wee purplish sacs remaining at her feet.

As we watched, she nosed around and started to ingest

another. The corner in which she sat was quite bare, I noticed. None of the usual pellets and shreds of paper. Maybe she'd eaten all that, too.

"There were five," Mr. Brueggeman said hoarsely. "Five, I think, maybe six . . ."

Lucille and I looked at each other. "Oh, wow," or so we'd have thought if people had been thinking "Oh, wow" then. Or "Shit oh dear," which has always seemed to me to show a nice blend of surprise with mild concern, but people weren't into that yet either.

"Oh, my," I said, finally. Then Lucille poked me, and we started to giggle, embarrassed for Mr. Brueggeman and maybe a little for Genevieve, too. Then we more or less backed out the door and hightailed it upstairs.

But I must say, I was impressed.

By Genevieve's appetite, for one thing. You wouldn't have thought she'd have had room! And, for another thing, her tidiness. She really won the big N for Neatness. Why, she'd been neater about this whole complicated business than she'd ever been in her ordinary day-in day-out living, which was always pretty messy; and you had to admire this, though I suppose we can all rise to a crisis and be neat if we have to. There was also an admirable self-sufficiency about it. A functioning closed ecosystem, I suppose they'd call it now.

And so Lucille and I went back to bed, where we finished the rest of the fudge. We also decided that I was right about the merits of a square pan. That is, Lucille finally admitted I was right, for I had known it all along. When you pour fudge into a square brownie pan, all the pieces come out square and true, if you cut neatly. But on a round plate you'll always get those silly-shaped pieces at the edge of the circle, which makes the fudge harder to divide.

As for that early-morning biology session, whether or not we learned from Genevieve whatever it was we were supposed to learn, I don't know. I suppose several lessons could have been drawn from it. Like, you don't always do a thing right the first time. (I had noticed this myself, my first time out with finger bowls.) Or like, keep your cool, no matter what.

Genevieve had shown admirable poise, especially for such a public *accouchement*.

Certainly I drew no antimaternal Philip Wylie-esque conclusions; I am sure of that. I did, however, find the spectacle unique. As someone remarked years later about sex, that there's nothing like it—some things better, some things worse, but nothing *like* it—I think I'd have said there was nothing quite like motherhood either; this was my distinct impression. And having been a mother myself now for a fair number of years, I can't say I've turned up any evidence yet to contradict it.

6

A Pride of Crumpets

*or Little Lessons from
Everyday Life*

I have frequently reflected that if there is one thing well calculated to win you a poke in the mouth if not a one-way ticket to the Bermuda Triangle, it is complaining about an overabundance of something that most people haven't enough of.

Watching a television talk show the other day while an entirely gorgeous actress-model was complaining of all the problems you have when you are an entirely gorgeous actress-model, I was able to control my sobs. I felt the same way, too, about a millionaire's autobiography I leafed through recently. Oceans of money, he had; money coming out of his ears, money out the kazoo (as we say in Hawaii), or money (as we would have put it in McKinleyville) up the gum stump, though such was our hero's nobility of character that he wasn't about to lay any of his burden on anyone else. Yet he, too, was asking for sympathy, and, as I say, these things can be hard to put up with politely.

As a consequence, I know that I tread on delicate ground when I say that we are somewhat oversupplied with drawer space in our new kitchen.

"Room to put things in," we had asked of Uwe. And Uwe had come through gallantly indeed, with colors flying and with twenty-two—count them—kitchen drawers. At least, that was the number according to my husband's latest survey. I didn't ask for a recount for fear he'd find another one, and, as it is, I may never see the barbecue skewers again.

The trouble is, of course, that we now have twenty-two drawers to lose things among instead of our former three. With three it had been fairly simple. I knew that if my favorite big wooden spoon wasn't in a bowl or a pot stirring something, it was soaking in the sink or it was reposing in one of the three drawers or else on the counter top, in plain sight.

But now it is apt to be anywhere. In the top drawer nearest the stove because it's good for stirring soup. Or in the big side drawer where the bread pans are because it's good for mixing dough. Or in the drawer where the other big spoons and the soup ladle are supposed to be because this, too, has a certain logic, depending on how I'm feeling as I put things away. Or in any of the eighteen drawers remaining; and one brown oak drawer-front looks remarkably like another.

Having duplicate tools is no real help either. How often can you find an exact duplicate? There is always a favorite— one spoon that fits the hand the best, one bowl that's the perfect size for nearly anything, one knife that stays the sharpest. . . . It's like recipes. Though I have several different recipes for a cheese soufflé, a lemon pudding, whole-wheat bread, and so on, there is always one that I like far and away the best. So why don't I edit the file and throw away the also-rans? Beats me.

At any rate, I know I should do something intelligent about the drawer situation before too long: take strong affirmative action and declare that the eggbeater lives *here*, the big wooden spoon lives *here*. If I don't, they are going to freeze in place one of these days—an illogical place, more than likely—and stay there. Things will do that.

Well, hard cheese. I'll tell it to the chaplain.

What occasioned my thinking along these lines was six crumpet rings that surfaced the other day, after an absence of several months. I found them in residence at the back of a drawer containing mainly bottle openers and nutpicks. (Other people cook and clean up in my kitchen sometimes, because we let our occasional house guests fend for themselves for breakfast and lunch. Although I lose some items this way, it is better than being a nonstop short-order cook, and things seldom stay lost for keeps.)

It was nice to see my crumpet rings again, though I can't say I missed them. Crumpet rings are not something I use every day in the week. But just putting them away with the muffin tins had me thinking about crumpets. Specifically, it had me remembering with great clarity my first taste of a hot buttered one, at my piano teacher's tea table, some eons ago in McKinleyville, as well as the somewhat painful developments that preceded that memorable moment. And here I must digress a little.

It has often occurred to me that most people experience at least once in a lifetime what I think of as the Aha Reaction. To something. To a paintbrush or a scalpel, a book or a printing press, a tennis racquet or an eggbeater or a miter box—to any of a thousand different things. At the very first sight of this whatever-it-is, there is a gut feeling of "Aha! I bet I can do something with *that*." And it generally turns out that they can, and do. It may take time. Then again, it may not. Sometimes, only a couple of practice dips and a side roll and they're heading for Paris.

It is also possible, unfortunately, to mistake fox-fire for the true blaze; to mistake for an Aha what is in reality only a Ho-hum.

This is the way it was with me and the piano in the fifth grade. I had long admired the flair and sparkle that our school music teacher brought to the keyboard every Monday afternoon. I had also swallowed whole those magazine ads in which they laughed when somebody sat down to the piano (I couldn't know how prophetic this part was, in my case), only to listen in hushed awe as the somebody swung into a glorious cadenza or some smashing jazz. Wow. I couldn't wait. This was for me. I had the piano bug bad. I *had* to learn how to play the thing.

And so, because I wouldn't shut up about wanting one, and also, I suppose, because a piano was a nice respectable object to have around, tangible and audible evidence of culture in the home, my parents bought a big black upright. And it took me approximately thirty seconds after it hit the house to realize that I didn't want any part of it; that it would, moreover, take me approximately three hundred years of hard practice before I'd ever be able to make any kind of a decent noise on it. And the heck with it.

That's what *I* thought.

Not so, my parents. You wanted a piano, you've got a piano, now learn to play it, was their uncompromising position. A favorite expression of my father's was, "When you say A, you've got to say B."

I didn't exactly see why. Couldn't you just say, "Excuse it, please, I was only kidding," and let B go hang?

Apparently not. And B, in this instance, meant piano lessons from Mrs. Smedley, who was McKinleyville's piano teacher.

It would be hard, I think, to devise a program of piano instruction more likely to instill a loathing of the piano* in the child than Mrs. Smedley's, particularly if the child happened to be predisposed in that direction anyway. The main reason was Czerny.

Czerny, Karl Czerny, was the distinguished Austrian pian-

* To this day I even hate the way a piano looks. There is nothing uglier than an upright piano except a grand piano. If you ever noticed, gazing down from the second balcony, say, onto a closed grand piano, it looks just like a big piece of liver.

ist and composer who composed, among other things, piano exercises that Mrs. Smedley just loved. Czerny taught Liszt and Thalberg, but he didn't teach me. Every Wednesday afternoon I tripped, stumbled, flailed about, and eventually spread-eagled all over his *School of Fingering,* an exercise book bound in dullest pale green and full of sixteenth notes. Sixteeenth notes are the fast ones. They have to be played thirty-two times faster than half notes, which you didn't run into very often in Czerny, and they had to be played, always, to the infernal Chinese water torture of the ever-ticking metronome.

Mrs. Smedley herself was all right, actually. She was a short pouter pigeon of a middle-aged lady with a complicated coiffeur, a face like a rosy wrinkled persimmon, and pretty little hands with tapered fingers. She also had considerable patience.

Piano lessons at Mrs. Smedley's were held in her small darkish living room. Darkish and cool, and on the mantel was an ormolu clock with the world's slowest minute hand. Above the mantel hung Franz Hals's *Laughing Cavalier,* and I knew why he was laughing, all right—he wasn't taking a piano lesson; you were.

There was also a baby grand piano, at which you sat. On its high right-hand shelf was the metronome, and on its high left-hand shelf was a taffy-colored bust of Beethoven, regarding you with what seemed to be nausea.

This living room, or music room, was separated from Mrs. Smedley's dining room by floor-to-ceiling velvet draperies, which were called—I had it on good authority from an older pupil—pore-tears. And the Smedleys were undoubtedly rich, for not only did they have pore-tears, but they also had a maid, a bumpy-faced girl named Mary, from the country, which meant nearby. (Go a few blocks in any direction, then, and you were fresh out of McKinleyville.)

She was a real maid, though, no doubt of it, because, afternoons, she always wore a black dress with white collar and cuffs, just like in the movies.

Mary was the first maid in my somewhat limited experience, and the infrequent times she came into the music room during my lesson would have thrown me quite off my stride had I had one. As it was, I would just stop and start over, which I was forever doing anyway.

I thought a lot about Mary when I should have been concentrating on things like keeping the fourth knuckle of each hand—that's the pinky knuckle—higher than the other knuckles as I played, which is an anatomically abnormal, if not impossible, thing to do. Mrs. Smedley could do it and her daughter could do it and I was sure they were the only two people in the world who *could* do it.

However, this maid business opened my eyes to another and finer world. Imagine! I could see it plain as day. You'd never have to pick up your pajamas or make your bed or clean up the mess you made in the sink or anywhere else. I would live in a long blue satin housecoat; I could see that, too, in rich detail, the slithery blue gleam of it as I snuggled into the chaise longue, which our house didn't contain one of either.

"Bring me a peanut butter sandwich," I would say, "and a chocolate malted, please." And when she brought them, I would thank her. I would always be polite, I decided. Polite but firm.

"Why don't we have a maid?" I asked my mother.

"Oh, heavens, I couldn't stand having somebody underfoot all the time," she said briskly.

I didn't see why she'd have to be underfoot all the time or even any of the time. She'd be somewhere doing the dirty work while we were somewhere else having fun is the way I read it. I knew better than to argue with my mother, of course, at least over things like that. Still, when I saw Mrs. Smedley's Mary bustling around with her feather duster, and, most of all, when I saw her setting the tea table in the dining room behind those velvet curtains, as I was on my way to the bathroom, I could see what a lot we were missing. (Mrs. Smedley must have thought I had a real bladder dysfunction, because once I became aware of the tea table I went to the bathroom a lot.)

That tea table was something. It is true that this was my first acquaintance with a tea table. Indeed, it came as news to me that certain people sat down to drink tea and eat good things *at five o'clock in the afternoon*. (Didn't they know it would spoil their appetites? Or didn't they care? And if not, how perfectly splendid!)

However, as I recall that tea table now, it seems to stand up nicely beside all the tea tables I've seen since. It didn't groan, it purred fatly under its luscious load of cakes and little sandwiches.

I learned later that it was Mrs. Smedley's glamorous widowed daughter who was mainly responsible for these wonders. This daughter, a Mrs. Smedley-Cowles, had married an Englishman, who was killed in the war, the one they call the Great War. She had studied piano in Europe, even played on the concert stage, before she came back to McKinleyville to live near her mother. And besides being an accomplished pianist, she loved to bake, specifically English things: scones, plum cakes, shortbread. And crumpets, which were usually heaped high in a shallow silver bowl, toasted, with melted butter filling up all the little craters, all ready to be loaded with strawberry preserves. How come I knew they were crumpets and what you did to them is that one Wednesday afternoon I forgot my music case. When I went back for it, I caught Mr. Smedley applying a great dollop of jam to one of them, and he said, "I do like a little crumpet with my jam."

But he didn't offer me anything—not from stinginess, I am sure; it just didn't occur to him. He was a little wafty anyway, an odd, benign, and elderly gentleman who moved tentatively about with a cane. He had a great many wrinkles but his hair was jet black—a toupee, as I learned later, because once it was on backwards when he came into the music room. Mrs. Smedley had hurried him out on that occasion, and when he came back in, he looked like he always did, which is how I knew.

Now, this tea table wasn't set for Smedleys exclusively, as a rule. I had heard from older pupils that if your lesson had been an exceptionally good one, you would quite possibly be invited to stay (or come back) for tea.

But this was nowhere in my horoscope. Indeed, there was no danger whatsoever of my ever having a good lesson, let alone an exceptionally good lesson. How could I possibly have a good lesson? Most weeks, I hadn't touched the piano since leaving Mrs. Smedley's the last time. Due to circumstances completely within my control, I never practiced; I just lied a lot.

"Did you do your practicing?" my mother would ask.

"Yes," I would say.

"When?"

And I would name a time when she had been away from the house. Or "After school, on the gym piano," I'd say. Craftily, too, I would ask her for permission to practice at times when I knew she wanted to listen to the radio undisturbed, like Dr. Fosdick time on Sunday afternoons. "Can't you wait till later, honey?" she would ask. And later, feeling remiss for having put me off, or perhaps just forgetting, she like as not wouldn't pursue it.

Thus, wholly unprepared and unarmed except for wild optimism and uncommon nerve, I'd go to the weekly Wednesday afternoon lesson, hoping (with an eye to the tea table) for a good one, which it never was. Half the time Mrs. Smedley was disappointed and the other half annoyed. Either way, I felt bad about it and I would leave full of resolve: a whole hour's practice, without fail, *every day*. But resolution was fleeting. By the time I got home I didn't care doodelysquat, and next Wednesday would be just like always.

I have reflected, since then, that Mrs. Smedley's glamorous piano-playing daughter was undoubtedly another cause, however unwitting, of my total inadequacy at the Steinway. For it was Mrs. Smedley's custom to have her daughter perform for you, at least once, whatever piece of music you were currently working on, so you would know how it was supposed to sound. (God knows you'd never find out from listening to yourself.) And Mrs. Smedley simply wanted to give us a standard of excellence to aim at, I am sure, like the farmer putting the ostrich egg in the henhouse.

However, with me it worked in reverse. The same fire that hardens the egg will melt the butter; and much depends on the personality type, whether you customarily rise to a challenge or whether you sink. For as long as I can remember, I have been a sinker. One challenge, and I drop like a rock.

Accordingly, this flashy lady was all I needed. Drama, emotion, verve—Mrs. Smedley-Cowles had them all, and she played with a bravura that had to be seen and heard to be believed. Also I knew *I'd* never have those marvelous long incredibly agile fingers, those sparkling rings, that heaving bosom, that gorgeous pile of auburn hair, let alone that total command of the keyboard.

Flash, crash, ripple, smash! And she never had to look to see what her hands were doing (because they were always doing the right things, that's why), never had to stop and start over, stop-and-start-over, stop-and-start-over. . . .

Which was, as I have mentioned, my basic style. But please believe me when I say that stopping and starting over isn't nearly so bad as not ever being able to stop in the first place, as I learned at the Spring Recital in the Presbyterian Church, the awful afternoon that lived in my mind as the Day Opal Quit and I Couldn't.

All right. Recitals.

Now, everyone is entitled to his own personal opinion as to what was the worst part of being a child; and indeed there are numerous contenders.

Perhaps it was always having to eat what They said you should eat. Or always having to live by Their time clocks, not your own. Or it may have been physical education, and the gummy feel of the hockey-stick handles, and the funky smell of the showers.

Or perhaps you'd nominate one of the good old-fashioned family remedies for one of the good old-fashioned family ailments, like the common cold. For instance, our own family specialized in a head-cold therapy originated, I believe, by the Marquis de Sade. First, they'd pump saltwater up your nose till the entire sinus cavity was an open wound. Now it was all ready for the big syringeful of evil, black, stinging Argyrol they'd shoot up there next, till it ran dark and bitter and metallic down your throat and you'd spit black for days.

Still, on my own list, I suppose the first worst would be that cruel and unusual punishment known as the Piano Recital. One of the loveliest things about being grown up is the knowledge that never again will I have to go through the miserable business of performing in Mrs. Smedley's Annual Piano Recital at McKinleyville's First Presbyterian Church.

"Why do we have to have dumb recitals?" I remember asking my Idaho grandmother, who was visiting us as D-day grew near.

"So you can become accustomed to playing for people, dear," she said.

"But I'm never going to play for people, Grandma," I said.

"Of course you will," she said. In her era, young ladies would entertain the assembled company after dinner with "Swanee River" or "Flow Gently," and who says there's anything wrong with television? "That is the main reason you are learning the piano, dear—to give pleasure."

Well, though I loved my grandmother, I recognized this for the twaddle it was. I was fully aware that the only thing about my piano playing that gave pleasure was that longed-for moment when I stopped. And, as I say, when I found myself in the truly hellish position of not being *able* to stop . . .

Cut now to an interior shot, First Presbyterian Church, on the particular spring Saturday afternoon under discussion.

Two large dank funeral ferns hold down the two front corners of the small platform brought in for the occasion. The pulpit, now sporting a sizable cut-glass bowl of big red flowers, has been moved ten feet due west to make room for the grand piano. A few latecomers straggle down the aisle now to find places beside the punctual parents and other relatives already seated and looking like Death Row. And here is Mrs. Smedley, opulent in brown chiffon with a brown glass-bead bodice, and here is Mrs. Smedley-Cowles, too, suave in mauve velvet with a great many gold chains.

As I remember, there were sixteen pupils in all, five of us in the Lower-Intermediate Group: Freem Fuller, Opal Henking, Ellen Bishop, Barry O'Donnell, and me.

We performers sat in the two front rows, where Barry kept us in stitches, of course, with his various drolleries. He was a year older now, as we all were, and still Terrible. Freem Fuller had discovered in the nick of time that afternoon the PLEASE KICK ME HARD sign that Barry had managed to stick on the seat of his pants. Now Barry was sailing paper airplanes he made out of the recital programs and asking whoever showed up if they'd like to occupew the pie.

So we were laughing, as I say, at least as hard as you can laugh when you have a terminal case of the clammy-damps and a herd of butterflies kicking holes in the lining of your stomach. What if you *forgot?* That was the most terrible and the likeliest possibility, for Mrs. Smedley was a purist who allowed no music on the stand.

If for none other than humanitarian reasons, I should have been first up. Logically, too, this was indicated, because I was such an easy act to follow. Next to me, anyone looked good. But it was more equitable, Mrs. Smedley felt, for us to draw numbers out of a bowl. So we did that, and I drew —wouldn't you know?—Number 5, with the first spot going to Freem Fuller.

Freem got us off to a roaring start. He was an intense black-haired boy with a wild cowlick and big ears. At school he did everything hard—ran hard, talked hard, pressed so hard on the blackboard he'd break the chalk, sat down so hard it rattled the whole bolted-together row of desks, and he probably had ulcers by age twelve. Anyway, Freem lit into the "Marche Militaire" like he expected a counterattack, and it never had a prayer. The audience clapped loud and long.

Barry O'Donnell was next, and he was okay—just dashed off whatever it was, plenty of mistakes but *he* didn't care. And then, fittingly enough, came Ellen Bishop, looking so pretty in her white net dress over a pink slip *with silk pumps dyed to match the slip* that she could have just sat and picked her nose and made a hit. But of course she didn't; she played a very pretty little tune, maybe "The Primrose Waltz," and played it very prettily, too.

Well, and then came Opal. Opal Henking. She was the one from the Ozarks. Opal was chunkily built, and she had several natural talents like rope skipping and Junior Traffic Patrol, though piano playing wasn't among them, any more than it was among mine. But she tried harder. (She actually *did* practice on the school gym piano.)

Today, however, was not Opal's day. Or perhaps it was, at that; her day to—at least—take a stand.

Her selection was "A Day in Venice" by—well, by whoever wrote "A Day in Venice." And she was well into it, doing all right with the expression, the pauses, the trilly parts, when—suddenly—she drew a blank.

Stopped.

Frowned.

Lifted her hands from the keyboard.

Started over, and this time she covered only a half-dozen measures before she stopped again. And scowled at the audience. "A Day in Venice" had segued right into an afternoon in McKinleyville.

"I can't do it," she muttered. And slid off the piano bench. And stalked away, out the back door, presumably, and home.

Well! There was a collective gasp from us kids. This was unheard of. Because whatever you did, you didn't quit. Quitting was—well, you just didn't quit, that's all. *Quitter* was the dirtiest word in the book, and stick-to-itiveness was the godliest, in every one of the heroic tales we had been suckled on.

The little Dutch boy, remember? He'd keep his finger in the hole in the dike in all that freezing water, just forever. And Elsie Dinsmore, sitting on the piano bench, that day when her sacrilegious father insisted that she play the piano on the Sabbath—just sitting there till she fainted (all frail and pale and adorable). *She'd* hung in there. Yes, and Robert

Bruce, who learned perseverance from the patient spider, then went out and licked the British. Try, try again. Everybody said that, all the time. Trying was a good thing. Quitting was a crummy thing.

Yet Opal had quit. And even walked off. We couldn't believe it. And we couldn't keep from sneaking a peek at her mother and father either, their faces turning a dull red as they stood up, to walk stiffly back up the aisle and out. Oh, boy, would Opal ever catch it when she got home. She wouldn't be sitting down on a piano bench or anything else for a while.

Though there was no time to think about that now, for it was my turn to play "Amaryllis."

I wonder if people still play "Amaryllis." I hope not, though I am quite possibly prejudiced. It is simply an innocent little tune that goes GAGC, GAG; AAGA, and now four quickies—GFED, EC. Next comes a harder part and you go back to some more GAGCs and repeat.

And I repeated. Oh, indeed I did. I repeated and I kept right on repeating, because I was stuck and couldn't come unstuck. A broken record, it was, an endless series of identical plinks. I couldn't get out of the GAGC groove, couldn't shift into the next phrase, and couldn't quit playing it either, and, quite frankly, I don't think it had anything to do with the inspirational example of Robby Bruce; I think it was an involuntary reflex sort of a thing, like the hiccups.

But no matter. I only know I continued, hopelessly locked into it, as spring blossomed pinkly into summer and summer ripened redly into fall. . . . Where will *you* spend eternity? I could have answered that.

Then someone laughed. Then everyone was laughing. And finally Mrs. Smedley came up and patted me, saying, "That's fine, dear. I think we can stop now." Then everybody clapped and laughed some more, and, blushing redder than the peonies on the pulpit, I went back to my seat.

"Don't you worry. You hung in there, and that's what counts," my father said stoutly as we walked home later. And my mother hugged me and said I'd done just fine.

But what little kid wouldn't rather be stoned than laughed at? It was a dark, dark day.

However, on the following Wednesday—and I have to admit it—things picked up. Back in Mrs. Smedley's living room I had my standard submediocre piano lesson, but Mrs. Smedley didn't seem to mind. Well aware, I am sure, that I'd never touch "Amaryllis" again—I'd have hanged first—she had me warm up on the easiest Czerny. Then, after she'd given me a new piece to work on for the coming week, she said, "I hope you can stay today for tea."

So I had officially made it. At long last, there I was by invitation, on the right side of the pore-tears where all the good things to eat were, not just sneaking a look at them on my way back from the bathroom.

We sat down to the table, the Smedleys and I, and it was immediately apparent that Mrs. Smedley-Cowles and Mary had outdone themselves. There were tiny ham sandwiches, chicken sandwiches, cucumber sandwiches. And rich scones and raisin cookies and butterscotch bars. *And* crumpets, my first crumpets. Mr. Smedley kindly insisted on piling the strawberry preserves on mine himself.

And I wasn't disappointed. There was something immensely comforting, I found, about a crumpet—so comforting that I've never forgotten about them and have even learned to make them myself against those times when I have no other source of supply.

At any rate, on that long-ago Wednesday afternoon, I did a workmanlike job on everything in sight, and Mrs. Smedley might have taken comfort from my expertise at the tea table if not at the pianoforte. At least I was good at something.

And indeed, after the recital, the relationship between Mrs. Smedley and me seemed to have altered for the better in some subtle fashion I could sense if not understand. She probably felt sorry for me. But besides that, I think she had given up; and a touch of realistic fatalism can, of course, improve nearly any relationship. I was never going to change. Never going to improve. So be it.

And so things continued. . . .

But for a long time afterward I wondered about the merits of persistence. Because, going way back, had Elsie Dinsmore really won? I wasn't so sure. It's true that her antics on the piano bench attracted the attention of a Mr. Travilla, who eventually married her, but he was an unbelievable creep, even I could see that. And Robert Bruce could possibly have retired to some safe part of the world that had never heard of him, but no, thanks to the patient spider he had to fight still another big bloody war. And the little Dutch boy. They never told us if he ever got his circulation back, but I'll bet he didn't; I'll bet they had to chop that finger right off. . . .

And to come right down to cases, who'd really come out ahead after the piano recital? Opal? Or me? The longer I thought about it, the more I thought it was probably Opal.

Opal wasn't so dumb. She had faced facts. It is true, her quitting had had some unpleasant little side effects. She got a good lambasting, all right; I knew that because she told us all about it later. But the things she liked to do best you do standing up anyhow—jumping rope, Traffic Patrol. . . . *And* she got to quit taking piano lessons, forever and ever amen.

And me? What had been the rewards of my persistence? Well, crumpets. Otherwise, there I was every Wednesday afternoon, back at the same old stand in Mrs. Smedley's dark little parlor, guilt and all, clock and all, stop-and-start-over under Beethoven's level stare, the Cavalier endlessly snickering over the mantel, and still Czerny up to here and up the gum stump. It didn't seem to me that I had bettered my basic situation one bit.

That A and B business of my father's. I thought about that too. Apparently, the big thing was to be very very careful before you ever said A in the first place. There seemed no doubt about that. And today, looking about my kitchen, with its rich new embarrassment of drawer space, and thinking of our old piano, I believe another moral is probably implicit here, too: when you ask for anything, duck.

7

Of Irish Stews and Birthday Cakes

and Some Other Disillusionments in Assorted Sizes

As I may have pointed out earlier, for it has a warmly familiar ring, you can't trust anyone quite all the way; and I regret to say that this also goes, or went, for McKinleyville's First Presbyterian Church.

It was a shattering moment when I discovered this at a tender age, though no more so than another that happened about the same time in the McKinleyville Airdome Movie Theater, and still another that occurred much later along, about six months after I was married. These three are the bleakest disillusionments I can remember; and though it means playing hob with the time frame, I think I'd better put them down, for we may not pass this way again.

What had me thinking along these lines was, oddly enough, an Irish stew I was putting together the other morning, driven by conscience, not appetite, for it was right after breakfast. (This new kitchen of ours reminds me disconcertingly sometimes of a Saint Bernard dog who once owned us. When we'd start out the door, he would lay a long sorrowful look on us as well as a reproachful paw, so that half the time we'd have to take him along. This kitchen occasionally gives me a similar feeling—that I should do something about it, or with it, or even in it.)

The stew I was making, pictured in a food magazine, was a beautiful stew—truly a jeweled paradigm of stews, with its pearly onions and glistening wedges of pale-emerald cabbage and slabs of ruby beef, all artfully presented in a two-hundred-dollar Belleek bowl. If you've ever noticed, the flossier food magazines expect us all to be properly ethnic at all times—serve the steak-and-kidney pie from a Crown Derby pie plate and the tacos on a black Oaxacan platter and the egg rolls on something out of the T'ang dynasty.

But when my own stew was done, it would—I strongly suspected—look like onions, cabbage, and corned beef that had been cooked more or less together and served from the convenient ovenproof $14.98 ceramic casserole dish that I customarily cook it in. Which is exactly the way it turned out.

Accordingly, even though it had me reflecting about disillusionments in general, I can't honestly say it was one. Too often I've noticed the dependable disparity between the magazine picture, sheer poetry, and my own production, which is generally solid prose.

For genuine disillusionment you need surprise: for instance, surprise of the sort you find traveling, when it comes to those regional delicacies you read about and hear about but so seldom encounter once you get there.

For instance. Right here on my island, I know of only one restaurant that customarily serves poi; and this comes as rather a disillusioning surprise to many a visitor. Poi is as Hawaiian as the hula, and so why isn't it available anywhere?

But it isn't. Thus, aware of that fact and knowing the way the world goes, why, when I travel to the heart of the shoo-fly pie and Dutch cruller country, am I disillusioned to find neither shoo-fly pie nor Dutch crullers on the menu? ("We got Danish, apple, or cherry; we just pop it into the microwave," said the cute little waitress in the Amish costume.)

And why is there no wild rice on the menu in Minneapolis? Or a single fresh trout served in the charming little restaurant beside the World's Best Trout Stream? Or an orange to be found anywhere in the whole of the big Beverly Hills Hotel?

I know I shouldn't be surprised at these things, and yet I always am.

Then take South Carolina, where I recently spent a pleasant but fruitless interval searching for the beaten biscuits that turned up hot and delectable in the Chamber of Commerce handouts but never on my plate. Though everything else quite lived up to advance notices, from the Spanish moss that festooned Miss Essie's plantation to the she-crab soup, preceded by a whiskey at the bah and accompanied by fahn wahns—vintage wahns, our host said—not to mention Southern gallantry ("May Ah be the thorn between two roses?" he asked, sitting down between his wife and me). Yet nowhere was a beaten biscuit to be found.

How come, and why? Back in the days when they beat them by hand for at least two hours, the South had more beaten biscuits than your hound dog had fleas. But now, with all our electric mixers, food processors, beaters . . .

Well, alleged progress abounds in ironies. Why didn't they invent tumble-dry fabrics before they invented the voluminous petticoats women used to wear? But no, it was the other way around. And the more magic fabrics and driers we have, the fewer clothes we wear.

Consider, as well, the farm wife who used to cook all day on one stove for twenty people. Now she cooks about three hours a week, all told, for herself and her husband (the hired man is one with the great bony-plated Stegosaurus, and both sons are away at Vassar), with the help of two and a half ovens plus enough magical electric-electronic equipment to power a midtown restaurant.

And let's consider just one more Southern mystery: the perplexing case of the gallberry honey. In Charleston I asked for some.

"*What?*" said the waitress, who obviously hadn't read the Chamber of Commerce poopsheet. She stared.

"I understand you're famous for gallberry honey around here," I said.

"Never heard of it," she said, regarding me with a suspicious eye.

I have a dark foreboding that if I ever make it to the land of milk and honey and finally sit down to tie my napkin around my neck and place my order, they'll say, "Milk and . . . how was that again?"

Oh, there are many kinds of disillusionment when it comes to food, and how often it does! There is the way coffee never tastes as good as it smells (bacon does, roast turkey does, coffee doesn't) and the way French pastries are never so delectable as they look. And there is the way a mere word can affect your anticipation of something and hence, at least by a little, its taste.

For instance, as Emlyn Williams has pointed out, "I have come to realize that in Britain food is tinned, while in America it is canned. Is it not possible that this could make a subtle difference to the flavor? *Peut-être.*"

No *peut-être* about it, if you ask me, though Mr. Williams and I would probably disagree as to which word improves the taste of the product. I am reasonably sure that Williams, being Welsh, prefers tinned. But when I hear, say, "tinned salmon," I can almost taste the tin, like biting hard on a piece of aluminum foil, and I shudder. If I can't have my salmon fresh, please, preferably poached with a touch of tarragon, I'll take the canned.

The British give bad names to good food anyway. Surely innards are more appealing than offal. And then they have their boiled sweets, flummeries, and fools, their treacle tarts and their toads—anyone for boiled tinned toads?—not to mention their bangers and mash and their fish paste, their bubble and squeak and their rumbledy-thumps, their suet pudding and their Wet Nelly and their plonk. In fact, the British make good things sound bad quite as effectively as other people make bad food sound good. The *chipolata* that intrigued me the other evening in an otherwise pleasant Italian restaurant turned out to be a wishy-washy egg custard over canned fruit, a truly expendable dessert.

So there went another small illusion. When it rains in Ireland you can call it Dublin Dew or Galway Mist or Irish Confetti, but it still gets you wet. And Anything du Barry on a menu still gets you cauliflower.

However, as I started to say, one of my larger disillusionments with food is connected with the church, back in good old McKinleyville.

When I visited there for the first time after twenty-five years away, I learned that the McKinleyville First Presbyterian had turned into a mortuary, and my first thought was, How could they tell? I had attended it briefly—its Sunday school, that is—and there wasn't much difference even then.

It was a small, squat, brownstone church, the First Presbyterian was, featuring hard shiny yellow pews and a general over-all stuffiness, as of bad breath in unaired rooms where nothing jolly ever happens, though it was a perfect setting for funerals and piano recitals. (This had been, as you may remember, the scene of my triumph with "Amaryllis.")

My Sunday-school teacher was a frizzle-haired, elderly dumpling of a woman shaped like a melting snowman, and she usually sported dark wet half moons under her arms. She also had red, sore-looking, indented half moons on the sides of her nose, where her eyeglasses must have pinched badly. Though we never saw her wearing her eyeglasses, her nose never seemed to get any better. She taught us in the back room, while our parents held down the hard shiny yellow pews out in the dreary front part, and her name was Mrs. Cooley.

The back room was just as dreary, and so was the Sunday-school class routine, as I recall it. There was roll call and an opening hymn, generally "Yes, Jesus Loves Me," and then some of the short-form catechism ("Who made you?" "God made me." "Who is God?" "God is the Father, Son, and the Holy Ghost," and some other questions and answers which I forget). Next we would salute the flag, pledging allegiance to the country for Widget Stanns, whoever she was. Then Mrs. Cooley would read us a Bible story, after which we'd do the Lord's Prayer and put a penny in the collection plate and that was that.

Unless a child had had a birthday during the preceding week—in which case, said Cooley, we would celebrate on the following Sunday, with a cake and everything. She mentioned this not long after I had been enrolled in the class, and it just so happened that my seventh birthday was actually programed to fall on that very coming Sunday itself!

Well, I don't know how I ever managed to make it through the week. The special birthday dinner that Mama would cook for me on the following Sunday (everything I loved the most, which meant lamb chops and fried sweet potatoes and Brown Bettina) paled to nothing beside the gastronomical delights I expected, through some manic flight of fevered fancy, to be wallowing in, courtesy the First Presbyterian Church and Mrs. Cooley. In fact, could she have looked inside my head and seen that troupe of impossibly delicious dancing sugarplums, it would probably have driven her straight to the sacramental grape juice. For, as it turned out, the First Presbyterian's ideas of a birthday celebration were a good long way from mine.

The following Sunday I was early, naturally—put on my green best dress with the shirring, left home well ahead of my family, and ran all the way so I could cool my heels for half an hour outside the Sunday-school door till Mrs. Cooley showed up to let me in. As she eventually did, though she appeared without any boxes or bundles. This rocked me a little. Still, she remembered to say "Happy Birthday," and that was encouraging.

As I remember, we followed the usual Sunday-school class routine that day—roll call, hymn, catechism, and so on, clear down to a Bible story I didn't hear a word of—and my suspense had built to a zingy new high by the time Mrs. Cooley shut the book and finally got down to business.

"Today," she announced, "is Peggy's birthday. So shall we all sing the birthday song, children, while I bring in the cake?"

Accordingly, all nine little catechumens lifted their voices in "Happy Birthday to Peggy," as Mrs. Cooley headed for the cupboard in the back and opened its door. In a moment, perspiring nicely, she brought forth and placed before me a magnificent three-tiered lavishly frosted white birthday cake adorned with eight pink candles (that included one to grow on), all lit and burning brightly.

But no plates. No cake knife either.

I must have looked as baffled as I felt, because Mrs. Cooley explained kindly, "Oh no, dear, it's not to eat. This is the plaster cake we use all the time. But you can make a wish and blow out the candles."

Can you believe it? A phony cake! Solid plaster of Paris, or maybe plaster of Paris over concrete, it was that heavy. *All* phony, including the luscious-looking frosting.

Talk about your whited sepulchres! Talk about your dis- illusionments!

Well, what the heck. I blew. What else could you do with a cake like that? It was too heavy to throw and too hard to kick. And then—get this now—Mrs. Cooley passed the collec- tion plate, explaining that it was customary for the Birthday Child to contribute an additional penny for each year of his age instead of the usual one cent.

Hot ziggety damn. Some birthday party. As if a cake I couldn't eat wasn't bad enough, now they wanted a nickel I didn't have, though Mrs. Cooley generously allowed that I could bring it with me on the following Sunday. And maybe this was her idea of a big time, and maybe John Knox him- self was rubbing his hands and beaming, up there in his tidy Presbyterian corner of heaven (which I've pictured ever since furnished with hard shiny yellow pews).

But it sure wasn't my idea of a big time or even a very nice Sunday school; and whether or not I even went back there at all, I don't recall, though in retrospect my connection with the whole scene was satisfyingly brief.

What I do remember clearly is how hopping mad my grandpa got when I told him about it, the next summer vacation in Kansas, where we customarily visited for a few weeks each year. I suppose he took it personally, having been a Presbyterian minister at one time himself. Anyway, he was a raging tide—sputtered, frothed, fumed—then marched me straight down to the town's best bakery to choose whatever cake my piggish little heart desired (which turned out to be, if memory serves, a marshmallow-frosted Chocolate Swirl).

Moreover, being a staunch advocate of moderation in everything, including moderation, Grandpa said the whole cake was mine alone, which earned him some hard looks from my brother, Jack. But at practically the same time he got Jack a whole quart of ice cream, which he said was all for him, thus earning Grandpa some hard looks from me.

And then Mama, who didn't want two puking moppets on her hands all night, said, Nonsense, the whole family would eat the whole works for dinner. So there was another disillusionment thrown in for free as I learned that your very own mother isn't above doing you in.

Disillusionments.

Of course there were the inevitable childish bubbles that were busted—the academic ones, like learning in the fourth grade that George Washington had not, after all, cut down the cherry tree, though this probably isn't a patch on what the tots are learning about him today in this era of biography that's not only warts-and-all but, often enough, all warts. And in arithmetic I remember feeling a trifle let down on learning that the product of one times one is only one. All that multiplying and you're still not a bit further ahead. . . .

However, it seems to me that too much is made of the emotional impact when some smart-ass third-grade know-it-all blows the whistle on the Easter Bunny and so on. I can't believe these moments are all that traumatic. At least they weren't for me.

———

Like Santa Claus. It was my observant brother, Jack, who noticed one Christmas Eve that Santa Claus was wearing brown shoes just like Daddy's. Excitedly, Jack relayed this blockbuster to me.

But I took it calmly. It was, after all, only an interesting coincidence. Even when we finally figured out that Santa Claus was indeed Daddy, it simply upped Daddy in my estimation. Daddy, the giver of all good gifts.

A far bigger jolt, about the same time, was learning that my father would never, after all, become President of the United States.

That this would inevitably happen, someday, had been one of my comfortable certainties, along with the basic wickedness of all Democrats, rich people, Fords, whiskey, and spiders, and the basic goodness of all Republicans, poor people, Chevrolets, orange phosphates, and frogs, who occasionally turn into princes. Life is so very simple when you have no facts to confuse you.

And so one night I asked him point-blank—I suppose I was getting tired of waiting around for us to do our White House number—when it would happen; and he informed me, kindly but with a positiveness that left no room for doubt, that it wasn't going to happen at all.

Now, you might well wonder why I would have entertained such a curious notion in the first place, my father being a school man, with never a political connection or inclination to his name. But I had been serenely sure of it, because he did, after all, know everything. And the smartest man in the world naturally and inevitably ends up being President, right?

Well, no . . .

But after pursuing the subject of disillusionment for this little way, I begin to wonder where its boundaries are. If it displaces a former fond misconception, any come-to-realize is actually a disillusionment, isn't it?

There was a man I was going out with, some years ago, a

fairly short man. One night, happening to notice his shoes on the floor, empty, no feet in there filling them up, I thought they looked odd. Then I realized that they were elevator shoes, with a good additional inch or so built into the deceptively low heels.

Now *there* was a come-to-realize for me; I mean a truly disillusioning surprise. Not that I minded his being short. What I minded was *his* minding, to the extent those elevators seemed to attest, and nothing was quite the same afterward. Presently I stopped seeing him, though it's true that that wasn't the only reason. He also had a disconcerting habit of seeing famous people in wallpaper patterns and clouds, was forever yelling, "Hey, look quick, right there. There's Winston Churchill" (or Groucho Marx or whoever) — "see? See the cigar? . . ." I never could find any of them, and I just didn't think I'd be able to handle this on a year-in year-out basis.

Disillusionments.

Well, and then there was Mrs. Smedley-Cowles. Some piano player, all right, till I heard Rachmaninoff. And eventually I came to realize that there are some rotten poor people in this world and even some good Democrats, and orange phosphates make some people sick, and frogs don't turn into princes half as often as princes turn into frogs. And the house I grew up in wasn't the big place I thought it was and neither was McKinleyville.

> *Last winter I went down to my native town, where I found the streets much narrower and shorter than I thought I had left them, inhabited by a new race of people, to whom I was very little known.*
>
> —JAMES BOSWELL

Indeed, it is sometimes a fine line between disillusionment and enlightenment. Perhaps this is the way of it: a disillusionment is always an enlightenment—that is to say, educational, though it isn't necessarily true the other way around.

And then I remember a summer evening at the McKinley-ville Airdome Movie Theater, not too long after the President business—an exceptionally humid evening, as I recall it, the air virtually fungoid with the thick sweet smell of penny candy being chewed and drooled, for most of the little mouths stayed open most of the time, open and exuding a rich, tropical, dark-brown essence of Bananamels commingled with Walnettos that overpowered even the smell of the popcorn.

This particular movie, the one that occasioned a memorable disillusionment, or, anyway, confrontation with things as they so bleakly were, was an epic of Revolutionary days. In the course of it, the gorgeous blond heroine barely escaped defloration by a villainous redcoat, only to be tied to a tree (plenty of kindling heaped around her, too) by some bad-tempered Iroquois, and then saved in time's preciset nick by the handsomest chunk of beefcake that ever drove a horse—clear-eyed, square-jawed, flowing locks, seven feet tall and every inch gorgeous, leather pants, fringe on the deerskin jacket, manly shirt open clear to the manly navel—whewww!

And suddenly—I don't know why or where it came from—a sad sort of wisdom seeped into my very bones. Spellbound, glassy-eyed, rhythmically chewing away at my caramel cud, somehow I saw in a burst of revelation that life, for me, was simply not going to hold any such sixteen-cylinder moment.

I remember crying myself to sleep that night over the knowledge, with Mama trying to comfort me, and of course I couldn't tell her where it hurt. (There is your dividing line, by the way, between child and nonchild—when the first trouble happens that Mama can't fix.)

But I knew what I was grieving for, all right. It was the unattainable towers of Camelot, though I'd never heard of them. Oh, I might get married someday, sure. Might have children and all that, sure. But never—I knew it with a crystal certainty—never would I know the total romantic terror of being imperiled by lecherous Englishmen and wicked Indians, or the total ecstasy of being rescued and—of course—eventually wed by a tall, tawny, absolute hundred-percent sugarbritches like this one.

Well, as it turned out, I was wrong, in a way. That is, I eventually learned that ecstasy isn't exclusive to Camelot or to MGM, and that glorious blondes and Lochinvars luckily don't have a corner on romance.

And yet, in another way I was absolutely correct. Both the Englishmen and the Indians I've happened to meet have been singularly well behaved; and the only thing a man has ever saved me from,* besides the supposed miseries of a spinster's lot, was a piece of beefsteak I recently choked on, at dinner. If my husband hadn't remembered the Heimlich maneuver at the appropriate moment, this book would be gravely shorter than it is.

I give him full points for saving me, too. It was a realer rescue from a realer peril than my long-ago heroine enjoyed —just not quite so romantic. Still, it cheers me to remember it by its other name—the Heimlich Hug.

And so we come to the third major disillusionment I mentioned earlier: my disillusionment with domesticity, back when I was first married, a time that I'll return to later but want to touch on here.

For reasons that are obscure to me now, and despite considerable evidence to the contrary, I believed when I was first married that the spirit-warming, life-sustaining properties of home-baked cookies and flowers in a blue bowl and fresh curtains blowing in a lilac-scented breeze would all add up to live-happily-ever-after, and then I discovered that somehow they didn't. As millions of women have done before me, I pulled domesticity over my head like a blanket and found I was still cold. And so I started writing, and eventually, after my first published story burst into oblivion,

* Of course there was Jack on Halloween, but brothers don't count.

everything was all right, or at least never got so wrong that it couldn't in some fashion be fixed.

Thus another illusion bit the dust, and a good thing, too. Some illusions you don't need.

Yet, some you do. At least, there are some that I need to hang onto if I am to get any work done.

Early mornings are an especially vulnerable time for me, because that is when I work. When I am writing something, I drive to my office, most mornings very early, to get away from the clamorous house. (A sex difference they don't mention is that a man can work at home just fine, never derailed by the sight of a dull copper pot or a cluttered table top or a new kitchen. But I can't. The Bettina Mystique dies hard.)

So I drive the eight miles to work, down the narrow black highway that separates the ocean from the Mountains of the Moon, my headlights shoving back the dark the way a snow-plow pushes snow. Sometimes the stars are still out, a great black meadowful, and I wonder if anyone else is awake up there. Some astronomer said, "Sometimes I think we're alone. Sometimes I think we're not. In either case, the thought is quite staggering. . . ."

Four-thirty A.M. is a good time. Not many people are up and about—at least, down here. Though the island wakes a bit earlier than the mainland does (school keeps from eight to two, not nine to three, to provide better surfing hours), most people aren't stirring yet. The houses are dark and so are the big resort hotels, where guests are resting the tired muscles, getting ready for another hard day's play.

The people who *are* up and about, I regard with suspicion. What is a decent citizen doing up at this hour? Well, going to work the way I am, I suppose. On the way to open a hotel kitchen or activate a gas pump or swab out a rest room or unlock a cash register. And I enjoy meeting them, in a way—the oncoming cars, I mean. I like to dim my distance lights momentarily, like the tip of a hat, a small but pleasant courtesy that doesn't have to be followed up.

And there are animals about, in the dark out there. Mongooses sleek across the road like a child's pull-toy pulled so fast the wheels blur. And nearly always there is at least one cat or dog, like a child's discarded teddy bear, thrown to the side of the highway, just visible in the headlights, the stuffing spilling out, red stuffing. . . .

So I drive through the dark velvet air, dark now but lightening fast, the palm trees becoming gradually sharp-etched, like a black-and-white snapshot developing in the fluid and then (by some process that would certainly surprise the photographer) magically coming up colored, blue water and pink banners of cloud over the mountain, everything fresh as the first morning in the Garden of Eden.

And I think of all the projects that have undoubtedly been started or furthered in the past twelve hours around the world by how many millions of people. How many millions have found an idea, handled a crisis, solved a problem, patched a quarrel, started a painting or a clinic or a treaty or a song or a garden or a baby or a ballet or a business, cleaned a room or a street—whatever. Gone about the business of the world, I mean. And there I am, about to start something myself, probably a new paragraph, and it all seems plausible, possible, even worth doing.

That is when I mustn't make the disillusioning mistake I made yesterday morning, turning on the car radio. I wanted the time, but I got the news; and I found out that I was wrong, that all those things don't count. All that happened worth noting was that a prisoner hanged himself in the State Pen, five nurses were busted for drug possession, an old lady was mugged and raped in Seattle, six congressmen are being investigated for graft, Cambodians are starving, the oil picture looks worse than ever, another plane was hijacked out of Atlanta, baby-seal-clubbing season is upon us again, the nuclear-waste issue is bubbling with a vengeance, and some radio comic asked his little boy what he wants to do if he grows up. There went my illusions, the stuffing all spilled out, like the little animals along the highway. I didn't get any work done yesterday.

So I protect my illusions as far as possible, at least when I am working, because, I suppose, I agree with Martin Luther, who said that if he knew the world were to end tomorrow, he would still plant his little apple tree. Apple tree, paragraph, gas pump, whatever it is, it's still the only game in town.

8

Of Copper Bowls and Kansas

and a Snapshot or Two from the Family Album

A few mornings ago at the kitchen sink, I was polishing a big copper bowl that manifestly needed it, one that customarily hangs over the counter to the right of the window. This island air tarnishes copper so fast that you could polish it every day, depending on your standards and your good sense.

Well, brass and silver, too. My grandpa's silver tea ball, shaped like a miniature Georgian teapot, hangs in the kitchen window, sometimes gleaming in the morning sunshine, but semitarnished, I'm afraid, most of the time. If you had very good sense indeed, you'd hang up no brass, silver, or copper objects at all—you'd hide them, a procedure I've recommended more than once in various writings on the subject.

However, in the kitchen's formative stages, Uwe had spoken to us with enthusiasm of room accessories. This is a popular decorating term for objects that are generally a nuisance—things that require watering or dusting or polishing or, in extreme cases, insuring, though this kind is usually spelled *objets*. I could sense that he expected us to get some, because naturally he wanted us to live up to his kitchen. Moreover, this large copper bowl had come from a pedigreed kitchen boutique as a Christmas gift. It was meant to whip egg whites in—supposedly something about the copper swells the volume—and also to hang up. Uwe would approve, I was sure.

So humor the man, I thought, and took the path of uneasy compromise: hung it up and forgot it. I seldom use it for egg whites because it doesn't blow them up enough to get excited about, and so I generally don't notice it needs polishing unless we are expecting company. Then, when I look around the place with a critical eye, sure enough.

I was reading as I polished, for with all this new counter space, my cookbook holder can stay out in the open all the time now, right where I want it. This book holder is a clear acrylic affair that keeps a book upright, open, and safe from spatters. It often holds books other than cookbooks, too, because occasional snippets of reading time do come along in a kitchen—minutes when you are doing a job like polishing, or waiting for something to rise or pull itself together or otherwise do whatever it is supposed to do.

It's true that it would be reasonable to use these random minutes for random jobs, like polishing the toaster or grating some bread crumbs. But that kind of efficiency isn't my natural gait. Besides, I recently adopted for my own a good motto I saw somewhere, on a barroom mirror or possibly a washroom wall: "The time you enjoyed wasting wasn't wasted." I think I'll have that printed some day on a T-shirt or the bedroom ceiling.

On this particular morning, the bookstand held a book of Everett Allen's that I was rereading, open to a page containing a paragraph I had underlined:

> . . . *mostly we have a habit of doing things*
> *while we are thinking of what we are going to*
> *do next, or what we should have done before.*

> *That way, we never really know what anything
> is, or feels like, or smells like, or tastes like. . . .*

And how true that is, I thought. The present is so seldom sufficient. Almost always, we want to enrich it with the past or the future or both at once, never simply accepting and experiencing the moment for itself alone.

Moreover, I thought, I could very well take those words as a gentle rebuke right now. Reading while polishing is a good example of what he is talking about, isn't it? And therefore, why didn't I quit reading and start concentrating on that bowl's essence—get down to its Is-ness, its *Istigkeit*, its very quiddity?

And so, putting my mind on my work, I tried hard to experience the experience. I polished, and, while polishing, made myself think about the solid roundness of the bowl, about the feel of it and the smell of it, about the harsh metallic smell of the copper, or is it the tarnish or the polish that smells that way? . . .

And I thought, I shouldn't polish too hard or it will have that new, raw, pink, chafed baby-bottom look that I don't like, but if I stop rubbing it now, it will look spotty. And then I thought, Well, polished copper is like a haircut anyway—you have to live with it a couple of days before it's really comfortable.

And then I thought about electrons, how the bowl is composed of billions of dancing electrons all holding hands just as I am composed of billions of dancing electrons all holding hands, only it apparently has better-quality electrons, at least sturdier ones. After all, this bowl could last another five hundred years, and I don't really expect to, at least with my present set of electrons.

And then I wondered about reincarnation, does anyone ever get reincarnated as a copper bowl? Or does it always have to be another person or animal or something like that? And then I noticed that the tarnish was really disappearing now and so was my manicure.

And then I thought, Maybe a copper bowl just doesn't have enough quiddity to think about, at least for very long at a time. And I reflected that it was a good thing the bowl was getting brighter, because my thoughts weren't, and if I didn't finish the job pretty soon I would likely run out of thoughts altogether. Then I would have to start all over with the solid roundness of the bowl and so on, my thoughts going round and round like those rum-dum processionary caterpillars that follow each other, nose to rear, around and around forever amen and won't break ranks even though they're starving to death and a juicy mulberry leaf is placed within easy reach, the merest inch off the path. . . .

That's the trouble with housework all right, I reflected further; your head is likely to get as dull as the copper does, if you spend much time at it every day. . . .

And so I washed the copper bowl in hot suds, rinsed it, dried it, gave it a rub for luck, and hung it back up, appreciating the gleam against the blue tile but wishing I had remembered to leave a small tarnished place so I could see how much I had accomplished, the way my grandma Em used to do, back in Ganister, Kansas. She also liked to leave a smudgy square inch or two on any windowpane she happened to wash, so she could keep right on appreciating the improvement. (It is a quirk that runs in the family. My brother once objected to washing his neck, which had acquired that small-boy gray-flannel look, because then nobody would be able to see how clean he'd got his face.)

Well, there is something to be said for contrast in these areas. Today, I know, you're supposed to nibble away at the housecleaning all the time, so the place always looks about the same. While that is undoubtedly sensible, I'm not sure that it is as emotionally satisfying as the old-fashioned cathartic kind of a job that used to happen every spring.

Now, my grandma Em kept house and never let the house keep her: never let it keep her forever *at* it, I mean, as so many women did then. For one thing, she expected you to clean up after yourself to a reasonable extent—remove the mud you brought in, give the washbowl an occasional swipe with the cleaning rag, and so on. Too, whoever was last up made all the beds, which may be why I've been an early riser all my life.

I know Em would have approved the words I saw recently on a public rest-room wall:

> *Those whom the Good Lord has enabled to drop things on the floor She has also graced with the ability to bend over and pick them up.*

But she'd have paid scant mind to whoever said "Women's work is never done." It was done all right, so far as she was concerned, for she predated Parkinson in her gut feel for the basic truth that any housekeeping job will expand to fill all the time you've got, if you let it.

Hence, she seldom let it. Her real life was books, cats, and her husband—my grandpa Ben; and she kept her priorities clearly in mind.

"It'll keep," she'd say, of a dusty shelf or an andiron that wanted polishing. But some things wouldn't, like a library book half read but due back tomorrow, or a walk with Ben on the night of the new moon.

He liked it that way, too, though he would joke about it. "You can eat off Em's floor," Ben would say; "there's a lot of good stuff down there." And she'd laugh. "Ben, you're a caution!" she'd say. That was one of her favorite words.

But perhaps I should stop here and explain about Ganister, Kansas, for I find it hard to separate Em and Ben from the place where they lived. And I was thinking this morning, Take the banana frond out of the southeast corner of the Hawaiian landscape that's framed by my kitchen window, and it could almost be a Kansas cornfield rolling up and away to the horizon. Hillier, perhaps, but the same glossy apple-green. Corn and cane look remarkably alike to me, when the crop is young.

Kansas is the large, neat, rectangular state right next to Missouri, on the Rocky Mountain side of it. Kansas is yellow on the map, I suppose because of all the corn and wheat. The town of Ganister, my mother's home base, was on the right side—still is, so far as I know—quite close to the Kansas-

Missouri border. However, because our home town of Mc-Kinleyville was way over on the right side of Missouri, the two towns were a whole state apart.

I couldn't have been older than seven when I checked this out in the geography book, to find out why our annual summer trek from McKinleyville to Ganister took so long. That was back when geography came in miles, colors, and shapes out of geography books, instead of in hours and time zones out of travel agents. (Idaho, where my other grandmother lived, used to be an attractive pink state shaped like a sock you'd hang up for Christmas. Now it's—I don't know what it is, except five and three-quarter air hours from where I am sitting.)

Anyway, from our house in McKinleyville to Grandpa's in Ganister was a good day and a half's work—about three hundred and fifty miles in a car that did thirty m.p.h. if you really—as the phrase went—stepped on 'er. And, of course, another reason it took so long was that I wanted so much to be there, to see Grandma and Grandpa and Aunt Liz Noah. She was my favorite aunt*—great-aunt, actually—and she lived only a few blocks away.

And so, each summer we would chug over to Ganister, my parents and brother and I, and when the bad-smelling air began to seem virtually tangible, air you could reach out and grab a big brown handful of, we knew there were only sixty miles to go. The smell came from the stockyards in the Kansas Citys.

There are two Kansas Citys, one of them in Missouri. This was confusing, and because we always drove straight through or around them, I never learned to tell them apart. I knew only that one of them didn't amount to a hill of beans and the other one did—never learned which one did or didn't,

---

* I must confess that this is always pronounced *ant* in my mind, the short *a* instead of the broad, because that is the way we always pronounced it in McKinleyville, even though Miss Leffler tried to break us of it in the eighth grade, explaining that ants bit and aunts knit. But it was too late. Though I have trained myself to *aunt* now, I secretly think it sounds (as we would have put it then) la-di-da. It is the same way with kids. Tell a kid a million times to say *child* because a kid is a baby goat, but a kid is still a kid and a kid knows it.

though, or which smelled the worse, for that matter, or even which one everything was up to date in, as I heard that it indeed was, some twenty years later. (These early confusions persist; I have never been entirely sure about leeward and windward either, and whether cement is made out of concrete or is it vice versa, and whether the Nile flows up or down.)

Ganister, on the other hand, smelled unfailingly fine when we got there, smelled of high noon and clover, rain and sweet new hay curing in the sun, of dew and buttercups, and fence-row daisies, and lingering dusk, and some horse manure. Ganister had a livery stable, and a few die-hards still kept a horse and buggy.

It was a town of nearly eight thousand people, not so big you'd ever feel lost, yet large enough so that you had cultural advantages, as Em was always quick to point out. The Chautauqua came every summer, and the Crystal Theater movie house was open for business around the year.

Ganister had the big four-story Grand Osage Hotel, too, on downtown Main Street, where you'd eat in the Coffee Shop (Booths for Ladies) on special occasions. Right beside the cash register, a big dish of pink and green sugar mints was approximately centered under the fly-studded sticky-paper strips fluttering from the ceiling.

There were also big slow-moving fans and waitresses. They were kind, comfortable women who had been there for years and took their time and kidded the customers and almost remembered which grade you were in, every summer.

It was a town full of trees, Ganister was. Maples, to begin with, according to Grandpa, till the evil green maple worms came along. So then they planted elm trees, which didn't solve the worm problem, only changed the variety. Some days, just walking down the street you'd have to carry an umbrella to keep the little black measuring worms from dropping into your hair from the branches overhead. They'd even drop down the chimney, and I remember Grandma muttering as she swept them out of the hearth.

Ganister also had two graveyards, one called Highland and another one that was on the west edge of town. I can't remember its name, but I know that it bore the weight of

Em's total disapproval. Damp, it was, she always said; damp and low and too near the railroad (why that should be in its disfavor, I don't know) as well as too close to the river. Never, said Grandma, would she lie quiet in so inferior a graveyard. Give her Highland or nothing. (And she eventually got Highland, bless her heart . . . high and sunny and green and quiet, in her rightful place beside Ben.)

Ganister was a town of frame houses: white ones, brown ones, green ones, usually two-storied and front-porched. If there were brick houses, I wasn't aware of it. I think any available bricks went into the streets and the sidewalks, where green moss grew quietly between them, and my father said that what you did in Ganister on Saturday nights was listen to it grow. He would sometimes add that in the hot humid daytimes, you could also watch the labels slide off the catsup bottles. Like many men, he was dutiful about visits to the in-laws, though not overly enthusiastic.

Grandpa's house was white with green trim, set well back in a big yard full of elm trees wearing sticky white belly-bands so the grubs couldn't crawl up. The yard was also full of croquet wickets that could send you sprawling in the dusk of a summer night.

As I remember, the lawn was mainly crab grass and dandelions. Grandpa wasn't much of a gardener, never had been. If Jeff-next-door didn't mow the lawn and weed the flower beds, they went unmowed and unweeded. But Grandpa rationalized well, and Grandma once told me about a time, before he'd left the ministry, when he made some of his church members more than a little uneasy.

His rectory yard, it seems, had finally grown so ratty that people were starting to talk; and so Grandpa made it the subject of a Sunday sermon, taking as his text, "Judge not lest ye be judged," or something of the sort. Who but the Good Lord Himself, my grandpa asked righteously, could tell a saint from a sinner? Equally, who but the Good Lord Himself could tell a good green thing from a bad green thing, could say truly which was flower and which was weed? Moreover, wasn't a weed an equal treasure in His sight? As the

Lord loves poor people—else why did He create so many—doesn't He love weeds, too? And snails and bugs and aphides? They are equally His creatures. Yet there stands the gardener, with murder in his heart and a spray can of poison in his hand. . . .

Oh, it was a powerful sermon, studded with solid Biblical references and quotes, and the gardening congregation slunk out looking at each other sideways, as Grandma said, about to go turn their hoes into eggbeaters, till a suspicion gradually flowered among them that they had been gently had.

That had been years ago, of course, long before I was born. Grandpa still didn't give a hoot about yard work though, and Ben and Em's life together was mainly indoor-oriented. That is what I mainly remember, the house cool and a little dim, the shades often drawn against the hot summer sun, Em sitting in her rocker, reading, and usually with a cat in her lap.

She was a compact little person, my grandma was, plump and smooth and round as a grape. Or like a classic English roly-poly, that's it—like a good jam pudding. I've always liked Em's style, the tilt of her kilt—or the hang of her blanket, I suppose I could say with equal accuracy. Mainly Scotch-Irish, she insisted she was part Indian, too, though I don't think anyone ever knew which part or how much. She tended to alter the ratio, it was said, when she was miffed at Grandpa. This didn't happen often, but on the rare occasions it did, she'd bump it up to a good fifty percent Blackfoot, to put as much genetic distance between them as possible.

I remember asking Grandpa in private once if she really was part Indian (she looked it), hoping she was, because then I'd be part Indian, too; and he said, "Of course. Don't you remember the day we found the old Indian war whoops up in the attic?" That was Ben for you. (*He* didn't look Indian; he looked like a balder, jollier John Greenleaf Whittier, or, better, like a tall benevolent gnome. All his hair had mysteriously fallen out when he was about sixty, but his white beard was lovely. More pixie than patriarchal, it went well with his shiny pate and his very bright blue eyes.)

The few pictures I have of Grandma Em show a younger woman than I ever knew. Straight black hair, skin that is a trifle olive, snapping black eyes, and a firm though full-lipped and pretty mouth. If her stoicism was any indication, Grandma had some Indian in her all right. It is part of the family annals how she was in labor for two days producing my mother—a breech presentation out in the country in a January blizzard with Grandpa away, the doctor unreachable, her only help a thirteen-year-old (my aunt Liz Noah), who couldn't do much but locate the aspirin and hold her hand. Grandma bit her lip clear through in two places, but never screamed—it would have frightened little Liz—and all she'd ever say about it later was that it smarted some.

(Or could those stoic genes have come from the Scotch-Irish side as well? Only recently, I was reading in Flora Thompson's *Lark Rise to Candleford* about rural Britons circa the late 1880s, of how it was a great source of pride not to flinch. "A woman would say, 'I set up wi' my poor old mother six nights runnin'; never had me clothes off. But I didn't flinch, an' I pulled her through, for she didn't flinch neither.' Or a young wife would say to the midwife after her first confinement, 'I didn't flinch, did I? Oh, I do hope I didn't flinch.'")

Em hadn't flinched.

She always sat erect, too, straight as a good Indian arrow. "Sit tall!" she would say if we slumped at the table, and I have no trouble picturing her as the schoolteacher she was before she was married. First thing in the morning, a former pupil of hers told Mama, Em would say to the slouched and drowsy class, "Let's see some talls!" and magically they'd shoot up like jack-in-the-boxes. . . .

Em was a good manager. Well, being married to Grandpa she had to be. They lived on a Presbyterian minister's meager pay for nearly twenty years after they were married, and then when Ben left the ministry for the mortgage company (whether for financial or theological reasons, I never exactly knew), it didn't make that much difference to the family exchequer.

So Grandma kept house on a no-frills basis. She could make a dollar do the work of three, and Ben would occasionally complain that she squeezed those nickels till the Indians war danced. (Ben himself was more like his sister Liz, who would often remind me, before she sent me to the grocer's, "Now don't buy like poor people!" Not just two bananas, she meant, but a bunch of bananas. Not ten cents' worth of this, but a good half-dollar's worth.)

Em didn't care though. She figured that what she saved with her little economies allowed Ben to eat better than he would have otherwise, and Ben liked to eat well. So when he caught her being frugal, and sang out the old rhyme

> *Get up, get up, you sleepy-head,*
> *Get up, you lazy sinner—*
> *We need the sheet for a tablecloth*
> *Or we'll all be late for dinner*

she'd only laugh and go right ahead doing whatever it was, melting candle stubs to pour over jelly or making her own turpentine-and-beeswax furniture polish or tying up soap scraps in little muslin bags.

Grandma didn't own a lot of kitchen utensils, I remember. I think she'd have laughed at the present-day passion for arcane single-purpose widgets—our clam forks and strawberry shuckers, our egg punchers and artichoke shears, our corn tongs and lemon-zest scrapers and American-cheese slicers (not to be confused with our Swiss-cheese slicers) . . . .

Whatever Em kept around had to do at least two things and preferably six. Even a rock wasn't just a rock; it was a paperweight or a curtain weight or a doorstop, it could start a wall or a jack rabbit, it could plug a mousehole, and if it was a small rock, she'd drop it with some others in the bottom of the double boiler to alert her before the pan boiled dry.

Broomsticks. She collected them the way people collect sea shells, and she used them in all sorts of inventive ways: tied a feather to one, I remember, for tickling high cobwebs, put a cup hook on the end of another for squiggling weeds out from between the sidewalk bricks, glued a magnet to another for picking up pins, used one to poke holes in her vegetable garden for dropping seeds into. . . .

She often said she could set up housekeeping with a clutch of broomsticks, a jar of vaseline, and a bottle of good white vinegar, and I haven't a doubt of it.

She certainly wasn't acquisitive. Like so many people then, she seemed reasonably content with what she had. Of course, there weren't so many new things to want, and shopping wasn't the avocation it is today. You seldom bought things, for, like Queen Mary and her hats, you had them; and housekeeping to Em meant taking reasonable care of them till they wore out, unless you wore out first, which was highly probable.

About the only thing besides the cat population that I remember changing in Em and Ben's house was the kitchen-table oilcloth. No wonder, since the kitchen table was a versatile and well-used object. All by itself it was the Chopping Center, Mixing Center, Pastry Center, breakfast table, lunch table, and, often, desk, where Grandma wrote her letters and grocery lists, and where Grandpa, back in his preaching days, wrote many a sermon, too.

That kitchen-table oilcloth always remained a trifle longer than it should have, till it was crosshatched with hair-fine knife scratches and worn nearly through at the corners, four fuzzy gray thin spots. I think she purposely left the old piece in place till we arrived each summer so that we, too, could enjoy the remarkable transformation when she replaced it with the fine shiny new one. Perhaps it would be brave red cherry clusters and green leaves this time, to replace the faded old blue-and-brown teapots (though the teapots had been beautiful, too, when they were new).

So you took Em's house as you found it, and you also took Em as you found her, which was probably, as I have said, in her rocker, reading, with a cat in her lap, any time of the day. One Monday morning when a neighbor came over to borrow some soap, saying jocularly, "Why, Mrs. Mac, don't you know it's washday?," Grandma said, "Washday, my foot," and went on with her book, but not before she'd given the lady a dark look that had her backing right out of the parlor, forgetting what she'd come for. Washday, to Em, was when she felt like washing.

I might add that "my foot" came into her conversation so frequently it became endemic to our family. As in "Do you want a sandwich?" "Sandwich, my foot; I want my dinner." Or "He's busy." "Busy, my foot; he's asleep." Now I look at the phrase, I realize for the first time that foot was simply a bowdlerization of a more personal part of the anatomy, through the same pasteurization process that had turned most strong language then into a child's garden of curses. There was never a profane thorn or a bramble in this particular doggoned, dingbusted, golderned place and time of which I speak.

I'll take that back. Except for Aunt Liz Noah, I mean, who sometimes had a salty tongue. She'd never have said "H-e-double-toothpicks," as we did in the fourth grade; she came right out with a Hell, sometimes, and even Damn and the Devil without saying "Pardon my French." But then, she had lived in New York.

If I'd said those words, I'd have caught the Old Harry from Grandma. The closest she ever came to indelicate language was when she said firmly, on rare occasions, "If he doesn't like it, he can sit on it." And I am sure she'd never have believed for a minute that *foot,* in "sandwich, my foot" meant anything but foot. She'd have wondered what in the mischief you were talking about. "Oh, fudge!" she'd have said, rocking comfortably and rubbing the cat in that special little erogenous zone around the ears.

Cats. They were an enduring part of the scene. Toms and tabbies, calicoes and tigers, mainly alley but once in a while with a little Persian additive. Seldom fewer than five, often as many as fifteen, they all lived in the barn (there was a barn behind the house because South Main Street had been wide-open country not too long before), and a totally mouse-free barn it was, though the cats all had house privileges.

Mainly they roosted high, on mantels, bookcases, and the top of the wardrobe, where old Grizel liked to have her kittens. At Grandma's, you could always expect to find a cat sitting fatly in some unexpected place, like the middle of the dining table. Mama never forgot the time Grandma's favorite of the moment, a handsome tiger named Mr. Rochester, was curled up there the night the Latin teacher came to dinner. Grandma wouldn't budge him either.

"That's our center-puss," Grandpa remarked offhandedly; *he* didn't care, but Mama nearly died of embarrassment. I've reflected since then that parents embarrass their children probably more than the other way around. I don't know why we should blush so hard for our parents—we didn't rear them—and yet we do.

Em always named her cats after her current literary heroes and heroines, and her tastes in literature were unswervingly romantic.

"That's a real nice little story," she would say approvingly of *Stella Dallas* or *Freckles* or the like. She was well into Olive Higgins Prouty and Gene Stratton Porter and Kathleen Norris at about the time I began reading. Accordingly, there were some four-footed Stephens and Laurels and Davids leaping about, padding around, and purring. Before that, the picture had been more classical. One time when Mama was growing up, Grandma's horny old Sentimental Tommy turned into Mr. Heathcliff overnight.

And so Em housecleaned to her own drumbeat—swept or dusted or didn't, as the spirit moved—except for once a year, when she hired a girl, and then they'd make the fur fly. Grandpa would see to it that he was elsewhere, till he got the All Clear that Em was once again back in her rocker, reading her nice little stories.

All in all, Em and Ben got along remarkably well, though they were certainly different. Ben loved horses and cold weather; Em loved cats and warmth. Ben loved crowds and noise; Em loved solitude and quiet. Thus, as Ben was fond of pointing out, between the two of them they could stand anything. And after a spot of real trouble early in their marriage, which I'll come to in just a minute, the only other problem I ever heard about was the minor one of Ben's comb, back before all his hair fell out. Maybe a marriage is lucky, at that, to have a dependable small lightning rod like this one to draw the heat away from possible larger issues.

As I have indicated, Em was a loving and a dutiful wife. She kept the house quite as well as Ben wanted it kept, cooked what Ben liked to eat, nursed him vigorously when he was sick—according to Ben you had to get well in self-defense—and was undoubtedly a jolly little bundle in the connubial bed.

To repeat, she was a loving and dutiful wife, in every respect but one.

"I don't mind doing for a man," she often said, "but I won't clean his comb." It was a simple declaration of policy, like "We don't do windows."

Now, normally, this wouldn't or shouldn't have caused any trouble. Except that Ben didn't do combs either, and Em had to look at his, for there it always was beside her bottle of Florida Water and her mother's silver hair-combings bowl with the hole in the lid, and her silver hand mirror, its silver heavily, creamily swirled on the back like poured penuche; there that comb everlastingly was, all gummy and disgusting, on top of the chiffonier. (And I wonder whatever happened to the chiffonier, pronounced shiffen-ear. Long gone, I suppose, along with the Macassar oil Ben used to put on his hair while he still had it, and which was largely responsible for the comb's deplorable condition.)

As I have said, it wasn't a throwaway age. Once you had a comb, you took care of it; for combs were moderately expensive, made of horn or tortoise shell, which weren't supposed to be washed.

Therefore, what you did (or your wife did, if her name wasn't Em) was brush between its little teeth with a brush that supposedly reamed the stuff out but never got it all. So then you went to work on it with tiny twists of tissue, this being a revolting as well as a time-consuming operation, bad enough if it were your own comb, and if it were someone else's, just one huckleberry too much.

And so she explained the situation to him as she saw it. If he didn't clean his comb, he would have to buy a new one, because she was going to throw it away. And he made it equally clear to her that she was hollering down a drainpipe; he wasn't about to clean his comb. He then started ordering expensive combs by the dozen from Caswell-Massey in New York.

Thus it happened that every month or so Em would pick up his comb in gingerly fashion with a gloved hand. Holding it delicately between thumb and forefinger, as one might carry a cockroach by one antenna, she would bring it to Ben as he worked on his accounts in the back room.

"I assume you won't be needing this?" she would say with gentle courtesy as she dropped it into the wastebasket.

"Not at all, thank you," he would say, with equal *politesse*. And there it went, another half a dollar, which I am sure curdled them both, but especially Em. Fifty cents would buy a lot of good things then. But neither Em nor Ben ever gave an inch.

However, this was but a minor flaw in an amber otherwise clear as the lucent crab-apple jelly Em put up in quantity every fall.

Now, Aunt Liz Noah's house was eight blocks away from Em and Ben's—five down South Main Street, right on Locust for three, and there it was on the corner, the white house with the front door she'd painted blue. She lived alone, if you don't count her myna bird, Captain Anderson, and I used to love to go there. The house was older than Grandpa's house—after all, he and Liz Noah had grown up in it—and smaller, though it had more porch, virtually a wraparound porch, which I considered perfectly splendid.

But then everything about Liz Noah was perfectly splendid, from the look of her thin tanned arms (mine being incurably round and pink) when she'd sit forward talking at supper, elbows on the table, chin on both fists, to the way her dark hair grew, a fine mane of it, some silver streaks now but never a cowlick. She had a strong aquiline nose and deep-set somber eyes. Her square boyish-looking hands were frequently paint-smudged, and she always wore the same rough gold-nugget earrings in her ears. I think they had been a wedding present from her husband.

She was a handsome woman, though that didn't occur to me then (handsome was for men, pretty was for women and girls). Built lean and tall, she looked exactly right in her customary old riding pants and shirt.

She was Grandpa's younger sister and therefore my great-aunt. But "Great-Aunt Liz Noah" was cumbersome, and she didn't mind the short form. Ever since she'd married John Noah she'd been Liz Noah (run together, Liznoah), to avoid confusion with the family's other two Lizes.

This had happened late along, when she was about thirty-five. Up till then she'd been a cheerful old maid living in New York's Greenwich Village—certainly a bohemian life by Ganister standards—painting pictures and illustrating books. But when she met big John Noah, a splendid-looking actor on the New York stage, it was a glorious, fast, head-over-heels romance. They were married in Ganister, honeymooned in Italy, and resettled in the Village, where she presently gave birth to a beautiful baby girl.

They christened her Littlepage, a favorite old name from John's side of the family; and the baby wasn't quite three when the tragedy occurred—certainly the most heartbreaking thing that has ever happened in our family. Littlepage and John Noah died together in a theater fire on West 45th Street.

It almost killed Liz Noah. She was still in the hospital, with a breakdown, when her parents, with remarkable unanimity, began their deaths back in Ganister. A long, old, arduous dying it turned out to be, too, though it probably saved their daughter. She suddenly regained her equilibrium, packed her grief, her pictures, her bags, and a trunkful of big-city hats, to come back to the house she'd grown up in, turn the dining room into another bedroom, and take care of her mother and father. (And yet for all this, I think I've laughed with Aunt Liz Noah more than with anyone.)

After they died, she stayed there and gradually constructed —with some care, I imagine—a workable life for herself: reading, painting. Two mornings a week, summers, she gave free drawing lessons to kids in the bandstand of the small Ganister park. I would watch, feeling proud and proprietary and a little jealous. She was *my* aunt Liz Noah. Then in late afternoons, Kansas weather permitting, she would usually ride old Kiwani Girl, an amiable chestnut mare she and Ben had had for years. They'd go for miles, exploring the low hills and fuzzy pastures southwest of town.

Of course, all Ganister knew of Aunt Liz Noah's tragedy. My mother told me of the time a neighbor stopped by to chat with Em, years after it had happened, and started wallowing in it, unaware that Aunt Liz Noah was within earshot on the porch.

"I just don't see how she can live with the memory," this woman said, with the complacent air some people adopt for situations like this, as though they themselves couldn't possibly, as though they themselves were far too fine-grained, too sensitive. And Aunt Liz Noah suddenly appeared from the porch then.

"You don't live with it," she said carefully but matter-of-factly. "You live around it. On the edges."

The woman was discomfited, of course, though Aunt Liz Noah hadn't meant to embarrass her, I am sure; only to explain.

Anyway, Grandma liked her to eat with them whenever she would, because you couldn't trust Liz Noah to feed herself. Either she would forget to eat or she would just tunnel her absent-minded way through a pot of stew or a case of cornflakes—day after day simply eating one thing exclusively till it was gone. (You'd have thought she was a daughter instead of a sister-in-law, the way Em fussed, though Em wasn't so very much older, only seemed so, completely gray-haired as she was, and increasingly round.)

I can see us all now at the supper table at Grandpa's house, those long-ago summer evenings, Em in a fresh apron, Ben in a jacket and tie, even if he hadn't worn one all day, and sitting tall. Em never had to tell Ben to sit tall, even when he was, as he put it, older than two turtles and a redwood tree. Then there would be my mother and father, Jack and me, and Aunt Liz Noah, looking like a tall proud stork.

And I can hear the intermittent husky rasp of the locusts outside in the deepening dusk, and see the big framed litho on the opposite dining-room wall, a family eating, and beneath the picture, the old Scottish grace:

> *Some hae meat and canna eat*
> *And some wad eat that want it;*
> *But we hae meat and we can eat*
> *And sae the Lord be thankit.*

I can also smell the heartening down-home smell of bread being toasted—whole wheat for Em and the rest of us ("peasant toast," Ben called it, said it was what the nobles used to give the peasants and after that the peasants would stay away) and white for him. There would also be a platter of thick-sliced red tomatoes, another of cold meat, and usually a willowware bowl of Em's watermelon pickles. Kansas was good watermelon country.

At the supper table at Grandma and Grandpa's we talked a lot about food, and this would annoy Mama. She thought we should talk about what she considered larger issues.

Grandpa would say, "Good tomatoes, Em. Red Gems, aren't they?"

And Em would say no, she hadn't planted any Red Gems this year, they'd done so badly last year, remember? These were the Improved Hawley's Finest. Then maybe Jack would say they were good, they didn't have as many seeds as the other kind did.

Then Grandpa might comment on the bread situation, like it was a shame you couldn't find good salt-risen any more. And then Liz Noah would wink at me (it was a joke between us, how predictably this food talk bugged Mama) and say she'd like some more of Em's apricot jam, it was exceptionally good apricot jam, had she maybe spiked it with a little orange rind? And, barely able to restrain my giggles, I'd contribute a sparkler, like I loved apricot jam but I just hated orange marmalade. . . .

And then Mama would explode, sure enough, with a "For heaven's *sake,* can't we ever talk about anything at this table except what we're eating?" And then Daddy would get into the act with "Sure, we can talk about what we'll be eating tomorrow."

And always, at the supper table, there was the business with the tea.

"Would you like your tea now, Ben?" Em would invariably ask after the blessing. Without waiting for an answer she would open his silver tea ball—the one that hangs in my kitchen window now—and start filling it from the box of China tea.

"If that's the best you can do," Ben would say, or words to that effect.

Then she would say, with a cautionary-loving-indulgent inflection I can hear to this day, "Now, Ben. . . ." And of course I wondered what this was all about, till I heard the story of it one night after dinner, in the kitchen, while Em and Mama and Aunt Liz Noah and I were washing, wiping, and putting away.

(And I would like to ask, parenthetically, what has happened to leisurely talk like this since the advent of the automatic dishwasher? And can we really do without it? It seems to me it must be how the records of the race have survived since time out of mind, before reading and writing—racial records being, after all, only family histories somewhat extended and intertwined with other family histories. It was women cleaning up after a meal, while the men slept it off or mended nets or honed hunting knives, and talking family talk with an occasional child listening in, most probably a female child who was unconsciously recording, to pass it along in her turn. Family gossip and anecdote, who was born when, married who, took after who . . .)

I remember Em's eagle eye for visible traces of various ancestors in the newer twigs of the family tree—the Mc-Questen ear lobes, the Johnstone temper, the Bracken eye fold. I had apparently played no favorites—drawn Grandpa's forehead, they agreed, and Great-grandma's hair, and Daddy's nose, and Mama's eyes (her grandmother's before her), and I've thought since, If I had it to do over again . . .

But you can't escape heredity, they said.

"What *is* heredity?" I asked once.

"Well . . ." and here Aunt Liz Noah dropped one eyelid in a remarkably droll wink that was a special talent of hers—a way of dropping that eyelid, smooth as a rolled-down window shade while the other eye stayed stark-staring open. "Well, it's like this," she explained. "If your grandma didn't have any children and your mother didn't have any children, then you probably inherit a tendency not to have any children and you probably won't have any children either. That's heredity." Which made the picture perfectly clear momentarily, till it clouded up again.

And so it was on one of those Ganister nights, the men elsewhere, probably on the front porch counting the Fords go by, the women washing up in the kitchen, that I learned the significance of that nightly exchange over the silver tea ball, and heard for the first time about my great-great-uncle Reet. Reet had had his troubles, God love him, as Liz Noah would say, usually adding, "if there is a God and He isn't blind with tears."

It seems that my great-great-uncle Reet was . . . was . . .

Well, let me put it this way: every family has its scattering of skeletons—you'll admit that—and ours is no exception. For example, I give you Cousin Ralph, a pinsetter in a bowling alley at age fifty. But he was so incompetent he didn't have to wait for technology to displace him; the management did. Just tied the can on, as Ralph delicately put it in a letter asking for a loan to tide him over.

And there was Jeannine, a female relative in Ganister who married a stable hand. This was before I was born, so I didn't make it to the wedding, though I heard later how flustered the bride's family was, simply didn't know which way to look. I mean, democracy is all well and good, but after all. As my father murmured to my mother during the "Here comes the groom" part, they weren't just kidding.

Oh, we have our embarrassments all right, including a relative who regularly sends out a long Xeroxed Christmas letter, regaling a mailing list of hundreds with each and every tiny adventure from holidays to hemorrhoids that was enjoyed by each and every member of her immediate family during the entire preceding year.

However, of the whole lot, Ben's and Liz Noah's young uncle Reet wins the Oscar, the Emmy, and the solid-gold horse and buggy. He is the big blushing red apple on the family fig tree—so embarrassing to us, as a matter of fact, that we boast about him now, as people are apt to do about some old reprobate of an ancestor who managed to get himself hanged as a horse thief, providing it happened long enough ago.

Now, Reet drank hard likker by the gallon, or so it was said, and as a young man he wasn't too particular about where he pleasured himself. In fact, his claim to being the Number 1 skeleton in our ancestral bone yard is that he acquired Carrie, his lawfully wedded wife, in a Chicago whorehouse. He married her—eagerly, I have always imagined—and brought her down to Ganister, where he worked for the Santa Fe railroad. ("Poor Reet" is what the women in the family mostly called him, but not the men.)

Aunt Carrie was a dish, a doll, whatever they called a mighty pretty girl back in the late 1880s. Even in the faded daguerreotype I have, you can't miss the lustrous black curls, the camellia skin, and in the large dark eyes a certain margin for mischief.

However, the point I want to make concerns the bad influence Reet had on Ben. Reet wasn't married yet but Ben and Em had been man and wife for a couple of years. And the fact is, Reet and Ben used to go out and hell around together and get drunk.

Just how they managed to do it in Kansas, I don't know. The W.C.T.U. was waxing fat and happy then in a state that had never been exactly famous for Dionysian revelry anyway. It is true that the initials T.A.N.S. hadn't started appearing on social invitations yet, indicating that it would be an occasion of Total Abstinence, No Smoking; but the only reason, I am sure, is that in Em and Ben's day, decent people wouldn't have expected anything else.

But where there's a will there's a way. Reet found a source for the sauce, and judging by the old photograph I have of him, I'm not surprised. With a raunchy black derby pushed far back on his head, a black cigar held casually between slender and elegant fingers, and a knowledgeable, twinkling eye, he looks like a teller of tall tales, an appreciator of fair women, and a man who could find his way blindfolded to the nearest bar just any time at all.

Ben would, accordingly, roll in with his scuppers awash. And next morning, when he woke up with a king-size hangover, or what was familiarly known in Kansas at the time as the red-eyed snozzle-wobbles, he wouldn't even bother to answer when Em pointed out, somewhat unnecessarily, "Ben, you've been drinking again."

Thus it was that one freezing winter night when Benjamin had stayed out clear up to ten o'clock, Em decided that the time had come to take a stand. So she put on her bonnet and shawl and then swaddled their eight-month-old baby girl, my mother, in all the warm things she could find. And then she planted the two of them on the hatrack-bench in the front hall to await his arrival. She met him on the front porch as he lurched up, singing; and "A Baby's Prayer at Twilight" it was not.

"Ben," she interrupted, "you are again under the influence of liquor, and I have had all that the baby and I can put up with. We are going over to Lucy's"—Lucy being her best friend, who lived a block or two away. And she continued, "I will not live with a drunkard." (Alcoholics had yet to be invented.)

As my mother told it to me, this hit him right between the eyes. Basically a good boy, with all the makings of an upstanding citizen, Ben didn't care at all for the idea of, to put it bluntly, Splitsville. Nor did he like the mental picture of his solid little strong-minded wife heading into the cold night with Baby Ruth.

And so the strategy worked. Between tears and hiccups, Ben vowed a solemn vow: as of that very minute, he would abandon the wide-and-curvy for the good old Presbyterian straight-and-narrow. He would neither drink nor gamble, wouldn't even swear; he threw that one in for good measure.

Em took him at his word, and eventually Ben even joined the ministry; eventually got out of it, too. But he kept his pledge, and after that evening, Em and Ben went happily up the hill and down the farther sunlit slope together, with scarcely a cloudlet to darken the genial affection between them.

I wish the years had been as kind to Carrie and Reet. But they were not, not the Kansas years, at any rate, and it is a merry-go-sorry tale. Carrie found Ganister a place good neither to visit nor to live in; and perhaps I should add a postscript about this.

That it didn't work out should have surprised no one, really. This was then, remember, not now. Now it would be different. At least, in the California town I left for Hawaii, Carrie's experience would be considered an extra and desirable dimension. She would be asked to head a workshop in Creative Sex Play, or, at the very least, run an "Ask Carrie" column in the local paper.

But, as I say, this wasn't now, and I've always thought Reet must have had rocks in his head in addition to the evident stars in his eyes when he brought his bride back to his own hometown that green May morning in 1886. How in the world could he have expected the good women of Ganister to cotton to Carrie?

Even had they known nothing about her, the reception would have probably been frosty, if only because she was so pretty. Having the clothes to go with it didn't help either. Em said with relish that Carrie made the rest of them look like they'd crawled out of the missionary barrel. But the town knew—or at any rate learned—about her colorful Chicago connection shortly after the couple arrived.

It was the long arm of coincidence—wouldn't you know it?—that upset the apple cart. It just so happened that the county assessor, who lived in Ganister, had enjoyed Carrie's Chicago hospitality on a business trip the previous year. And of course he wouldn't want *his* wife associating with a woman who was no better than she should be, as I believe the phrase went. (I'd love to know how the little sneak managed to give his wife the information without explaining how he got it.)

Anyway, what happened was—nothing. Carrie and Reet set up housekeeping in a nice little bungalow on South Main Street, where Carrie scrubbed and polished and made curtains and baked good things to eat for people who never came. Not a visit or a social call or an invitation, except for Em's. (Aunt Liz Noah was in New York then.) So Em and Ben had them over often for afternoons and suppers, and that was the size of their social life, except for, possibly, an occasional chilly nod from someone in church.

And so the weeks turned into months and the year rolled along, till it was nearly time for the Aid Society's annual pre-Christmas Bake Sale. Everyone who had a cookstove was urged to contribute at least something, all proceeds going to the mission.

Accordingly, Carrie baked a beautiful Lady Baltimore cake, which was politely delivered to the church by Reet himself, and promptly returned the same day, with exquisite courtesy, by the Aid Society president herself, who thanked Carrie for the loan of the cake, which, she explained carefully, no one had seemed to want.

Silently, Carrie accepted it. But Reet, who was there, told the lady she could go plumb straight to hell and take the Aid Society with her, and he showed her the door. According to family legend, they started packing the same night, and shortly after that they headed west, bag and baggage, lock, stock, and barrel.

Em missed her. "She was a good woman," she always said, and she got out of the Aid Society.

It was the last Ganister saw of Carrie and Reet. A few letters came from Denver, eventually, and one from somewhere in California. Then two of Em's were returned, "Unknown at This Address," and no one ever heard anything more.

I've wondered, often, what happened to them. And of course I have invented various endings. Some sorry ones:

Reet could have begun to resent Carrie, illogically, for the snubs and the slights and the forced move. And she could have resented him right back: after all, whose idea was it to get married in the first place? Or possibly her wifely status eventually went to her head and she became a perfect lady in the bedroom? Or perhaps she found virtue increasingly dull work and Reet learned that though you can take a girl out of the whorehouse, you can't . . . well . . .

But I'd rather not think in those directions. I would rather believe they eventually found a warm sunny place to put down roots—Albuquerque? San Diego?—anyway, a more genial all-around climate than Ganister's had proved, for them, to be. And it occurred to me only this morning, as I was thinking about a certain westward-ho compulsion that seems to have affected various members of our Middle Western clan, it is just possible that Carrie and Reet made it all the way to Hawaii. This would have been in the 1890s, well before Hilton and McDonald's and United Airlines discovered the Sandwich Islands, but about the same time that Mark Twain did, when he called them surely the loveliest fleet of islands that lies anchored in any ocean.

Perhaps Reet and Carrie found their own enchanted isle to settle on, here, under the waving palms, where the friendly folk probably never heard of a Lady Baltimore cake, but where the native guitars pour their special honey into the soft air, sweet as guava syrup on a coconut waffle.

Perhaps they settled on the very island where I live. And perhaps, one of these mornings, strolling down a dusty palm-shaded road within sound of the surf, I'll find myself passing the time of day with some easygoing kamaaina leaning on the lawn mower in his front yard, and we'll start a little easygoing talk-story, swapping names and mainland ties, the way you do.

And then he'll say, "Reet McQuesten? Really? Why, that just so happened to be my grandfather's name!"

So I have decided that that's what I am going to believe. After all, the most all-around, practical, long-wearing illusions are the ones that you weave yourself.

9

Joy Cometh in the Morning

or My Grandpa Was a Very Kindly Man

Though I haven't told Uwe so, I do feel a trifle uneasy, sometimes, about the modern equipment in this new kitchen of ours—that is, about its philosophic implications.

Very probably I won't mention it to him either. He wouldn't thank me, I'm sure, and anyway I don't know what he could do about it, short of starting over and replacing everything with period pieces from fifty years ago, like the Congoleum rug on the kitchen floor in Grandma and Grandpa's house, or their stove-and-burner unit on its tall skinny legs, or the chip-prone porcelain sink, or the icebox with the dishpan underneath to catch the drips—all stunning, expensive camp now, collectors' items that I know we couldn't afford.

Why didn't these things stay in the family? Why did we let them get away? Why weren't they handed down like the set of sterling flatware (complete service for twelve, mind you) which the congregation gave Grandpa when he left the ministry?

Well, I think I know the answer: because back then, few people foresaw the tidal wave of nostalgia that was going to come surging out of the seventies and eighties to backwash over the twenties and thirties and all their artifacts—a wistful it-is-to-weep nostalgia for those (in spite of everything) safe and innocent quaint old days before the TV dinner and the polyester pantsuit, before pollution and the Pill, before acid rain and the aerosol can and the computer and the moon shot and the Bomb, before quarks and psi particles and the primal scream.

And so when Em finally acquired a new G.E. refrigerator, with its brace of ice-cube trays and the proud round gun turret on top, she was delighted to see the last of her old zinc-lined icebox—gave it to the Salvation Army store, as I remember, down on Lower Main. (Now I think of it, I had the zinc-lined kind myself when I was first married, and I couldn't wait to get rid of it either.)

But what bothers me, when I let it, is the way our new kitchen conforms so completely to the tenor of the times—our modern propensity, I mean, for cleaving to the sin and escaping the penalty. Go ahead, drive like a maniac, we'll protect you with air bags! Go on, drink your sweet soda, we took out the sugar! Type sloppy, IBM will correct you; be rude, we'll excuse you for your insecurities; be spendthrift, there's always a credit card . . . all these things being wholly at odds with the moral climate I grew up in, where if you sinned, you suffered, and the retribution was approximately immediate. Drive crazy, you got hurt. Be a pig, you got sick. Type sloppy, you typed it over. Be rude, you got smacked. Be extravagant, you went broke.

In this new kitchen of ours, though, you can get away with almost anything. In this kitchen you could be an absolute slob and no one would ever know.

Examine, for instance, the floor, which is paved with maple-sugar-colored tile flecked with ivory—a marvelous combination, as I happen to know, having lived at one time with a plain dark-floored kitchen where a spatter of flour showed bright as dandruff on a blue serge suit. If you ever noticed, it isn't the dark-colored things, it is the light ones, that are customarily slopped about in a kitchen. It's the flour, the sugar, the cornmeal, the baking powder, the crumbs. On this amiable new floor of ours I think I could lose a cup of each and no one the wiser.

Consider our big new competent dishwasher. I used to cook with a certain prudent foresight, rinsing as I went, making one knife, one spoon do the work of three. But no more; and it is rather impressive, the number of utensils I can involve just to make a tuna sandwich.

Take a look, too, at My Mother the Oven, how she cleans up after me! I needn't be careful any more to see that food doesn't spill over and bake onto the oven floor, the way I used to be, way back before ovens learned to clean themselves up, way back when I knew that otherwise I'd have the devil's own time getting the stuff off. No more. All I do now is move a lever and set two dials to get the oven as clean as new, all ready for me to let something boil over in it again.

And then there is the big new reefer I've mentioned before, standing tall, proud, and sufficient unto itself—a far cry from the stubby little icebox, the old oaken icebox, the old zinc-lined icebox I was just talking about.

In retrospect, I think the main purpose of that zinc lining was to store up various succulent flavors like old fish and onions and cantaloupe, reissuing them with a fine impartiality to any impressionable items you may have forgotten to cover tightly, like the butter or the cream.

In fact, there were several things you had to remember with the old ice-powered icebox. It was a commitment and an ongoing pain in the rear, though it certainly kept you on your toes. You had to remember to turn the ice card around, the one in the window informing the iceman that you wanted 25-50-75-or-100 pounds of ice, and you had to be there when he arrived or otherwise arrange it somehow so he could make the drop. And always, like the beat-beat-beat of the tom-tom came the drip-drip-drip of the ice melting away into the drip pan, which required punctual emptying the way a baby needs changing, though when you forgot and the drip-drip-drip became ominously inaudible, you could generally count on the lady downstairs to remind you before her ceiling quite fell in.

But this automated reefer now! It doesn't expect me to remember a thing. It keeps itself at the proper temperature, it doesn't (as we noted earlier) jostle the eggs, it gives personalized attention to the butter, vegetables, and fruit, it never needs defrosting. . . .

And neither, of course, does our big new freezer—a fact that rather baffles me in the face of its extravagant coldness. I would expect ice to pile up like glaciers. But no. Open the door and jump back, or you'll freeze solid in the white vapor pouring out, great rolling clouds of it. This is a sub-zero freezer, colder than a banker's eye or an Eskimo cookout, colder than anything I know of, always excepting the absolutely coldest thing on my personal planet, which is the padlock on my grandpa's barn door on a February morning, back in Ganister, Kansas.

But now that I've said this, I find it necessary (if it is true that you must say B once you've said A) to stop for a minute in order to dig my way out of an untidy windfall of memories that are somehow interconnected.

Scraps and bits about Grandpa: it was his barn, certainly, and his padlock.

Scraps and bits about the Seventh-Grade English Club, of which I was president, this being only the biggest Happening since who flung the chunk, bigger even than having my poem about rats printed in *The Auntie Teebee Magazine** (*Rats are very dirty things / They're full of bugs and lice / And never never wash their paws / Which isn't very nice.*)

And both Grandpa and the English Club are somehow commingled with the traumatic period of the statewide Junior

* *Auntie Teebee* was a mimeographed giveaway health monthly for grade schools, which took a strong stand against tuberculosis. Years later I realized that Auntie really meant Anti-, though at the time I thought that she was just a nice old lady.

High Speech Contest, when Freem Fuller got the blight and I found myself wearing his mantle, only slightly heavier to my shoulders than a concrete chubby.

I would like to figure out what is the curious glue that holds these various things together in my mind.

To repeat, Grandpa—that's Ben—looms large in this account, not only his barn and padlock, but the sort of person he was; and I feel I should emphasize here that Grandpa was, first and foremost, a very kindly man.

"I hate to kill anything before breakfast; it starts the day off wrong," he explained once, and I can see him now in that old Kansas kitchen, scooping a spider out of the sink before he shooed it out the door and went back to tending his coffee.

Which took some doing. I should perhaps explain that he liked his coffee blowed-and-saucered, though he'd never have said blowed-and-saucered without putting quotation marks around it. (I come from a long line of simple but grammatical folk.)

But that's what he'd do, every morning at the oilcloth-covered kitchen table: pour part of his coffee into the cup's saucer, blow it to the perfect, comfortable, drinkable temperature, and then drink it, holding the saucer properly between the thumb and third finger of each hand. This left the problem of where to set the cup down, since coffee had doubtless dribbled down the side of it after pouring. And that is the raison d'être of a dozen little white scallop-edged Haviland dishes I inherited: to set a sloppy cup in.

(Actually they are not good for much else either, and that is why they live on a high cabinet shelf in our new kitchen now. They're too small for anything except what we don't like very well, like bread pudding—same principle as the string-saver's collection of Pieces Too Short to Use, or my own box of Pencil Stubs Too Short to Sharpen.)

But back to Grandpa.

Yes, a kindly man. And also a religious man, in his way. Though he had left the ministry well before I was born, he still tithed, always a tenth of what he had to the church, and he still visited the sick, which took more out of him than the sick would ever have suspected.

I especially remember going with him a time or two to visit a former parishioner who now lived at The Elms. This was Ganister's Convalescent Home (where people seldom convalesced) or call it Rest Home or Nursing Home or Old Folks' Home—no matter—which was located a few blocks down South Main Street, almost midway between Ben and Em's place and Aunt Liz Noah's. A large swinging sign outside said THE ELMS', which always had Grandpa snorting and muttering, "The Elms' *what?*" The ubiquitous idiot apostrophe always bothered Grandpa a lot.

It was a big old barely remodeled Kansas Victorian house that even then was something of an eyesore—peeling mustard-colored paint, and tall weeds growing nearly through the floorboards of the porch. The porch was generally cluttered with wheelchairs, most of them occupied by impossibly old people, their eyes open but mostly empty, their mouths open and often empty, too.

We'd go in, Grandpa and I, and I wouldn't know which way to look because whatever your eye landed on would embarrass you—tubes attached to people, and bedpans here and there, and strange-shaped bottles. (I learned early that if I breathed through my mouth I wouldn't smell anything.)

Old old people in bathrobes drifted around, often into the wrong places, according to Mrs. Hendrickson, the large harried woman who ran the home. She couldn't keep her Mentals separate from her Blinds and her Seniles, she'd say accusingly to Grandpa, she just couldn't, that's all, without more room and more money. And Grandpa could only shake his head in sympathy and agree. It was a private nursing home, no state or county funds, and the only financial help it got besides the woefully inadequate monthly fees was the annual Elks' Club Benefit Picnic.

I remember asking Grandpa once, after one of those visits, if he and Grandma would have to go there. And he said no, you'd only go there if you had neither chick nor child to take care of you. This set my mind at ease, and it didn't occur to either one of us then, I am sure, that Aunt Liz Noah had neither chick nor child.

Grandpa would also visit the sick at home, which was hard

on him, for he was squeamish—hated messes, just couldn't help it. But more people died at home in those days than do now, from mysterious and inexorable and often messy things. When Grandpa came back from some sorry sickbed visit, he would usually have a migraine headache. But he would always go again.

A kindly man.

Yes, and, even better, a first-rate grandpa, the kind that took you seriously and lightly all together in just the right proportions, a truly accomplished grandpa, who could give lessons in the gentle art today if he were around and able to get the boys in from the nineteenth hole.

Of course, it would help if they would shed the bright polyester pants and the golf shoes and dress like grandpas, too. It was a comfortable feature of those days, how people dressed their age and gender, instead of the omni-age omni-sex life style we follow now, with everyone wearing everything. I was reflecting on this only the other day as I climbed into my beach rompers.

Back then, grandpas wore dark three-piece suits in the wintertime and two-piece seersucker suits in the summertime (which went nicely with the stiff Maurice Chevalier straw hat). And they wore well-polished black shoes with oddly bulbous toes, low shoes in the summer, ankle-high in the winter. At least, my grandpa did. And whenever he took off his suit jacket you could see the broad rubber bands that kept his shirt sleeves up. Perhaps shirts weren't sleeve-sized then, or maybe Grandpa had short arms.

And grandpas carried canes or walking sticks. Fuddy-duddies or curmudgeons used theirs to lean on or to threaten whippersnappers and flibbertigibbets with. (And where in the world did all the fuddy-duddies and curmudgeons and whippersnappers and flibbertigibbets *go?*) But Grandpa used his cane to poke things with or run along picket fences. It made a highly satisfactory noise.

As I say, he was a first-rate grandpa. For instance, as a Tooth Fairy—Gnome—he stood alone. Paid way over scale, Grandpa did, a whole heavy half-dollar invariably wrapped in an invisible-ink note, usually some terrible tooth joke. (*How do you say farewell to a tooth? Bye, Cuspid!*) And once, in exchange for a lateral incisor, I found a pink handkerchief tucked into a toy megaphone, which he explained was for crying out loud. Oh, he was a formidable Tooth Gnome! And on the one Halloween visit we ever made to Ganister, when I was of an age to be scared out of my Mary Janes by pop-up snakes and skeletons dithering on strings, he had concocted a memorable Museum of Horrors out in the barn. And on the Fourth of July he'd have more Red Devils and cherry bombs at the ready than anybody.

Best of all, though, were the walks we'd take after supper. Fine old serendipitous times they were, those walks with Grandpa in the summer dusk. We would play walking games: look up till he said, *"Down!"* and then name ten things you'd seen up there—a rag of cloud, a bird on a wire, a first star. Now look down till he said, *"Up!"* Seed pods, a sudden mushroom, a Ganister *Sentinel* lost and yellowing under a porch.

Then Grandpa's nose might start to itch, which meant we were nearing hidden treasure. Sure enough, under a bush or a rock we'd find a shiny nickel or a marble or a stick of gum or a genuine imitation emerald ring just my size.

Before we went back home, we would usually stop at the confectioner's for a quart of peach ice cream—it always seemed to be peach season—to eat on the front porch.

And Grandma would say with approval, "I do think young Homer makes better ice cream than his father did." (Old Homer Fudge had recently passed the confectionary along to his son, and who says names aren't destiny?)

And Grandpa would say, consideringly, "Well now, I don't know about that. The old man never held back on the peaches. Sometimes I think young Homer cuts a few corners."

And Grandma would say comfortably, "Oh, I don't think so, Ben. . . . But remember that praline ice cream we got in Kansas City?" She never failed to mention this marvelous praline ice cream they'd had on their honeymoon.

And Jack would say, "Why don't they make root-beer ice cream?" (This was well before Thirty-one Flavors.) And I'd say, "And peanut-butter ice cream!" "And cranberry-jelly-and-turkey ice cream," Jack would say, warming to his work, "and spaghetti ice cream and hot-dog ice cream and . . ."

And maybe I would ask, "If you work in an ice-cream store, can you eat all the ice cream you want to?" But I probably wouldn't get it out before my mother would say impatiently, "Can't we ever talk about anything except what we're eating?" And my father would say, "Well, we could talk about what we ate yesterday. . . ."

As I mentioned earlier, in the matter of the parsonage lawn, Grandpa wasn't above playing a mild practical joke. There had been the Aunt Heck episode, too, which Grandma told me about years later, for it happened well before I was born.

Aunt Heck was a shirttail relative who lived across the state. Apparently she was one of these positive people, the sort that knows everything, notices everything, remembers everything, and has you feeling like an insensitive clod because you didn't know or notice or remember it yourself. She was right ninety-five percent of the time, too, which isn't a lovable batting average in matters like this; and Grandpa made up his mind, one time, that he'd give her something to think about.

This was when he and Em first moved into the house on Main Street, when South Main was still virtually country. Their lot was a former cornfield, and there wasn't even a lawn yet, only bone-bare ground.

So when Aunt Heck wrote that she was coming through to stay overnight on her way to Florida, Grandpa got himself a portable tree from a theatrical supply house in Kansas City— a truly remarkable tree, about twenty feet tall, though it couldn't have weighed twenty pounds, for it was mainly papier-mâché. But Em said it looked realer than most trees do. Instead of roots it had a long sharp spike for easy transplanting.

Accordingly, Grandpa stuck it in the ground by the front door before he went down to the depot to fetch Aunt Heck one crisp autumn afternoon. Her sharp eyes didn't miss it either, and later, at dinner, when Grandpa was bemoaning his tree-less acre, she said, "Well, at least you've got that nice little elm out in front."

At which Grandpa looked puzzled. "What are you talking about?" he said.

"Your elm tree. By the front door," she said crisply.

"There isn't one," Grandpa said. And of course there wasn't, when she strode impatiently out to look, for he had already stowed it away in the barn.

She came back in, muttering. "I'd have sworn . . ." she said.

"You've had a long day, Heck," Grandpa said, sympathetically. Then the next morning, before anyone else was up, he replaced the tree by the front door, and Em stood beside it, waving, as Ben drove their visitor back to the depot after breakfast. Aunt Heck didn't say a word the whole way, he reported later, just kept shaking her head like a dog with burrs in its ears.

The following Sunday, Em told me, Grandpa made an extra-large contribution to the Poor Box. I suppose if he'd been Catholic, he'd have taken the whole thing to confession. But being the minister of his own Presbyterian church, he had to confess to himself—conduct unbecoming to the clergy, I suppose—and make reparation of a sort. Though Grandpa wasn't a folly-and-imminent-hellfire sort of a preacher, neither was he in favor of the sin without the punishment. (I don't think he'd have quite approved of my self-cleaning oven.) Still, I think he felt that occasionally the sin *with* the punishment was a fair-enough bargain: eat the whole pie if you have to, but don't dodge the bellyache.

Not that Grandpa ever talked about these things to me. He never lectured. The only advice he ever gave me, that I remember, was never to murder anybody, because that could lead to setting fires and telling fibs, and the next thing, he said, I'd be rude to the teacher and even late to school. So I never murdered anybody.

As I think I've said elsewhere, I never knew why or how Grandpa got into the mortgage business, which must have had its unpleasant aspects, too, like foreclosures (though be-

ing a very small mortgage company it couldn't have fore-
closed very hard). Nor did I ever know exactly why he left
the ministry.

His sermons were good. It's true that he caught some flak
now and again for certain of his attitudes or interpretations.
Grandpa felt that "Love one another" should be retranslated
into "Put up with one another," on the theory that we have
to crawl a good while before we can walk, and he had no
reluctance about saying so. And he had his own categorical
imperative: Solve your problem without making one for
somebody else. His was a practical approach, all right, more
Unitarian than Presbyterian, I think. But his congregation
liked him, and they didn't want him to go. I know that, and
if I had any doubts, there is the valedictory set of sterling
flatware they gave him, to set my mind at ease. Not a nig-
gardly service for six, mind you, or a namby-pamby compromise eight, but a solid, affirmative, all-out twelve.

I think he just wasn't quite tailored for it; and I know
Grandma always believed the afternoon he spent with the
extremely proper wife of a Kansas City elder had hastened his
decision.

This lady had come from Kansas City on some mission or
other from her husband. When it was taken care of, Grandpa
drove her around, in the buggy behind Old Favorite, to see
some of the high spots of the town, like the cemetery. Then,
trotting briskly back home down Main Street, the horse suddenly stopped cold, right in the middle of downtown Ganister, to take care of a personal matter of utmost urgency.

I don't know just how much water a horse can hold, and I
don't think Grandpa knew exactly either, though he esti-
mated it later at about two hundred gallons. It was a Niagara,
he said, flashing bright in the sunshine, a flood of dimensions
heretofore known only to Noah-son-of-Lamech, but no Ararat
in sight, only the townsfolk, some of them taking considerable
pleasure in the plight of the prim-looking red-faced lady, who
apparently had never seen a horse relieve himself, and the
minister, who—after watching Old Favorite for a good while
in the immemorially earnest, comical, spraddled position of a
horse urinating—found himself laughing his head off.

Old Favorite went right on. As Grandpa put it later, shaking his head, "Him peed powerful." (He sometimes had his own way of putting things.) He also said that the Kansas City lady seemed to regard it as all his fault; you'd think he had arranged it in advance. And Grandpa added, with a gleam in his eye, that if he'd met her first, he just might have.

I suppose Grandpa himself felt that he wasn't quite ministerial material, and he was probably right. I think he found too many things funny, which could be a handicap in a minister, as in a lover. There are mysteries that can be dissipated or quite frightened away by an untimely guffaw.

But I think it is time I turned my attention to the English Club now, and to the Speech Contest, which is how Grandpa got in here in the first place.

The fact is, if I hadn't been president of the Seventh Grade English Club, maybe I wouldn't have gotten so big for my britches that I volunteered to take Freem Fuller's place in the speech contest when Freem got encephalitis. Yes, and if my father hadn't been acquiring a reputation as a speaker, maybe I'd have had the nerve to back out while the backing was good. Yes, and if your aunt had wheels she'd be a scooter. If me no ifs, my mother would say. Ifs butter no parsnips. Unfortunately.

This English Club, now.

Well, it was democratic. In fact, everybody in the class was in it. In fact, it wasn't a club. Miss Leffler, our teacher, presumably felt that "English Club" had more appeal than "writing class," which is what it actually was.

Each Monday there was an assignment: write five hundred words of dialogue, narrative, description, *something*, and each Friday Miss Leffler would sit at a pupil's desk in the back row while I—elected head of it, probably because of being best speller—took over *her* desk, calling upon each student to read his work aloud.

That is really all I did, and yet I doubt if our nation's president-elect approaches the inaugural platform with any more profound sense of responsibility than I felt every time I picked up the gavel to open the meeting and start calling upon each of my classmates, in any order I cared to, to stand up and deliver. Then at year's end, we selected by vote each student's best work, to be included in a mimeographed booklet for which I did the typing.

(For a long time, my copy stayed with me. But I have moved too often since the seventh grade, and I am sorry to report that it disappeared along the way. Lost somewhere in the bright tumble of the years is Augie Barnes's memorable discussion of mackerel fishing in Newfoundland's cold waters, in which Augie managed to spell mackerel eight different ways, *macrel* to *makerol,* without once hitting it right. Gone, too, is Opal Henking's report on her main after-school avocation, cleverly entitled "How I raised my chickens from scratch." And I'd love to read, just one more time, Ernie Olinger's moving vignette entitled "The Day I Threw Up." This had been at a movie house, into the lap of the portly gentleman sitting beside him, when Ernie was eight years old, before his mother could hustle him out. It was simply a matter of too much popcorn.)

Looking back, I just can't understand why I put my hand up—I was certainly the only one who did—when Miss Leffler asked without much hope if someone would care to take Freem's place as our grade's contender in the February oratorical competition, after Freem got sick.

This contest meant a lot to Miss Leffler—we all knew that. She was very big on speech and dramatic emphasis, and sometimes she would elocute a poem for us, like "The Highwayman." She'd do it really well, too, with thrillingly deep chest tones, though we'd all be squirming with embarrassment at the romantic bits, like when the heroine plaited a dark-red love-knot into her long black hair, because Miss Leffler just didn't look the part. Her pale tan hair was stiffly marcelled, and she had a nose like a sweet potato, while high on one cheek, at the end of a fragile stalk, was a tiny wart that trembled like a harebell at any breeze or whenever she moved her head. We used to wonder if it would blow off or fall off someday, but so far as I know it never did. She also wore peculiar-looking shoes, which she explained was because she had a high arch. The way she said it gave it a lot of status, and I have been respectful ever since in the presence of a high arch.

Miss Leffler had already had two winners in this annual competition, and Freem had been practically a shoo-in for a third. He was a natural—we all knew that, too—and I certainly wasn't. And surely I knew that standing in front of a classroom, calling on kids to read papers, was a far cry from standing on a platform in front of God knows how many people and making a speech about the League of Nations, which happened to be the assigned topic.

I suppose I volunteered for the same reason men run for president or volunteer for other do-or-die missions: insanity, temporary or otherwise. Delusions of competence, dreams of glory, or an idiot certainty that the time will never really come, that nothing bad can ever happen to *you* . . .

Well, and then there was the fact of my father's oratory. As I have said, he was building quite a reputation around the state now as a good special-occasion speaker. Daddy orated in the good old-fashioned sense of the word—polished sentences, stately periods, and resounding rhetoric, usually building to a dramatic hush before he'd release the pigeons and unfurl the flag in a really smashing finale. I think perhaps I felt that having a father like this made me Freem's natural successor. I didn't realize, and Miss Leffler apparently didn't either, that Daddy hadn't passed along any of his platform smarts to me.

Finally, and most important, I yearned for approval. From anyone. And everyone. In vast amounts. And the pats on the head I'd gotten with the English Club presidency were habit-forming. Now I wanted more pats, a lot more, and I wanted them immediately. (Indeed, it has always plagued me, this hunger for pats, a hunger so strident that it sometimes has me volunteering earnestly to do kind, troublesome favors for people instead of just going ahead quietly and doing them. Thus I win their gratitude and collect the pats in advance; and this usually, to my shame, quite relieves me of the need or desire to follow through and do the kind, troublesome favors.)

Well, I started getting the pats, all right. Miss Leffler beamed and so did Daddy. "Good girl!" he said when I told him, and Mama called me a chip off the old block, and I basked and smirked. And Opal and Lucille and my other friends were openly envious and admiring, too. "I'd be so scared I'd *die!*" they said, and I smirked some more.

Oh, yes, I was getting the pats. Next, the school principal got me and the eighth-grade contestant up on the stage at Friday afternoon assembly, while the whole school stood and serenaded us with the McKinleyville school anthem,* which owed a heavy debt to the Wisconsin Fight Song but was nonetheless heady stuff.

Moreover—and here is the cincheroony—my mother had bought for me, at the after-Christmas sales, a perfectly splendid ensemble to make my speech in: an accordion-pleated MacDonald tartan skirt, a red silk blouse, a pair of black patent-leather pumps with almost inch-high heels, and my first pair of shiny real silk stockings.

Talk about committed! And as time wore on, I was nearly ready to be.

However, several weeks slipped by before I slid down to the end of that euphoric little rainbow; for in one of those casual eclipses of the mind—to use Sam Johnson's good phrase—I had quite overlooked the hard truth that there was, after all, considerable preparation to be done.

It was only when Miss Leffler asked me a few weeks later if I had finished writing my speech yet that I began getting intimations of impending disaster. (For some reason, it hadn't occurred to me that I would actually have to compose a speech and write it down.) And she said I'd better hurry so the high-school dramatic coach, who had volunteered to help, could start helping. Though the competition rules specified that the oration must be entirely the student's own work, coaching on delivery was permitted.

And so I dashed one off, but when I read it over a day or

* On, McKinleyville, on, McKinleyville,
  That's the school we're from!
  That is where we get our knowledge,
  Just as good as any college.
  Hail, McKinleyville, hail, McKinleyville,
  Let us shout hooray!
  We'll cheer Mc-Kin-ley-vi-ille
  An–y day!

two later, I could see—at least I needed no telling—that it was terrible. Whatever it is that a good speech needs—logic, pace, and point, not to mention beginning, middle, and end—it didn't have.

And so I rewrote it. And it was no better.

Then I stole and incorporated some ponderous paragraphs from a McKinleyville *Advocate* editorial. They didn't help either.

Then I rewrote it again and yet again, and it was still terrible, I mean a dog, I mean a real turkey. Oh, I knew it, with that quiet inner certainty that brooks no argument. And yet, the harder I labored over it, the worse it got.

Well, how could it have been otherwise? What did I know about the League of Nations? Only what the *World Book* said. And what did I care about the League of Nations? Not much. In fact, it could go slide down an Alp, so far as I was concerned, because for anyone growing up in that halcyon era between World War I and television, war wasn't real, it was purely academic.

War was history and belonged in history books, along with cave men and covered wagons. It was something that happened in Olden Times (which are any time before you were born), but certainly not now. I had read and wept over *All Quiet . . .* and I knew as clearly as I knew water is wet that people could never be that cruel and stupid again. And then, too, we weren't growing into a shrugging acceptance of it, as today's moppets must be, watching the daily six-ring television circus, rapes and riots, wars and murders, carnage and disaster. (And in this fashion does television help perpetuate what it pictures? "Watch thyself," the gods told Narcissus. And thus he was condemned.)

Then there was another thing that wasn't helping me any. Right from the beginning, I was aware that the high-school dramatic coach didn't think much of my speech either.

At our twice-weekly sessions, Miss Jacoby would make fretful suggestions: could I, possibly, brighten this part, the merest trifle? Couldn't I, well, strengthen that part, just the tiniest bit? And when I came to the business about raising the banner of enduring peace o'er all the world, would I—you could practically hear the "for God's sake" in her voice, though she never said it—would I please *raise* my arms and hands in a graceful gesture instead of lowering them as though I were shutting a trunk?

And so we struggled, Miss Jacoby and I, eventually evolving an elocutionary style that would at least "see me through," as she put it, adding with false jollity that now, if I would just forget my *self* (fat chance), everything would be hunky-dory, a favorite expression of hers. But I knew a bedside manner when I saw one, and I also knew that her misgivings were minimal compared with mine.

I have reflected, since then, that there is hardly a problem, no matter how complicated it is, that when looked at in the right way doesn't become still more complicated. I have further reflected that there are also some situations in this life that there is no graceful way out of. And there are also a few situations that there is no way out of at all, graceful or otherwise. When you find youself in one of these, you simply have to go through with it.

For instance, having a baby. Eventually you come to a point where you can only bear down, even though common sense tells you it's a ridiculous thing to do because obviously it is going to split you wide open. But being fresh out of options, you go ahead and bear down. Or consider the other side of that—the being born. You had no choices there either, if you remember. There was only one way to go, onward and outward. And I suppose dying is much the same.

So this was the bleak pass I had come to by February, living under a free-floating pall of gray misery, because there was no way I could get out of making that speech. And it remained terrible. As a speech-writer I was terrible, as a speaker I was a disaster, and February 12 now loomed like a great black whale on the horizon.

And the countdown began. On February 7, my brother was deposited with a friend in McKinleyville (school was out for a week because of the Teachers' Convention), and on February 8, bright and early, my mother and I took the train to Ganister. The plan was to visit briefly with Grandma and Grandpa, then go back halfway across Missouri to Columbia, the site of the convention, where Daddy already was, and where the speech contest was to happen, just in time for me to get up there and fall on my face.

Thus it was that on the unseasonably warm morning of February 10 I was sitting with Grandpa on the back stoop after breakfast, which had been Grandma's rye drop cakes—always a special-occasion item in our family.

These drop cakes are crisp, tender, golden-brown doughnutlike affairs made from a rye-flour batter which, once it is spooned into the hot cooking oil, seems to have a will of its own, as it bobbles and jiggles itself into funny shapes, often resembling baby chicks, and so we called them chickens.

The proper way to eat chickens was to dunk them in your own individual saucer of maple syrup, or else spread each bite with some of Grandma's Jampot Jam. This was Grandma's name for all those little bits left at the bottoms of jam and jelly jars, mixed together to save icebox space—an amiable blend of, say, apple jelly, currant jam, and strawberry preserves, with maybe a touch of cranberry, but seldom twice the same. Either way, with the syrup or the jam, it was hard to stop eating those chickens. Ordinarily, that is.

But on this particular morning I found it, on the contrary, hard to start. I wasn't hungry, and I had to force myself to eat my standard quota, though I felt it was necessary, because Grandma had made them specially for me.

And so Grandpa and I were sitting there, eating an after-breakfast tangerine and spitting out the seeds, *thup-thup-thup,* in our ongoing contest to see who could spit the farthest. But my heart wasn't in it, and presently when Grandpa got up and went out to his old desk in the barn, I followed him.

The barn smelled comfortably of old hay and dust and sunshine and cats. It hadn't housed a horse for some time, and Grandpa had rigged up a light and an electric fireplace in the former tack room. Though the air was remarkably gentle for a Kansas February, the warmth of the grate was welcome. Squatting near it while Grandpa sorted seed catalogs, I quizzed him.

"Grandpa, were you ever scared when you preached a sermon?" I asked.

He gave the matter some thought.

"Yes," he said.

"How did you, well, get over it?" I asked.

He thought about that, too. "I guess I never did," he said.

"What were you scared of?" I persisted.

"That it wouldn't be good enough," he said promptly. "Not enough seed corn in the gravel. Or that maybe I'd say something that would knock over somebody's applecart, some dang-fool thing I didn't mean, just to be smart."

I said, "Oh."

I was disappointed. Was *that* all? He didn't know what scared was, not the first little thing.

This was sophisticated scared that he was talking about; I mean surface scared. And maybe before I'd gotten myself into this mess I'd have said I knew what scared was, too, like ripping around the third curve on the River Park roller coaster, or playing the piano for a handful of parents in Mrs. Smedley's piano recital.

But this was different. Now, I was into the real stuff, I mean your genuine Basic Scared, your Basic Pea-green Scared, and locked in the Land of Heartsink. I was heading for the Fall-aparts, which are just the other side of Scream City. For I was going to (A) disgrace myself and my father in front of countless thousands—the auditorium I pictured was only slightly larger than Yankee Stadium—and (B) simultaneously let down Miss Leffler and the entire seventh-grade class, because I was undoubtedly going to (C) trip over my feet and fall flat on my head or (D) come up with a dry mouth that couldn't shape the words (this had even happened rehearsing with Miss Jacoby) or (E) draw a blank and stand there wordless, which had also happened, or (F) vomit.

And at that moment, overwhelmed by the positive likelihood of (F) and wishing to hell I hadn't eaten all those cute little chickens, I knew I was about to do just that, and I tried to run outdoors but couldn't quite make it in time.

Poor Grandpa! As I have said, he hated messes, and there I was, making a good one. But he held my head and eventually fetched water and a washcloth for me from the house (for both of us knew I'd be in for some drastic remedies if we told Grandma). Then he asked me what was bothering me so hard, and I told him.

Grandpa always listened well. With his bony shiny head slightly tilted, and his beard at a rakish angle, he'd regard you with an interested, lively, blue-eyed look that gave you confidence, made you feel you'd shown him an interesting new facet of something, something really worth thinking about.

"Would you like to go over your speech with me?" he asked, finally. "Nobody'd hear us out here. Maybe we could work on it a little."

I shook my head. It was too late for that. Rearranging deck chairs on the S.S. *Titanic,* that's all we'd be doing, and I knew it. Anyway, if I made any changes in that speech now, the whole thing would probably fall apart like a crisp little sun-baked mud pie. My grasp of it was tenuous enough as it was.

"Well, it might be a better speech than you think it is," he offered next, after a thoughtful pause.

But I knew it wasn't. Even allowing for the inevitable faint putrescence that sets in when something has been rewritten, rehashed, and rehearsed ad nauseam, I knew it wasn't.

There was another considering pause.

"Then maybe you'll just have to take your medicine," he said finally. "After all," he added, reasonably enough, "you did get yourself into this."

I nodded, miserably.

"And of course you could pray a little," he added as an afterthought.

I allowed that I guessed I could, though without much enthusiasm. I had prayed hard all the year before for a diamond ring and nothing had happened so far.

Still, I felt better for telling him. That afternoon I practiced some more, and I planned to pray some that night and then practice all the next day till Mama and I took the night train to Columbia. If I would rehearse it, say, two hundred times, I thought, then *surely* . . .

Early that evening it started to sprinkle, and then it rained hard. Late that night, the mercury plummeted to around 20°. The false spring was over. I was sleepily aware, sometime during the night, of Mama's padding in to pile more blankets on my bed, and the next day there was snow underglazed with solid sheet ice. It was what Grandpa called a growler of a day, the sullen, monochrome sky full of trouble, and snow blowing, flowing across the yard, a fine steady spray of it in an evil south wind, wind like a whip, and all hard ice where puddles had been the day before.

My brain felt like cold mush, but midmorning Grandpa went out with me to unlock the barn, so I could do my solo rehearsing there by the warm grate. On the way, we heard the sad caw of a sorrowing rain crow. I don't know what he was doing up and about on such a cold morning, besides freezing his tail off, but he certainly spoke for me. He sounded just like I felt. And, oh, was it cold! Frost was everywhere the snow wasn't, glistening on the fence and on the pump, and the padlock wore a thick frosty bloom like a peach.

"Look, it even covers up the keyhole," I said to Grandpa, who was searching through his big key ring for the key.

"Why don't you lick it off?" Grandpa suggested.

Well . . .

How do I explain this?

Because that is what I did. Being of allegedly sound though tiny mind, but also a mad creature of impulse—the same mad creature, come to think of it, who'd volunteered for the speech thing in the first place—and because the thick frost did look inviting, like snow, and Mama made lovely ice cream out of snow sometimes, adding real cream and vanilla . . .

I did. I licked the frost off.

That is, I tried to. And of course the instant my warm wet

tongue touched the frozen metal, it bonded like epoxy. I pulled away—again, tried to—and squawked like a stuck parrot as the blood poured out of my mouth, for I'd left part of the skin of my tongue behind. I still wasn't completely unstuck, but I knew better than to try that again.

Huddled as I was in ardent proximity to the lock, I caught a glimpse of Grandpa's stricken face as he said, "Don't move; I'll get some water," and he rushed for the house, returning in a flash with the teakettle, and Grandma not far behind. Between them both, Grandpa holding me and Grandma pouring the cool water, they worked me loose.

And how it hurt! Like sixty. That's what we always used to say, hurt like sixty, and I never did know how sixty acquired the pain quotient it apparently has. I'm sixty now and it doesn't hurt, at least not all that much. What about seventy? Or, in this case, would you go for eighty-five? It hurt like Billy Blue Blazes, that's what it hurt like.

But the really impressive thing was how it bled. The red torrent gushed. Then it bubbled, then it oozed, but it wouldn't stop. I'd never have dreamed there were so many capillaries in a square pink inch of tongue.

Grandma telephoned the doctor—my mother had taken the car, shopping—and the doctor said to pack it, to stanch the bleeding. So I had a mouthful of Grandpa's big clean white handkerchiefs when Grandma said to him, "Why on earth did you let the child do a thing like that?"

Let, she'd said. Ha!

"It was his idea," I tattled—started to tattle—tried to start to tattle, and that is when I discovered that I wasn't going to tattle anything, wasn't going to *say* anything, not anything at all, for a good long time. That is also when I began to experience a dawning, warming awareness, like the gently widening glory of a perfect sunrise. It was the beatific realization that I was indubitably and unquestionably out of the competition. There wouldn't be any speechmaking for me to do now. Not any at all.

The fact apparently occurred at the same time to Grandma, who was laboring under the delusion that this would be the disappointment of my life. "Sugar, you know you're not going to be able to make your speech now," she clucked. "And after all your hard work, too. But there'll be lots of other speeches; don't you worry. You'll see!"

Other speeches. That's what she thought.

But I nodded mutely and glanced over to Grandpa, busy at the kitchen table. He'd found some surgical gauze, which he was folding into big soft wads. In the dim light of the gray morning I couldn't see his face too well, but when he looked over at me I was almost sure I saw him wink—only a millisecond of a wink, the flick of a camera shutter, but I was almost positive. Then presently he went upstairs and had himself a migraine headache.

When Mama came home, she was appalled, of course, and I was comforted some more. Not that I needed comfort, for my heart was like a singing bird, oh, yes, it was! Especially when I heard her telephone my father in Columbia, who was to tell the competition judges to take my name off the list. I was off the hook, all right, and if not with any particular honor, at least without shame.

And so I've often wondered about this. It seemed to me that God or Grandpa or both had worked in curious ways their wonders to perform. . . .

Had Grandpa planned it? (But how could he have engineered that fast change in the weather?) And if he had known about the resultant gore and all the pain and the infection—because my tongue became infected, too, and hurt more and longer—would he still have had me lick the lock? Was it a spontaneous idea that he hadn't quite thought through? I suppose I will never know.

But as it worked out, it quite fitted his sin-and-penalty equation. I was off the hook, but I hadn't gotten off it scot-free. And it was therapeutic. My fevered yen for pats and strokes had vanished like spit in a hot skillet, and that clamorous little internal Me-me-me had—at least momentarily—shut up. I couldn't hear it at all, filled as I was with a quiet, humble, pure, and simple gratitude to whatever powers there be that now I didn't have to make that speech.

Yes, but an odd sequel to this episode happened exactly a dozen years later, and I would like to mention it, for it seems to bear out a certain mild fatalism that colors my thinking as I look back on some of these things. It may be that certain events are inescapable. Avoid them one time, they'll catch up with you the next. Perhaps we all have our appointments in Samarra, one way or another.

It happened on my first job after college, when I was asked to introduce the chief speaker at a large gathering, and it would have been highly impolitic to say no.

And so I made the mistake of memorizing what I was going to say, then made the additional mistake of walking to the microphone without a note in my hand.

Or a thought in my head, as it turned out. My lovely intro had vanished like the morning dew on the daisies, and I stood there helplessly silent, till the master of ceremonies bounded to the rescue and I was led gently away to the showers.

It was precisely what I had known was going to happen so long ago in the seventh grade. And it isn't true, by the way, that nothing is as bad as you think it's going to be. Some things are exactly as bad as you thought they were going to be, and some things are worse. This was.

However, by age twenty-four, the eggshell ego has had a chance to accrete more calcium than age twelve had, and it doesn't shatter quite so fast. It seems to me that some disasters are best postponed for a while if you can swing it, or if you are lucky enough to have someone around who can swing it for you. It is kinder to the emergent self that way. Which reminds me that, as I may have mentioned, my grandpa was a very kindly man.

10

Concerning
The Mither vs. Sin

and Some More Little Lessons,
Oh, Yes, Indeed

It rained for hours night before last, and a big noisy rain it was. This little island seldom does things by halves. In brilliant weather, the fresh hot postcard colors nearly fracture the eyes. Till the barometer drops, and then maybe it's the contrast that makes the days seem so mole-gray and wet, wetter even than the ninth wave. Louder, too, at least at our house, thanks to a broad-leafed rubber tree in the back yard. This rubber tree reaches to the upstairs bedroom window; and along about midnight the rain rattled on those leaves like rocks on a hundred tin roofs.

The next morning, looking out the window over the sink, I thought I'd never seen the yard so branchy and muddy and muddled. Disheveled is the word—used hard and put away dirty; and from the other side of the house the rest of the world looked the same way, an ocean the color of cocoa under a dishwater sky.

There is a story I read once and always remembered, a story about a superb housekeeper, her house immaculate from basement floor to attic lintel, who happened to glance out the window one day when a brisk autumn wind was whipping the brown leaves about, into the flower beds and hedges. She noticed some chewing gum mashed on the walk and some mud in the street, saw how the dead twigs lay untended in the gutter, how the loose dry grasses drifted like puffballs, and presently she was out there in a frenzy, attempting with broom, rake, mop, and bucket to clean up the sloppy old face of Mother Nature—sobbing, screaming, cursing as she swept, raked, scrubbed, trying to clean up with a teaspoon what old Ma kept dumping back on by the carload.

Let this be a lesson to us all.

Accordingly, I turned my attention indoors, to do a little low-key housecleaning. On gray days, surfaces always seem to look duller and corners more dubious. Even though you can spot the dust more easily on sunny days, I still think sunshine is more becoming, to places and people alike. And it was while I dusted a bit here and there and desmudged some white woodwork that I found myself thinking back— by no very great leap of the mind—to my Idaho grandmother, my paternal grandmother, known as The Mither, a gentle though strong-chinned lady, and a relentless housekeeper. Not that she was in the same manic boat as the woman in the story. But she certainly wasn't in my grandma Em's more casual little craft either; and it was thinking of The Mither, on this particular morning, that led me in some curious directions. Once you start hopscotching down Memory Lane, there is simply no telling what square you'll land on. I definitely would not have expected to start out with my nice moralizing grandma and end up with Marty (The Duke) Monelli in McKinleyville's vilest saloon. But that is the way the rock skipped. . . .

Now, The Mither often said that you might have to eat a peck of dirt in your lifetime, but you weren't going to find it at her house. She saw to that. She scrubbed all her floors, including the porches, once a week, and she damp-mopped her kitchen floor every single night, and she disinfected her wooden kitchen counters after every single meal. (The Mither always said it was better to live in a clean hovel than a dirty castle, though I knew I'd opt for the castle any day, if I ever got the chance to opt.)

I especially remember her kitchen sink, which she called, in as nice a little grandmotherly joke as you'll hear in a month of Sunday school, her sink of iniquity. The porcelain was discolored—had a big pale-yellow stain the shape of Australia that was apparently built in. She had scrubbed and scrubbed that sink to no avail, eventually going through the porcelain in places, so that rust took over, and my father finally bought her a new one. It isn't everyone who can scrub holes in a sink.

But I saw her in her own house only a time or two, and when I see her with my mind's eye now, it is always at our own house in McKinleyville, making her annual visit. And knitting. Always knitting, The Mither was, and looking exactly like a grandma as she did so, from her knob of iron-gray hair stabbed through and through with iron-gray hairpins to her dark-blue flower-printed housedresses right down to her honest black comfort shoes.

She was always called The Mither, and her husband, who died before I was born, had always been called The Feyther, for reasons I've never fully understood. Though we Brackens are mainly Irish, we've never worked at it; there's divil a bit o' the Irish brogue to the lot of us, nor any particular deep-down yen for corned beef and taties. But The Mither is what she was called; and always, unless you were addressing her directly, it was *The* Mither, never plain Mither without the article.

The Mither was a champion knitter, State Fair Blue Ribbon all the way. Knitting was what she did when she wasn't washing or scrubbing or polishing something. She knitted everything from antimacassars to skirts and jackets, with flocks of socks and table runners and doilies in between; and on her annual fall visit she would always teach me to knit (because I had invariably forgotten the little I'd learned the last time, my fondness for knitting being second only to my devotion to the piano).

Patiently, though, she would teach and reteach me, all the while dropping as many tidy moral precepts as I dropped stitches, for The Mither was a great moralizer. These were never the jolly kind, the eat-drink-and-be-merry kind, the never-trouble-trouble kind, but always the constructive or uplifting kind. Character-building. And she had as many as a bean-bag's got beans.

I liked it, though, hearing all those maxims and rules. I think most kids do. In fact, I think that most kids live in a kind of dumb search for *the* rule—it seems to me I did—I mean a polestar to steer by, a guy wire to hold down the tent in a high wind; and in this area I had high hopes for The Mither. Not that her nuggets were all twenty-four-karat, or her pearls all perfectly formed. But I had to grow up before I could distinguish the good ones from the not-so-good ones; and the trouble is that the older I grow, the less I know, so that about the only thing I'm really sure of any more is "You divide, I'll choose."

However, I must say that I've found The Mither's position on Habits to be quite sound. At least, my own experience corroborates her words. What she said was that when you uproot a bad habit, it will in all likelihood leave a great big hole; and if you don't plant a good habit in there immediately, another bad one will move in and take root.

She certainly was right about that. I know that when they took me off thumb-sucking, it was cold turkey. Nobody thought to replace it with a good habit, and so I just switched to ear-digging, nose-picking, and cowlick-twisting, then went on to head-scratching, pencil-biting, eyebrow-ruffling, and cuticle-worrying, till I finally graduated to smoking. I'd have saved a lot of fussing around if I'd gone straight to smoking in the first place, or, better yet, if they'd set me to whittling. And now that I've quit smoking, I suppose I'd better stuff a good habit into that cavity fast, or I'll find myself going right back down through the chairs again, straight back to thumb-sucking.

Another of The Mither's sound maxims that I remember was "Seek your salve where you got your sore." The first time I heard that one was when I was learning to ride a bicycle. Every time I fell off, she'd make me climb back on, scraped elbows and all, and I suppose it was a good thing. Otherwise I'd probably have settled almost immediately for the sour taste of failure and missed some good rides. I've found this to be a workable rule in other areas as well. When your true love proves not to be, the only real cure is another love, and when you've botched up a cake, better make another, better, one.

However, it is hard work being a child and on the receiving end of so much advice. Most of it must be taken on faith, and by the time you've learned better, it may be too late. Witness my brother, in the fifth grade. He was getting into a good many fist fights then, and The Mither recommended that when he found himself growing angry, he should count to ten and then say the Lord's Prayer. But as Jack learned in a hurry, it only gave the other fellow time to get his licks in first.

I also remember her telling me that it was just as easy to do it the right way, when she found me doing a fast sloppy job of something, like making a bed. Then she would unwittingly prove herself a liar as she demonstrated the right way, the mitered-corner hospital way, which was harder and took longer, too. In fact, for the record, I would like to say right here that I've never found anything whatsoever that is as easy to do the right way as the wrong way, and if there is such a thing I would like to know about it.

Now, a commodity that The Mither set great store by was virtue. In my autograph book she had copied out the longish verse that begins "Be good, sweet maid, and let who will be clever," ending with something about life's turning out to be one grand sweet song as a result of all this goodness. She often pointed out that virtue is its own reward, and said, "Be good and you will be happy," though even in my short span I had noticed that the reverse was as true, if not truer—that when I was happy I was much more likely to be good.

Whatever good was. Though I don't suppose I started pondering that until much later.

"Be good and you will be happy." I don't think The Mither was outstandingly happy, though she was certainly good—worked hard, scrubbed and knitted and cooked hard, gave to the poor, and sang alto in the church choir, which is understandable. Anyone married to my paternal grandfather would have sung alto.

He was a hard man, The Feyther was. When his son, my father, was married, he loaned him $100 for the honeymoon, at five percent, a good healthy rate of interest then. And early on in The Feyther's own marriage there had been an incident I have often wondered about.

One evening, when he lit an after-dinner cigar in the living room, The Mither informed him that from now on she would permit no cigar-smoking in the house, because it yellowed the curtains and dirtied the air. Upon which he rose and took his cigar with him down to the back room of the Twin Falls bank, where he worked, the bank he eventually owned and ran. That was the start of a regular nightly rendezvous for The Feyther and a handful of friends who likewise considered home a good place to stay away from. From then on, my grandfather spent every evening there save Thanksgiving and Christmas.

That is the story as I heard it from my father and mother, and from the available evidence it would seem that The Mither and The Feyther deserved each other.

Still, there must have been more to it. A cigar or two couldn't sink a marriage that was any kind of a marriage. Things are never that simple, and I would like to know what really happened. It seems to me that we all owe it to the galloping curiosity of our immediate descendants to leave some revealing family papers behind, to be opened, say, twenty-five years after we're dead, telling the bare-bones truth, the whole truth. . . . Or can you count on the immediate descendants' curiosity to be all that feverish? Is it barely possible they wouldn't give a damn?

But back to virtue.

I suppose we all mean different things by the word. Every philosopher seems to have his own definition, and certainly a thousand proverbs have virtue as a theme. I know that the one The Mither was so fond of—the one about virtue being its own reward—has never been, for me, very persuasive. It just doesn't seem to sell the product, and I remember thinking so even the first time I heard it, which was when I was grumbling to The Mither, during one of her visits, about that day's fifth-grade field trip to the St. Louis Art Museum.

That was the day Art Hoadley, Barry O'Donnell, and a few others got so obstreperous in the Egyptian Room that the museum finally kicked them out, to wait for the rest of us on the school bus with Mr. Jenkins, the driver. We learned later that after a while Mr. Jenkins, a genial soul, had driven them all to a lunch stand in the park and bought root beer and Chili Doggerinos all around. And there the rest of us were, stuck for two hours in the art museum, staring at dim pictures and crummy mummies and busted clay pots.

It just wasn't fair, I said. And that's when The Mither laid it on me. Virtue is its own reward, she said.

I persisted. Yes, but just *how?*

"The reward is feeling good because you know you did the right thing and didn't make trouble for people," The Mither explained gently.

Well, I couldn't exactly see that. I didn't feel good enough to notice it any. A Chili Doggerino would have made me feel a lot better, and it seemed to me there was something the matter with the virtue equation.

Or take the matter of the eighth-grade Shakespeare assignment, ten pages due the day after a Christmas vacation when it had snowed gloriously, everyone out sledding and skating. But I missed most of it, working hard on my paper. As it turned out, since I was the only one with a paper to hand in, the teacher gave me a kind look and the rest of the class a blanket extension. (Even if she hadn't, I thought, they'd still have had all that fun stashed away.)

Something was amiss. If that was the best that virtue had to offer, why not find something that paid a few dividends.

With sin, apparently, you at least had something nice to remember. Whereas, with virtue . . .

And so, as I rearranged the dust on that recent gray Hawaiian morning, it was thinking along these lines that led me back to a certain week in the blossomy month of May when I was a high-school junior and it was coming up Prom time.

Now, an interesting feature of the high-school Junior Prom in McKinleyville—possibly in other places, too—is, was, that you couldn't decide which was worse: going to it or not going to it.

Not going to it meant only one thing: you didn't have a date. This was a hideously embarrassing admission to have to make. Moreover, no matter how you lied about it—moribund parents, terminal grandparents, *everybody* sick, dying, or dead—everybody knew you lied.

Going to it, on the other hand, was just as bad. As everyone knows who has read the literature (which is voluminous), to all girls who weren't Ellen Bishop, that Midwestern fertility rite known as the Junior Prom was the pits, the shits, the trenches, the rack, and Room 101 in George Orwell's *1984* all put together.

One trouble was the foreknowledge of it. It wouldn't have been so bad if you could have trotted through the year in blithe ignorance, plumb up to Prom time and *then*—surprise! —got it all over you, like skipping happily down a country road and skidding in the cow plop. You can stand almost anything if it's unexpected and only once. But no, you knew for months and months beforehand that it was ahead of you. that large, fresh, steaming meadow muffin which you couldn't possibly avoid. And you knew precisely what was going to happen.

I mean, you knew exactly what the Junior Prom was going to be like, because you had already had a savory sample with the Valentine Heart Hop. Compared to it, an intimate get-together with Orwell's rats would have sounded good. And once again, there you'd be, standing around a crepe-paper-festooned gym, a silly smile pasted on your face (because the oaf who brought you had long since vanished into the middle distance), seeing fat little Chuckie Schwartz approaching with his built-in peanut butter breath, hoping he wasn't heading in your precise direction and then hoping, God help you, that he was.

Of course, this wasn't the way of it with Ellen Bishop and her group. This included Florence Ashenbrenner, who had developed (as they put it then) earlier than any of us and could also get the family car almost whenever she wanted it. It also included an exotic new addition to the McKinleyville High Junior Class, Marnie Lou Higbee, just up from the southland, a cute little Georgia peach who looked exactly like Janet Gaynor and talked almost exclusively in question marks. (Calling up about homework, she'd say, "This is Mahnie Lou? From school? An' Chewsdy Ah was home, heah? Jes' plain ole home with a cold? An' didn't get the French assahnment? . . . Ahnt you a *love?* . . .")

Well, naturally, among them they'd nailed down the cutest boys: Barry O'Donnell, who was still right up there—still belonged to Ellen, too—and Augie Barnes, now captain of the football team, plus a few seniors, including Burt Bailey, the male lead in the class play. Burt was terribly handsome, and did he ever think he was the oyster's ice skates (though most of us, secretly and individually, would have given an arm and a leg just to carry his coat).

As I say, Ellen and her revolving planetoids had nailed down the cutest boys, reserving the second-cutest for backups. And they'd all be out there in the middle of the dance floor on Prom night, extraordinarily busy. With each other.

For when the Ellen Bishops of the world were born, a good fairy who looked just like Billie Burke had flown in to hand out the Prom Queen buttons and then dump goodies all over the place, goodies like pert noses and skin that never got bumps and stockings that never wrinkled and an easy way of saying clever things to boys, and so on, plus an indefinable something, by a remarkable alchemy, turned even defects into plusses.

Like Ellen's false tooth, which I think I've mentioned.

For years the rest of us wished that *we'd* had a tooth knocked out; and if Ellen had had a wen or a bald spot or big ears or piano legs, we'd have wanted *them*. Also, this same peculiar magic made anything she said or did the in thing to say or do. That year, I remember, she was rubbing vaseline on her eyelids so they'd look all moist and shiny, and so all the rest of us did; and if she'd been applying diesel oil or cream cheese, we'd have done that, too.

Gone now, vanished with the snows of yesteryear was that halcyon time when we had accepted ourselves with reasonable serenity the way we were.

Now, spelling, who needed it? Maybe librarians did, or proofreaders or typesetters. But so far as social assets went, I mean those particular social assets that had the boys kicking the back of your seat at assembly or making kissing noises when you walked by or walking you home and stopping at Deagan's Drugstore—whatever the assets were that activated those little attentions, spelling wasn't among them.

Spelling. Among the social assets, it ranked right down there beside the shot put. As for fetching, it didn't fetch flies; and in this particular season of my discontent, when I was fifteen and a half years old, all in the world that I craved to be was Ellen Bishop.

And so, the toast of Deagan's Drugstore I was not. But, well, neither was Buzzy Kirmsey, the goalie on our field-hockey team; and this was of some minor comfort, of course, because Buzzy was now my best friend.

Buzzy was towheaded, with cheeks like ripe nectarines, and she was sturdily built. Not fat, I wouldn't say fat. But hefty. Maybe she should have been as careful about what she ate as she was about how she weighed herself. Buzzy wouldn't get on the scale in the first place unless she was stark naked; and even then, she'd park her wad of gum somewhere first and remove all her bobby pins and blow her nose. Then finally she'd step on the scale ve-e-ery cautiously, one toe at a time. But when it came to eating, she could polish off a grilled-cheese-french-fries-and-catsup with a double-thick-chocolate-malted faster than anyone I ever saw.

Buzzy had lively green eyes, and she was talented at thinking up interesting things to do. Sometimes on Saturdays we would go adventuring into downtown St. Louis. In retrospect I see these expeditions always in the wintertime, the long bus ride from McKinleyville into the seedy red-brick outskirts of the city, past old, angular, sooty brick buildings huddled under a dirty rosy-gray sky, the blue-shadowed gravelly snow in the street delicately soiled, like a doubtful shirt, and the big old two-decker bus lurching along down to 6th and Olive. Once downtown, our first stop was usually the big Famous & Barr store, where we would try on bridal gowns and bridesmaids' dresses; and one time we did that, Buzzy had tucked a small baby pillow up under her skirt in front. Laugh?

Buzzy hadn't been invited to the Prom. But I had. I had a date, to use the word loosely. I had a date, if you could call it that, a date that was only slightly better than a kick in the head. Carl Krepps had asked me. Carl was the math genius in our class, and I'm sure he grew up to invent the magnetic-core computer or something, but at this particular point he was a dreg. (All boys who weren't cute were dregs.)

Carl was skinny as a breadstick and he had pale eyes and damp hands. For some mysterious reason, his hands had always been damp, even as a little boy. In kindergarten ring-around-the-rosy, no one ever wanted to grab hold of Carl, and up through the grades we could easily spot his somewhat sweat-blistered test papers in the heap on the teacher's desk.

Even if Carl hadn't been something less than Clark Gable, the situation still wouldn't have been one to get excited about. Because I knew very well why he had asked me. He had asked me because his mother had lowered the boom and *made* him ask me. His mother and my mother were friends.

In fact, it had been one of those rotten maternal conspiracies from the word *go*. When Carl telephoned and I started to mumble some kind of an alibi, Mama had mouthed soundlessly at me, *"You—go—with—him!"* She had that look on her face that I knew better than to mess with. I knew she wouldn't take no for an answer, even though Carl would probably have loved to. I'm sure he didn't like me any better than I liked him.

What made this doubly annoying was that I had already

laid some face-saving groundwork that could have got me out of the whole thing. For the past three summers, when I had been in Ganister, a boy who lived a few doors down from Aunt Liz Noah's had been paying some attention to me. He would find out from her exactly when we were going to hit town, and that very evening—because he knew I always went over to see her the first night—he'd stroll by. And we would make some clumsy conversation, and then the next week or two while I was there we'd go for walks and an occasional soda or movie.

He even wrote to me several times after I got back home, letters I'd flash busily around school. The envelopes, I mean. The letters themselves I threw away. They positively throbbed with weather reports and baseball scores—he played first base on the Ganister High team. And he always signed them

Sincerly,
MONROE

Monroe. That was his name, pronounced MON-roe, the Mon to rhyme with Don. Monroe Deasey, and the big thing in his favor was that he'd never been near McKinleyville— never even been out of Ganister—so I could lie and brag about him all I wanted. Tall, dark, and dashing, he was, sort of a Hamlet–Heathcliff–Rhett Butler conglomerate. And I panted for him. Or so I said.

Actually, Monroe was barely a blip on my radar screen, and so far as classifications went, he'd have hardly made Dreg. When Billie Burke came flying in for *his* natal day, she'd forgotten to bring any decent chins along, and so she made up for it with Adam's apple. He was a beanpole with parched crab grass for hair and thick-lensed glasses that reduced his eyes to small blue dots, and he had the longest arms I ever saw on anybody. His hands dangled around his knees when they weren't dangling around me, though they weren't damp, I'll say that for them. I'd let him hold one of mine a couple of times at the movies, which is how I knew.

But as I say, I had given Monroe a great build-up, back

home in McKinleyville. Handsome? Wow! But jealous? Whewww! Why, if he ever heard that I'd gone out with anybody else . . .

And now all this had gone for nothing. Thanks to maternal solicitude, I was locked into the Junior Prom with Carl Krepps. And I could visualize, in exquisite haunting detail, that approaching Saturday night: just Carl and me, stumbling endlessly around that dance floor (assuming he didn't ditch me before the music even started), the two of us making sultry chit-chat about isosceles triangles, no doubt, with Carl's damp hands leaving moist dark marks on my blue taffeta back. And with Ellen and Florence and Marnie Lou probably tittering as we plodded by, around and around and around. . . . (But I'm sure I did them a disservice there, for they were far too busy in their own cozy little world.)

"Yes, but at least you got *asked*," Buzzy said, as I was glooming around about it one afternoon, when we were allegedly doing homework at my house.

"Yes and by who?" I said. (Fink that I was, I didn't mention the mother business. Even though being asked by a dreg was an indication that you were probably a dreg yourself, still there was at least a teaspoonful of status in being asked by anybody at all. You don't have to tell your best friend everything.)

"Well, you don't have to go," Buzzy said. "You could lie about it when your folks come home. Just don't go and say you did. Then we could go do something fun instead." (I was programed to stay at Buzzy's that entire weekend, the Prom being Saturday night, because Mama and Daddy were leaving Friday morning for Chicago, where he was to make a commencement speech.)

"Fat chance!" I said. I'd never get away with a lie like that, and I knew it. Not being superintendent's daughter, I wouldn't, never in all this world. Somebody would tattle for sure.

"Then let's do something fun anyway," Buzzy said practically. "I mean, the night before. I'll tell you what—" and she started batting her eyelids and chewing her gum fast, the

way she always did when she got excited—"Friday night let's
go out to Ye Olde Inne!"

As I have said, Buzzy was very good at thinking up interesting projects.

"Oh, boy!" I said. "Let's!"

Now, Ye Olde Inne was a roadhouse nestling in a grove of
maple trees, way out at the far rural end of the McKinleyville
trolley line. It resembled a cozy Anne Hathaway cottage, and
I had wondered if it was equally cozy on the inside, for I
knew it had a raunchy reputation. Before Repeal it had been
the county's busiest blind pig, and my father, as school superintendent, had done his best to have it closed down. But the
owners apparently had more political muscle than Daddy
did, and the place stayed open. Then when Prohibition
ended, they brought a big mahogany bar down from Chicago, enlarged the dance floor, and kept right on doing a land-
office business.

As I say, it was right at the end of the trolley line; getting
there would be no problem. Neither would sneaking out, for
Buzzy's parents were either remarkably dumb or extraordinarily trusting or totally unconcerned, and possibly a little
of each.

Accountants both, with a mutual office over their garage,
Mr. and Mrs. Kirmsey worked late and rose late. We had
learned that if we wore bathrobes over our clothes to say
good night in, we could then just slip out of them and out
the window, and the night was ours, if we could think of
something to do with it.

Up till now, our only real caper had been a couple of
banana splits at Deagan's, and, frankly, it hadn't been all
that great, because we'd run into Ellen and Marnie Lou.
There they were, sitting in the front booth with three boys,
talking about a movie they'd all just seen. So Buzzy and I
played it very cool—just nodded and kept on going, back to
the farthest-back booth, where we talked and laughed, pretty
loud and quite a lot.

No, our problem was financial. We'd both been caught

with our cash reserves way down, and this toot was going to cost money. We weren't sure just how much, because for one thing we didn't know how much a drink cost. And there were other areas of ignorance. Like the tenderfoot bellying up to the bar and hollering for a bourbon with whisky straight up on the rocks with branch water, we weren't too sure about what to order either, coming as we both did from teetotalling families. Still, there was always beer. Beer was easy and probably cheaper, too.

We solved the money thing with surprising ease, as it turned out, by pulling a couple of in-house burglaries. A large ad in the McKinleyville *Advocate* had announced that a Mr. Rufus Koenig was going to be at the McKinleyville Hotel for a week in Room #327, buying up old gold and silver. *Anything* gold or silver, the ad said, from inlays to eyeglass frames.

Accordingly, we rifled all the drawers in the house—her house and my house—for odd bits no one would ever miss (and, it turned out, no one ever did)—an old stickpin, a fountain-pen clip, a lone cuff link, a bit of tarnished silver key chain—and the affable Mr. Koenig gave us approximately a third of what it was worth, I am sure, or fourteen dollars, which we hoped would cover our immediate needs.

Thus it was that around nine-fifteen that Friday evening, we were on the trolley, Buzzy and I, heading for Ye Olde Inne and loaded for bear. We were wearing our shiny white-satin school chorus uniform blouses, with the balloon sleeves, and longish skirts, with our eyelids thoroughly vaselined, our mouths darkly lipsticked, and our fingernails totally unrecognizable, painted as they were with a violent mahogany-colored nail polish we had applied, with immense attention to the half-moons. (Half-moons were very big then. We spent most of our free time pushing back cuticle. It wasn't till a few years later that someone—possibly Wally Windsor or Loretta Young—decreed that the *entire* nail should be painted, and for many of us it was a joyous release. My half-moons were never anything to write home about.)

The McKinleyville trolley, known as the Dinky, was a small, unheated, uncooled Toonerville contraption with two high steps up to the varnished yellow straw seats inside. At the end of the line, the motorman would simply move his collection box to the other end of the car and head back to where he'd come from.

Actually, there were two Dinkies, plus a rail siding somewhere near the middle of the nine-mile route. They would start from either end, and the first car to reach the siding would shunt itself over to wait for what seemed a week till the other Dinky clanked past; otherwise they'd both have had to back up and start over again.

It was a delicately fragrant and gently luminous evening, fresh with lilac and forsythia, pearly with moonlight, surely a night to break the heart if you had a past to ponder or loves to mourn. But Buzzy and I hadn't. We felt just fine, riding along on the Dinky, *clinkety-clank,* with the sweet soft breezes pouring in the open window. The car was nearly empty; only the two of us, and two colored maids (you *said* colored maids then) going home, or somewhere.

We sat directly behind the motorman, a spry old fellow I'd never seen before. Which was fine; it meant he probably hadn't seen me before either. McKinleyville was just small enough that a trolley conductor might make it his business to find out what the superintendent's daughter was doing on a night like this at a dump like that, I mean a dump like the one we were shortly to be favoring with our presence and our fourteen dollars.

As we waited on the siding for the other Dinky to clank past, the motorman got chatty. "You girls going home?" he asked, and Buzzy said no, we were heading for Ye Olde Inne.

"You work out there?" he asked, and we poked each other. This was great. Then we *did* look old enough. We'd worried about that. I.D. cards hadn't been invented yet, but no bartender would serve a kid if he could help it. Of course, we were wearing high heels—highest we had, anyway, about an inch and a half high, and called (for reasons that escape me now) Cuban. And I was wearing my long brown hair up, in the McKinleyville version of a French twist, and Buzzy had sleeked hers back as well as she could, very severe. But all the same . . .

"Just once in a while," Buzzy answered casually, and we stifled our giggles.

And so we clinkety-clanked to the end of the line and clambered down out of the car.

"If you can't be good, be careful," the motorman sang out after us, the old rascal.

"I'll name it after you," Buzzy called back, completing the ritual. That Buzzy!

And so we entered Ye Olde Inne.

Well, the first thing I saw was that I couldn't see much. Black as a basement, that room was, except for a magnificent flashing jukebox, all rainbows and waterfalls, and a few candles on booths and tables. But presently my night vision got going, so that when Buzzy nudged me, pointing to the inside of Ye Olde Inne's front door, I could read the sign there that said YE OLDE OUTE.

As it developed, this rather set the tone of the establishment. On the bar mirror were numerous other hilarious placards printed in extremely Olde Englishe type, some stressing the total inadvisability of asking for credit, and one that said COME IN, WE'RE CLOSED beside another that said SORRY, WE'RE OPEN, and another that said THE MANAGEMENT IS NOT RESPONSIBLE. Smack in the middle, above the mirror, was a good big sign that said WELCOME TO YE OLDE GINTORIUM.

It was a large square room, mostly dance floor, red plastic booths around three sides, the bar against the other, and that glorious full-color, hi-tech Giant Wurlitzer in the corner. Only one couple was dancing—a beefy fellow nearly busting out of his white HANK'S GARAGE coveralls, with a pint-size redhead hanging around his neck like a locket, instead of placing her left hand daintily on his right shoulder, the way I had been taught.

But he didn't seem to mind, and they weren't exactly dancing anyway, just standing there wobbling to Bing Crosby's buh-buh-buh-blue of the night. It was punctually meeting the gold of the day, and it kept right on doing so most of the evening.

Heading for a booth and walking tall, Buzzy and I tried

to look as though we did this every night of the week.

The place wasn't too busy. It was early. Three men sat in the corner booth at the back, and in another, two uniformed bus drivers and a girl were drinking beer. A fat, balding bartender with his sleeves rolled up was chatting with a middle-aged couple at the bar, and that was about it.

Almost immediately, a wiry freckle-faced man in brown slacks and a tan pullover came across the room from behind the bar, lit the candle in the beer bottle (swollen with multicolored candle drips to the size of a small football), and said, "Hi, I'm Jerry. What'll it be?"

"Two beers, please," I said.

"Draft okay?" he asked.

"Okel-dokel," said Buzzy.

"A scuttle of suds for the ladies," he called over to the bar, and then went over to fetch it.

"A scuttle of suds" . . . That was cute. We had never heard that before.

The beer came in a pitcher accompanied by two frosty mugs. I had tasted beer only once before, at Lucille Brueggeman's house, and hadn't thought much of it. This seemed better.

So we sat, and sipped, and looked around. Jerry came back presently to bring us a bowl of popcorn and ask if everything was all right, and we said fine. Privately, though, I was beginning to experience a faint sense of anticlimax. I don't know just what I had expected. But still and all . . .

Suddenly and loudly, Buzzy belched. "Another precinct heard from," she said, with great nonchalance. Buzzy was the best belcher I have ever encountered, a real champion. She could dredge up a winner any time she felt like it, and this one must have rattled her back teeth. But after all. There's a time and a place. A woman in a booth ahead stood up and looked around.

"Buzzy!" I said. Embarrassed, I went over to the jukebox and fed it three nickels, punching and repunching Ellington's "It Don't Mean a Thing." (This being my brother's current passion, I knew it was an okay number to punch.) And it was right after that, dodging my way back across the dance floor, somewhat busier now, that I saw one of the three men in the back booth looking at me. Just staring. I looked away. Then when I looked back at him again, *he* looked away.

He was a stocky, square-built, older man, anyway twenty-five or six, dark-complected, as McKinleyville called olive-skinned, with dark curly hair. Very shortly then, Jerry came back across the room with another pitcher of beer.

"Compliments of The Duke," he said, and jerked a thumb toward the rear.

What were we supposed to do? Buzzy and I looked at each other. Then, with more presence of mind than I had, she said, "Will you thank him for us, please?" And the second he'd gone, she leaned across and stage-whispered, "Hey, you must've made a hit. What's he *like?*"

But almost the next thing we knew, he was right there beside the booth, so Buzzy got a good look.

"Excuse me," he said to her, and then he asked me to dance.

"Sure, that's okay," Buzzy said. "Go on," she said to me, and as I slid out of the bench she stage-whispered, "Don't let him blow in your ear!"

Trust Buzzy! It was a well and widely known fact or at any rate solid rumor that if you ever let a fellow blow in your ear, you would be putty in his hands, I mean a molten mass. But to come right out and say it like that . . . !

I don't think The Duke heard her, though. The Ellington record was loud. It was also fast, and I was glad when the music went back to the blue of the night, which was easier to dance to. Though it wouldn't have mattered. We didn't dance any more than Hank's Garage had—just stood there and shuffled. Dancing wasn't The Duke's specialty, he said, and it certainly wasn't mine.

Still, it was nice. He held me carefully and somehow delicately. His chest was solid as could be, and he smelled clean and spicy.

When the music ended, he steered me to the back booth, which was empty now. His friends had gone. I glanced over at Buzzy, who waved cheerfully. Jerry was sitting across from her now, so *that* was all right. (We never did figure out exactly who or what Jerry was. Owner? Waiter? Man Friday?)

"What would you like to drink?" The Duke asked. He was sitting across from me, regarding me steadily with his very dark eyes, eyes like dark-brown satin.

I looked at him, too. He would have a very heavy beard if he didn't shave—you could tell that—and his black hair was thick and glossy and not curly, really, just wavy. He was wearing a black shirt under a gray sports jacket, a really socko combination, and a thick gold little-finger ring set with a large green stone, maybe a bit flashy but it looked just right.

"What'll you have?" he asked again, and he added, oddly, "I like your style."

Style. Style, he said.

But I didn't have any. Oh, I wished I did! Style—I dimly suspected this but couldn't have proved it—was doing things your own way simply because that's the way you did things, and you were comfortable enough with yourself that this way was okay with you. And that sure wasn't me. I was trying to walk like my aunt Liz Noah and trying to look like Ellen Bishop (at least I had the shiny eyelids) and trying to hold my head like—like—maybe it was Norma Shearer.

Style. I didn't have any, not even drinkwise. All I could think of to say was that the rest of my beer was at the other table.

He dismissed that. "You don't want to drink any more of that stuff," he said.

He was drinking something clear as water, over ice. I couldn't tell what it was. And so I tried to think of something, but nothing occurred to me, till I noticed the sign on the bar mirror, BLOODY MARY, 60¢. Expensive, but I guessed he was paying.

"Oh, a Bloody Mary, I suppose," I said offhandedly to Jerry, who'd come over to take the order. I was feeling a slight pleasant buzz from the beer now, and I didn't know what a Bloody Mary was, but the name had dash. The Duke jerked a thumb toward his glass, for a refill.

"Vodka rocks and a Mary," Jerry sang out to the barman with an admirable economy of phrase, I thought, and a moment later he brought them over, mine an enormous catsup-colored lake, a great water goblet full.

Jerry grinned at me. "Don't worry, I'm putting ole Buzz to work," he said, and, sure enough, I saw her over there, delivering drinks to a couple at one of the tables. They were kidding her and she was kidding right back. Leave it to Buzzy!

I tried the Bloody Mary. It was strong and very spicy, but all right in small sips, and it kept improving.

I wish I could remember who said what, then, or just what conversational areas we covered. Of course we traded names. His was Marty Monelli, he said, but they called him The Duke. Sort of a trademark. And his business was jukeboxes and, well, other stuff, he said vaguely, but never said what the other stuff was. And he had a flat right around the corner, he said, nice little place, maybe I'd like to see it one of these times. . . .

And he asked how long I'd lived in McKinleyville, and I said twelve years, which was true—we'd moved there when I was three, though I wasn't going to say *that*. And he asked if I worked, and I replied (the saints forgive me) yes, and he asked at what, and I said sort of office work. Well, I did type bulletins for my father, sometimes, on a rainy Saturday. . . .

Mainly, I remember saying as little as possible, for fear I'd blow it. "A closed mouth gathers no foot." I don't know how often I'd heard my father say that. And so I was trying hard to look inscrutable and suave, as The Duke regarded me from across the table with this increasingly warm and appreciative look.

I've thought about it often since—about why The Duke picked me out. I suppose he was between girls, and I think now that I was probably prettier than I gave myself credit for. Of course, young is almost always pretty anyway, or so it seems to me now. And looking at my yearbook picture for that year, I see a girl who looks somewhat older than fifteen,

with a candid forehead and smooth skin and a gentle mouth
and a quantity of long brown hair.

And plump hands. ("Mama, you had fat hands!" my
daughter said when she saw the picture. "That was before
I'd worked my fingers to the bone for you, sweetie," I replied
smartly. Never hurts to remind them, once in a while.)

And so The Duke kept looking at me as though I had
something special. For him, I mean. Something he liked a
lot. As though I *were* something special. And I think even
the first time a girl gets a look like that, she recognizes it—
can distinguish it, I mean, from the sort of look that goes
with a whistle.

This was almost a loving look, and curiously shy. It was
almost shyly, too, that he came around the booth table after
a while and slid in beside me. And put his arm around me.
And kissed me—my first kiss, except for post office in the
sixth grade, in the coat closet with fat Charlie Mason, and
you certainly can't count that.

I mean it was my first genuine kiss.

I wonder if they remember first genuine kisses today. Or
do they only remember first genuine bedtimes? Or first
meaningful genuine bedtimes? The scenario has changed a
great deal while I wasn't looking.

Anyway, this was a good kiss.

Not a French kiss, or any other particular nationality that
I know of. And certainly not one of those miserable, wet,
spitty kisses. And even more certainly, not a platonic kiss.

It was a tentative kiss that became quickly less so. A firm
kiss, it was then, yes, tender and warm, and prophetic of even
more interesting things to come.

Which weren't long in coming.

"Does your mama ever see you nude?" he asked. Now he
was holding my hand—his own hand was nice and warm and
dry, not a bit damp, with crisp curly black hairs on the back
of it. He was kissing me again, so I couldn't answer for a
while, and he was also stroking my palm cozily with his
thumb. (Is the palm of your hand an erogenous zone? It must

depend on who is doing what to it, doesn't it? Otherwise, presidential nominees pressing the flesh at all those functions would be in a totally unglued state most of the time, wouldn't they?)

Nude. I wasn't sure I'd heard right. Come to that, all of a sudden I wasn't sure I was seeing right. I had not previously noticed that the bartender had an identical twin brother. There were also two Ye Olde Gintorium signs now, neatly side by side, and now the whole bar seemed about to slide apart into two bars, about to reproduce like an amoeba before my very eyes.

"Nude?" I repeated.

"Naked," he elaborated.

I shook my head. I was shy about those things. Even Mama hadn't seen me without clothes for years.

And then very quickly, before I realized what he was doing, or undoing, he'd undone the two top buttons of my white satin blouse and pulled down my bandeau—it was bandeau then, not a bra—and I found my chin resting on his dark wavy hair as he began to do something very strange.

What he began to do was—and I'm not sure I should tell about this, but, what the heck, I told Buzzy—what he started to do was, well, it was a very friendly, you might even say intimate thing that he started to do. What he started to do was suck with considerable enthusiasm at a place approximately in the middle—I mean the inside middle—of my, as it were, chest (my left chest). To provide me with a romantic and colorful little souvenir, as it turned out, though I wasn't aware at the time that this was what it was going to be.

It didn't hurt. In truth, it didn't make me feel any particular which way, including embarrassed. ("I'd of *died!*" Buzzy said with awe the next day when I showed her my memento, my love-blossom, monkey-bite, hickey, whatever-you-call-it—and a jim-dandy it was, looking for all the world like a large crushed mulberry. But then, Buzzy had always been embarrassed anyway about her superabundance of bust. And it is true that I had had a superabundance of beer and vodka-with-Worcestershire-sauce. And though I don't think anyone was paying attention—the place was pretty dark, after all, and there weren't many customers left now—I confess that I wasn't really looking.)

So I didn't mind, and The Duke seemed to be having a nice time, and he was still at it when Jerry came over, looking a little embarrassed but determined.

"Where's Buzzy?" I asked him, with commendable presence of mind, all things considered.

I guess he didn't hear me. He said, "Duke, we gotta talk."

It was obvious that The Duke didn't want to be interrupted. But Jerry's voice was urgent, and so The Duke said, "Wait a sec; I'll be back" and joined Jerry at the bar, where the two men conferred briefly, glancing now and again in my direction.

(It wasn't long, either, before I learned what it was about. Buzzy had blown the whistle; dropped the fact that I was only fifteen, and, possibly worse, the daughter of the superintendent of schools. And how could she have been so dumb? Well, she explained later that it must have been the beer. But I wasn't so sure. You never can tell about women. I had been having a better time than she was; I frankly believe it was just that simple. It hadn't really been all that jolly, delivering drinks, I suppose, and Jerry hadn't spent much time with her at all.)

Anyway, while The Duke was gone, I furtively wiped my, well, front, my rosy wet front, with a paper napkin. Then I rebuttoned my blouse, which was just as well, because when he came back he said shortly, "I better run you home."

Daddy must have had some clout, unfortunately, at that.

And so The Duke drove us home, me beside him in front, Jerry and Buzzy in the back, in a snaky long midnight-blue car that would have made my father's old black two-door sedan look like a penny waiting for change. Once, he turned, gave me a hard stare, and said, sounding aggrieved. "You didn't tell me you were only fifteen. Jeez."

"You didn't ask me," I said.

He didn't answer that, and I wasn't feeling conversational myself. The booze and the car motion were interacting to my considerable dismay, and also I had to go to the bathroom. I hadn't been to the bathroom all evening. Of course, if

Buzzy had been sitting in our booth, she and I probably would have gone to the bathroom together, because down the hallway at the right of the bar were two doors plainly marked YE VARLETS and YE WENCHES. But I didn't know how you disengaged yourself to go to the bathroom when you were all alone with a fellow. (In fact, this bathroom problem was one that girls devoted considerable thought and discussion to, on occasion, and I wish I could hear a tape of one of those conversations now. How could we possibly have spent so much time on it? What did we find to say? Today I doubt whether I could speculate that long on the origin of planets and who threw the overalls and how to avoid probate, all rolled into one.)

I wondered what Jerry and Buzzy were doing in the back seat. It was quiet back there. As it turned out, they were only sitting, Buzzy reported later, Jerry chain-smoking in a preoccupied way; and when we pulled up in front of the Kirmsey house, he was out like a gazelle to walk Buzzy up to the porch.

The Duke turned off the motor, leaving the humid leafy-green night loud with quiet. He put his arm around me. Then, apparently thinking better of it, he reached into an inside coat pocket. And said gruffly, "Here, take my card. If you ever feel like calling up . . ." He put it in my hand.

I didn't want to go in, in spite of everything. But Buzzy was standing on the stoop, holding the door open, and Jerry was heading back for the car.

And then I kissed The Duke, suddenly and hard. It was a good, solid, earnest, excellent kiss, if I do say so as shouldn't. I put a great deal into that kiss, or at least everything I knew how to put. Because I had a hunch it would be the very last one. For a couple of dozen good sound reasons, starting with my mother and ending with my father and featuring Louisa May Alcott somewhere in the middle, I was pretty sure I wouldn't be telephoning. And I suppose he knew that, too.

Once back in the house, in Buzzy's bedroom, I looked at the card he had given me, black ink on creamy stock, with lively touches of red.

> **MARTY (The Duke) MONELLI**
> "Duke of the Juke"
> Exclusive Wurlitzer Installation
> Maintenance—Repair
> CH 6049   OL 3562

I kept it for a long time.

One evening about two months later, Buzzy telephoned.

"Look at the paper!" she said in a hoarse whisper you could have heard across the street. "First section, page three."

And so I looked, picked up the *Advocate,* turned to page three, and saw him. The Duke. There he was; not a good picture, his five o'clock shadow more like eight o'clock or nine, but indubitably The Duke.

Martin Monelli, the caption said. According to the news story, Martin Monelli, 31 (*thirty-one!*) had been indicted in St. Louis for something I didn't understand, something about jukeboxes and a protection racket headquartered in Chicago. But it mentioned the remainder of the old Capone organization, and I understood that, all right. Everyone knew about Al Capone. And I'd had this sort of feeling about Marty anyway, I really had.

When I saw Buzzy the next day, of course we talked and talked. Buzzy just couldn't get over it.

"A gangster's moll," she said, with awe. "You could've been a gangster's moll."

"Naw . . ." I said modestly. But I was savoring the sound of it. You just better believe it.

Well, God bless The Duke. I never heard another word about him, but I hope he lived and loved for a long time, with both kneecaps intact. I hope he is sunning and sinning in some enchanting little Sicilian villa right now.

Because it was The Duke who got me through the Prom the following night; got me through it dream-fashion though slightly hung over and not feeling a thing, not even Carl Krepps's damp hands. I discovered that you can stand even a

Carl Krepps and a steamy high-school prom—even be kind to a fat little Chuckie Schwartz—when you've had a personal message from the larger world out there that it's really out there—a world that wouldn't necessarily know you were Best Speller, maybe wouldn't even mind if it did know. It began to seem barely possible there was life after high school.

Life. I had had, I felt, a sniff of the real thing. Indeed, I had had, you might well say, a snootful. It had been quite some evening. I had lied, stolen, got drunk, and been—I was almost certain—a loose woman, and I felt perfectly splendid, full of affection for everything and everyone. Virtue went down for the count, I can tell you, as I discovered that sin offered more rewards than you could shake a stick at.

It was something I'd have to think through, all right. Clearly, some X factors here were blurring the issue; and there were, as well, some terms that possibly needed redefining.

As a matter of fact, there still are, and I wish that The Mither were here. If only we could sit down together and talk it over now, I am sure we could figure it all out. She could also teach me once more how to knit, because I am still right where she left me the last time.

11

Mainly about
My Aunt Liz Noah

*or In One Ear and Half a Dozen
of the Other*

One recent summer afternoon, I was looking out my kitchen window—rather a cool, pale day it was, the wind flowing like water over the bending cane—when I suddenly experienced a quite unexpected moment of mourning, for all things brave and beautiful and funny that aren't around any more. I think it was brought on by a skirmish of birds in the back yard, a flock of myna birds asserting their territorial rights to a kiawe tree that a cardinal had already claimed; and it led me, as things so often do, right to my aunt Liz Noah. It also had me considering the somewhat unpromising business of growing old. I had never expected her to do that—I mean—and she rather let me down.

So far in these pages, I haven't said very much about my aunt Liz Noah, and that may be because there is too much to say. I know that hardly a day goes by that I don't remember her, for one reason or another, which seems to me to be a nice kind of immortality, really. Anyway I would like to think that when I've been dead and gone for thirty years, someone will think of me as often and for the most part as cheerfully as I think of her. (If she heard me say that, I know she'd wink that solemn wink of hers, one eyelid sliding down without disturbing the other in the slightest, and say something that would make me laugh.)

As she did on that summer night long ago, for instance, when I got dumped by, yes, by Monroe Deasey, that very same Monroe Deasey I've already mentioned, I mean Monroe Deasey, the chinless wonder. I might as well tell about that right here, because it is the last appearance he is going to make if I have anything to say about it, and as Responsible Person around here, I believe I do.

It was the summer vacation after the Junior Prom—after Marty Monelli, I mean—and I hadn't written to Monroe. Well, I seldom did; and even if writing to Monroe had been my Number One passionate avocation, The Duke would, of course, have wiped him clean off my slate. But I knew I'd be seeing Monroe anyway when I got to Ganister, my first night there and then some, just like always.

And so, quite as I expected, that first long, light summer dusk, as Aunt Liz Noah and I sipped iced coffee on her front porch, he came strolling by on schedule, wearing a dark-blue jacket and natty long white pants.

When I say strolling by, I mean just that. He gave us a casual wave of the hand and kept right on going.

Surprised? I was astonished. *Monroe?*

"He never did that before," I said stupidly.

There was a slight pause, Aunt Liz Noah regarding me with a look that grew steadily more doleful.

"That's what the farmer said when his horse died," she said.

I looked back at her. And suddenly it was very funny and we were both laughing, even as she gave me the brutal facts. It seems that Monroe was now—are you ready for this?—going with this very cute package named Dottie Imler, who was Ganister High's own version of Ellen Bishop. Monroe had made baseball history that year—most home runs, most runs batted in, most bases stolen, most everything—and he was now considered quite a catch.

It wasn't long before he reappeared, this time walking on the other side of the street. And, sure enough, hanging on his arm was little Dottie, all dark curls and pink cuddly sweater and flirty pink skirt, looking like she'd mislaid her pompons. Cute? And I must say, Monroe looked almost cute himself now, not half so ghastly. This was probably my first brush with the melancholy old retail truth that the merchandise always looks better when somebody else has her hand on it.

Not that I was really bruised, though; I'd had no emotional investment there. The only thing was, even as I laughed I could see that I'd have to do some heavy creative thinking before I went back home to McKinleyville, in order to oblige Buzzy Kirmsey, who was always avid for details of my hot nights with Monroe.

Well, I'd tell her we'd done the big renunciation scene on account of we were getting Too Serious. Too Serious was a good ace in the hole. Everybody knew what *that* meant. . . .

As I was saying, it was the birds in my Hawaiian back yard on a recent bright morning here that had me thinking back to those days. In particular I think it was a cardinal, who was looking rather like a rogue poinsettia as he swung from the branch of the kiawe tree.

These birds always seem out of place to me here. Back in McKinleyville, from my mother's kitchen window, you'd often spot a cardinal in the mulberry tree or the big oak (and often in the snow); and in Ganister, from Grandma's window, an occasional scarlet flutter in a cottonwood. But in a kiawe tree? Or a plumeria? And I suppose a born islander transplanted to the Middle West would probably wonder the same thing: what is that small bird doing so far from home? Wherever you see something the first time is where it belongs.

For of course it is equally cardinal country, here in the Islands. And myna bird country, too, as I was reminded only a minute later, watching this particular cardinal get dispossessed in a hurry by a myna bird, who flew in and talked him right out of his tree.

I could have predicted the outcome. Mynas usually get their own way. Then a whole delegation of them swooped in to join the first, and suddenly the quiet air was loud as a landladies' convention, all chatter and shriek. And it *was* a convention, I suppose, or at least a good big committee meeting. Mynas get together periodically, the way Congress does, to decide on joint plans and policy. Mynas run the island; any myna bird will tell you that.

Probably I should stop saying myna bird. You don't say eagle bird or robin bird. And yet it's gooney bird. . . .

Myna. Myna bird. I asked my husband. Which?

"Why don't you ask them?" he suggested. "They talk, don't they?"

And of course they do, nearly all the live-long day. But they speak only myna till they've been tutored in English; and even then, so much depends upon the input.

Back in Ganister, Aunt Liz Noah had a talking myna named Captain Anderson that she'd inherited from a seagoing friend of her husband's. During those long-ago summer vacations, I used to enjoy teaching him new things, at a fairly exorbitant time-cost per thing, it seems to me now, though of course I didn't care. When you're little, time stretches obligingly, and vacation is forever.

The Captain was a big glossy-black fellow with the myna's classically white-streaked wings and strong yellow legs. He also had an exceptionally fine, proud, fierce yellow beak, good for winkling bobby pins out of my hair as he rode around on my shoulder. When I tired of that, which was fairly soon, I would put him back in his cage and try to teach him something.

That was fun, though it was disconcerting the way he'd tilt his head and look at me, a you're-so-smart-why-can't-you-fly sort of look. Also, I wouldn't know for days whether or not a new phrase had registered. Then he might scream it for hours, or he might come up with another from a good five years back. Aunt Liz Noah and I decided that he had a bowl of alphabet soup where his brains ought to be—lots of letters down there but no telling what might bob to the surface, or when.

I remember one occasion, though, when his contribution was singularly appropriate.

Aunt Liz Noah liked her privacy. Her aversion to drop-in guests was known and respected by everyone in town, except for fat Mrs. Tobias, a great bore who lived down the street.

I well remember (because it became a family catch phrase) Mrs. T.'s way of prefacing dull remarks that no reasonable person would dispute with a roguish "I guess I'm terrible but . . ." As in "I guess I'm terrible but a happy family is more important to me than a spic-and-span house." Or "I guess I'm terrible but I think nigras have feelings, too." So you felt that you were expected to assure her that she wasn't a bit terrible, though you knew she didn't truly cross-her-heart think she was terrible either; and so what you really wanted to do was knock off this little *pas de deux* and hit her with something heavy.

Anyway, I happened to be there one afternoon when Mrs. Tobias dropped in and stayed and stayed, Aunt Liz Noah feeling restive—I knew that—though she never let it show. (She had a grave and unvarying courtesy; and I think that whoever defined a lady as someone who never hurts another's feelings unintentionally must surely have known her.)

But manners didn't hamper the Captain. When Mrs. Tobias finally lumbered to her feet and said she must be going, he said, loud and clear, "I'll drink to that!" which he'd picked up nobody knew where. It was a lovely effect.

The old Captain is long gone now. I wonder, if he were here, whether he would be able to chat with the mynas out there in my back yard, the ones making such a ruckus in the kiawe tree. Perhaps they speak only pidgin. Too, they look a bit small and dusty, not quite so big and satiny-black as I remember the Captain.

The truth is, though, most things seemed more so then. Bigger, brighter, louder, or . . . Sometimes I think of a song that was current years ago: *The grass is the greeniest / The scenes are the sceniest / The snows are the snowiest / The winds are the blowiest / The sun is the sunniest / The fun is the funniest / Way back home. . . .* Something like that, anyway, and that's how it seems, all right, everything more so. Warmer, colder, taller, smaller . . .

Or longer, like the eight blocks between Grandpa's house and Aunt Liz Noah's.

For one thing, these were such well-populated blocks, so full of things and people to think about along the way. You passed the chocolate-caramel lady's house, 50¢ a pound, 60¢ with nuts, sold from her back porch and made in her own kitchen, from the recipe she'd been offered $50,000 for and wouldn't take. This must have been the granddaddy of the legend one occasionally runs across now: the woman who innocently asks the chef for a recipe, usually for a dish requiring a package of something, like marshmallows, and he gives it to her, or so she thinks. Next thing she knows, she's being sued for $5,000 and has to pay up; and to revenge herself, she henceforth gives the recipe to everyone in sight. Legends like this have sold a great many marshmallows.

Then you'd pass the man-who'd-been-in-jail's house, we never knew for what, just that he'd been in jail, but the fact had you walking faster past it. And faster still past The Elms, the nursing home where I'd gone sometimes with Grandpa. Loony-looking old people in bathrobes would be shuffling around the side yard there on warm days, and when the wind was wrong you'd catch a chlorine-formaldehyde smell thick enough to slice.

And then past the corner lot where my brother played baseball, though only before and after meals. Of course he would be superbly unaware that I was walking by; nor did I know he was within miles of the place as I sailed on down the street, looking anywhere but there.

And finally to Aunt Liz Noah's, the house with the blue-painted front door that opened into a world different from Grandma's and Grandpa's and from the McKinleyville world, too.

In an ecru era, her walls were bright white and full of paintings, her own and other people's, along with woodcuts, lithographs, pencil sketches, some framed, some just tacked up. On the black-painted floors she had a few old Oriental rugs and not much furniture. There were books all over, on shelves and on tables, and a tall sprawl of magazines on the dining-room window seat, and the kitchen always looked as though she were moving in or moving out, you'd have been hard put to say which. As she ruefully remarked, she had a place for everything and something else was always in it—generally paints or brushes or penciled roughs or tissues.

Liz Noah was a good painter, and her work had hung in some good New York galleries as well as other places. What she mainly painted was horses—dawn-red horses, sky-blue horses, impressionist horses, Surrealist horses, and some very realistic individual horses, too. She would be commissioned sometimes to do horse portraits, Derby horses and so on. If a long shot loped in, she'd more than likely get a wire from the happy owner, which was terribly exciting to me, as any telegram was, though Liz Noah took it calmly. Then she'd go down to the bluegrass country or wherever the stable was, to meet the horse and photograph him, then come back home to do the actual painting.

She used the kitchen breakfast ell as a studio because the light was best there. To me, everything about her place was exactly right, from the rip-roaring Kandinsky on the wall behind the stove (Grandma had oilcloth tacked behind hers) to the red clay flowerpot full of soap cakes in the bathroom. At home or at Grandma's, either one, the extra soap wasn't kept out and visible. Only when the washbowl cake was finally worn to a slippery chip you could hardly pick up were you supposed to fish around in the back of the washbowl cabinet for the extra bar of green Palmolive. And Aunt Liz Noah's soap didn't smell soapy either, but smelled instead of cinnamon, sandalwood, jasmine.

There were other good things to do there besides play with Captain Anderson. I would go out back sometimes, a country block from the house, to wait for the afternoon Santa Fe freight train to roar and rattle past, and wave to the genial brakeman riding the caboose.

Then sometimes I'd weed a flower bed, to make points. Mainly I specialized in staying shrewdly out of eye range much of the time so she wouldn't grow sick of the sight of me, and, so far as I know, she never did. The only time I remember her being annoyed was one day when I was picky and restive, just over the summer flu, and cut up some of her good drawing paper for paper dolls. I can see her now, arms akimbo, stage Irish, and hear her "Sure an' you've been that aggravatin' only a mother could stand you an' her only hardly!" But then she gave me a great swoop of a hug and I knew everything was all right.

Her concentration was total when she painted. She wasn't aware of anything else—didn't hear the telephone ring or know I was there or when she'd eaten last. When she did eat again, it would be more of whatever she had a lot of—perhaps all meat loaf or all asparagus, depending on the season and the garden, or all eggs or all beans. Sometimes she'd bake a potful that would last for days. Once it was a splendid massive applesauce cake, dark and rich and heavily frosted.

Looking back now, I think her diet was reasonably adequate, at least for a good many years. She'd roughly balance the week, if not the meal or the day. But later she wasn't even doing that, and the enduring problem was that she didn't care.

I read a lot, too, at Aunt Liz Noah's, and her library partially mitigated the mental squalor my McKinleyville friends and I lived in, that cozy literary slum where Louisa May Alcott and Martha Finley were the spiritual den mothers.

Not that there weren't some good books at home. But home is home. The grass is often greener on other people's bookshelves, and it was at Liz Noah's that I first read Sherwood Anderson and Willa Cather and Edward Lear, Cabell and Frost and Housman and *Sherlock Holmes, archie and mehitabel* and Foxe's *Book of Martyrs,* and Emily Dickinson. There'd also be a current *New Yorker.* Aunt Liz Noah was quite possibly Ganister's sole subscriber.

I have heard that lonely people tend to underline. I suppose it is the not having someone across from them so they can say, "Listen! Listen to this! . . ." Now that I have some of her books, I am struck by the truth of it. She underlined often, and one marked passage in particular stays in my mind, in a book of voyages, among them one of Columbus's. There had been an endless time of violent storms alternating with doldrums, the men hungry, sick, or dying, when day after weary day the log's sole entry was a bleak "This day we sailed on." She had underlined that.

And then there were the hats, Liz Noah's hats from her life with John, the trunkful she'd brought back from New York. It was a family joke that she couldn't throw a hat away. She could found a Home for Elderly & Destitute Gentlehats, my father remarked once, and Aunt Liz Noah pointed out that she already had, right up there in the attic.

So she would let me play with them sometimes. I would forage hastily—the attic was stifling—and bring down half a dozen to model in front of the pier glass, looking like a mushroom in all of them, for they were all big marvelous hats designed for a tall woman. I remember a great coppery velour saucer of a hat, and another concoction of smoke-gray chiffon, and a glorious red velvet that seemed all tilt and feathers, and a still-crisp navy cartwheel brimming with red cherries.

And then when she stopped painting and felt like talking, there were the games we'd play, swinging idly in the glider on the cooler side of the porch.

Minister's Cats. He is an Ambitious cat who Aspires to the Arts, a Bad cat who Bothers Birds, a Cuddlesome Cat who Craves Companionship . . .

Or we'd make rhymes and limericks, or she would do funny spidery sketches to illustrate our growing collection of addled adages. "It's a wise child who spills his own milk." "A rolling stone seldom bites" . . . and if you think it impossible to depict a rolling stone in the very act of not biting, you just haven't seen Liz Noah's work. (I think she positioned it under the Wrong Tree we had developed, one time, for barking up.)

Or we would play Tough Choice, and tough choices they'd be. If you could have anything in the entire whole world you wanted, only first you had to have your hands cut off, would you? I remember, when I finally decided no, she said,

"Well, now, I didn't know you were so fond of your hands. Worth more than the Kohinoor diamond, are they? Why aren't you running around all day dancing and shouting, 'Look, I've got hands, I've got hands, I've got these wonderful hands that can do anything I'll teach 'em to do!!!' . . . H'mmm?" I couldn't answer that at all, though I've thought of it since.

Or if you could eat only one food for the rest of your life, what would it be? Or hear only one song—which? Or if you could save the whole town from exploding tomorrow by getting this terrible skin disease, would you? She asked me that once.

Those are hard decisions. "What kind of a skin disease?" I wanted to know.

She thought a minute. "Awful acne and gray mildew. For keeps."

Oh, boy. "All over?"

"All over," she said.

"Would they know I'd saved them?" I asked.

"No," she said. "But you'd know."

There it was again, good old Virtue, still being its own reward.

"Even Jesus got credit," I pointed out, and that made her laugh, though I hadn't thought to make her laugh. But I liked it when I did.

And we would wonder and ponder. Who would you be if you could be anyone who ever lived? Do butterflies have more fun than whales do? Are there more stars than grass blades? Are there more grass blades than grains of sand? What's on the moon? (I hope she wasn't following the moon shot from wherever she is, because what we imagined up there was a good deal better than what they found.) And what color is Nevertheless? Lavender? Or a shimmery gray-green? And what shape is Tuesday?

Then sometimes, strolling down the drowsing summer street to the soda fountain in the Grand Osage Hotel Coffee Shop, she would talk about some of the remarkable people who had once lived in these not-so-remarkable houses. The

Flotsams, who had all been born a hundred years old and then grew younger and younger, went from married to unmarried to littler and littler. And their neighbors, the Jetsams, born with their eyes on the backs of their elbows, so at movies they always had to sit with their backs to the movie screen, which must have been awfully uncomfortable, but it was funny to think of them all sitting there backward on their knees.

And once we arrived at the Osage fountain we always had the special Osage Orange Ice-Cream Soda, a luscious medley of rich vanilla ice cream, yellow as a four-egg custard, made with fresh orange juice and lots of fizz.

We had good times, Aunt Liz Noah and I, and I've learned, since, that someone to laugh with and wonder and speculate with is not to be found around every turn, and is to be valued. And I valued Aunt Liz Noah, though not really enough. Or so it seems to me now.

Well, the trouble is that growing up is a full-time job. I suppose it is natural, while you're busy with it, to shelve the elderly relatives you used to find fascinating. Or that is, to think about them only when you're there, so they come alive for you only when you show up, the way the refrigerator light goes on when you open the door. But, natural or not, it is a great shame, for they have generally died or otherwise disintegrated by the time you could enjoy being grown up together.

I know that after McKinleyville High, Ganister moved to a far meadow of my mind, buzzing with old sunny child-time summers but eons away and misty, seen through scrim.

It was only a few months after I'd gone away to college that Em and Ben both died, within a few weeks of each other. Sudden though it was, the pain of it was lessened for me by the distance and the new world I was trying to cope with. Moreover—no two ways about it—you expect grandparents to die, love them as you may, for they have been old as the pharaohs all your life.

Now Liz Noah was the only relative left in Ganister. And

I wrote to her, though infrequently and not for the most admirable of reasons. It was mainly when or because I needed my hand held.

At the small Ohio college I went to, it is rumored that academic courses were offered, lectures attended, and books studied. I even have, somewhere, a piece of parchment asserting that I completed whatever I was supposed to complete to get a Bachelor of Arts degree, though I can't imagine how I ever worked it in.

All I remember is boys who either loved me or didn't love me, that I either loved or didn't love, and with whom I never got in sync. So I was sometimes up, sometimes down, Oh, yes, Lord, and probably the only thing that made it bearable was knowing I was the only person who had ever felt this bad before.

The truth is, what I was looking for in college wasn't the Lost Chord or the Missing Link or some new elements to plug all those holes in the Periodic Table; I was looking for a husband. (And found one, too, though by a rather round-about route, and I'll get to that shortly.)

In this I wasn't unusual. The brisk winds of women's liberation weren't blowing then, though the winds of war were; and these may have given us additional impetus. But war or no war, for most girls growing up when I did, marriage-home-and-children was still the pot of gold at the end of the academic rainbow. Career girls, as professional women were usually called, were politely accepted, outwardly encouraged, and often admired, though I don't think my mother would have wanted her son to marry one.

But of course in that day you didn't go around hollering that you were husband-hunting any more than girls do now, though for different reasons. Today they are ashamed to admit they are looking for a husband if they are, and they generally are, because they've teethed on liberation, and open husband-hunting would be letting the side down. They are supposed to want to do something interesting, and being a wife doesn't qualify, though it must be admitted that catching a husband and then doing something about it is in reality more interesting than the things that many of them end up doing.

Equally, when I was young, you didn't go around hollering about it mainly because you knew that all the good husband material would gallop off into the tall uncut timber if you did. A fellow had to chase you till you caught him. Everyone knew that.

And so you concealed it, and I concealed it so well that I almost concealed it from myself. That is easily done when you don't know your own self; and I was so minimally acquainted with mine that I wouldn't have recognized her if we had bumped smack into each other on any familiar street.

In retrospect, it is as though I had put my life on Hold till I got that part of it settled, instead of the other way around, as it so often is today; and that part was either complicated or simplified—I can't decide which—by its being the pre-Pill, pre–New Morality era when, for most of us, wedding and bedding went in about that order. We expected Love-Marriage-and-Sex to happen in that sequence and then become inalterably fixed, like the three wheels on a sturdy tricycle. Though we knew they didn't always, that a couple of wheels might go square or even fall off, this was considered an aberration and not the norm.

But now it seems to have all come apart, that little tricycle has, and perhaps that's just as well, especially if there wasn't any tricycle there to begin with. Now it's Sex and/or Love and/or Marriage, and if disillusion sets in to sour the arrangement, whichever arrangement it is, you can call it a learning experience and buzz off.

At any rate, I was confusing love and lust in the immemorial feminine way without being able to give the lust a good go and find out; and through many a graceless fumbling and floundering in many a back seat, most of us remained dubiously but doggedly virgin, by means of, to quote the old limerick, "remembering Jesus, / venereal disesus, / and the chances of having a child." Besides being time-consuming, not to say frustrating, it was confusing and painful enough that I agree heartily with whoever said she'd rather be illegitimate than seventeen. Or eighteen or nineteen. And as Scott Fitzgerald once wrote of a bad patch he went through, it eventually turned out all right but for a different person. I believe they call it education.

And so in those years I wrote Aunt Liz Noah some long, undoubtedly tedious letters she always answered, though annoyingly often she'd have mislaid mine and forgotten most of what I told her, so I'd have to tell her again. ("It's my rotten memory," she explained when I saw her next. She viewed the business of growing old with a blend of amusement and wry distaste, and she said once that forgetting things is what gives old age a bad name, that and old age.)

And though I knew I should make allowances for it, I somehow kept expecting my life to have the same resonance for her that it had for me. Busy growing up, I suppose I didn't realize that growing old takes time and attention, too.

But she knew a howl of pain when she heard one. I remember her doing her best to comfort me long distance the year I was most thoroughly heart-scalded. In a book of Dorothy Parker's verse she sent, she'd tucked a note, ending, "Remember, I'm here, to be written to or not as the spirit moves, but if a good page of God-damn-its would help you, it wouldn't hurt me none. . . ." And I don't remember whether or not I availed myself of the opportunity, but I do remember something else, after I had mainly recovered and was belittling him, and me, and making fun of it all. "Don't de-value things like this," she wrote me, with unaccustomed gravity. "Just because it isn't doesn't mean it never was."

I have remembered that and been grateful to her for it, as for much else.

When an insurance man once told me that more accidents happen in the bedroom than anywhere else in the house, I thought he was making a poor joke. But no. He said the reason was that sometimes when older people get out of bed, they are awake but their legs aren't.

This was apparently the case with Liz Noah a spring or two later. Mama wrote me that one hot May afternoon, a neighbor happened to notice a quart of milk curdling on the Noah back porch. No one answered when Mrs. Ostigsen pounded the door. So she jimmied open a window, went in, and found Aunt Liz Noah lying on the bedroom floor in her pajamas.

"What are you doing down there?" asked Mrs. O.

"I like it down here," Aunt Liz Noah answered, with some asperity. "I'm going to grow potatoes under the bed."

"And she could've," Mrs. Ostigsen said with relish to anyone who'd listen, after Aunt Liz Noah was taken to the hospital with a broken hip. "Dust and fuzz under there, you never saw the beat of it."

The hip mended—no problem—and she went back home. And it was the summer after that, an August weekend between college and a job in Cleveland, that I visited her there.

It was a sultry time, the leaves on the big cottonwoods motionless in the still air. The place looked about the same, though the once-bright blue door was dull now, crazed and blistered in places by the hot Kansas sun.

On Aunt Liz Noah the years were showing, too. Especially her hands: knuckles newly swollen, one hand painfully massaging the fingers of the other all the while we talked. I'd known she wasn't painting, and now I knew why. Old age is only a collection of little infirmities you neglect to recover from—I read that somewhere—and Aunt Liz Noah was adding to her collection. And she was grayer, skinnier, frailer, nudging *old,* aging the way a day does, moving toward dusk and the dusk toward dark. But she still walked tall, still laughed. Some.

She was wearing the familiar faded khaki riding pants and a soft old blue cotton shirt. While she made our standard iced coffee, I noticed that her left earring was missing, one of the gold nuggets I'd never seen her without, and I asked her about it.

She touched her ear. "Oh, *no* . . ." she muttered, and left the room, but returned in a moment, the earring in her hand.

"Stupid!" she said briskly, putting it back on. "I was taking them off to polish and just forgot what I was doing. Midstream. I'm outliving my brains," she said, and added ruefully that she'd never thought breathing would be such a hard old habit to break.

"But you've probably been doing it all your life," I pointed out.

"That's right, I started young," she said wryly. "You know how it is; it seemed like a good idea at the time."

I think it was that same afternoon that she searched through the stacked books on the dining table for her Marcus Aurelius so she could read me a paragraph, which I would have forgotten forever if I hadn't come across it only recently, underlined in the little Modern Library volume that I inherited along with the rest of her books.

> *"Pass then through this little space of time conformably to nature, and end thy journey in content, just as an olive falls off when it is ripe, blessing nature who produced it, and thanking the tree on which it grew."*

"*But—*" she rapped the page smartly with her finger—"he was only fifty-nine when he wrote that. And that," she said, "isn't a very ripe old olive." Her left eyelid slid down in the old familiar way, and she regarded me quizzically. "But I suppose fifty-nine seems old to you?"

And of course it did, though I wasn't about to say so.

Mainly what we talked about that day was, of course, me, and what next. Our class had been graduated one sunny morning in late May, stepping out to the "Triumphal March" from *Aïda*, though the "Hesitation Waltz" would probably have been more appropriate. It didn't look even remotely like the best of all possible worlds, the one we were about to get into. And we were right. It wasn't long till the war started, I mean the real war, the big, rational, right war in which we all knew the good guys from the bad guys, the war we fought to make the world safe for future wars though we didn't know we were doing that at the time, which was probably just as well.

Anyway, I had a job that was to start in September, writing

copy for a small Cleveland advertising agency, and we talked about that. Aunt Liz had done some commercial work, too, early on.

While we talked, she kept getting up to straighten pictures. She would nudge one a quarter of an inch and barely sit down again before she'd be up, making some microscopic adjustment on another. Pictures hanging askew had always bothered her—I remember that—but never this much. I thought then, how easy it probably is for a whim to go from quirk to habit to compulsion till before you know it, it's a crotchet. . . .

She straightened a watercolor for the third time and I couldn't help mentioning it. "You just did that one," I said. "Twice."

"Did I?" She looked confused, and then cross at herself. "It's senility," she said flatly, and told me she had a new address, should anyone ask where she'd gone to. "Tell 'em Rackenruin," she said. "In the suburbs of Senility. Sneaking up on the inner city."

Senility. She'd said it.

"Yes, but 'if you know you're senile you ain't yet,' remember?" I said. I was quoting old Adolph, a former yard man of hers who had said many a quotable quote, and we'd often laughed with him as well as at him. But she didn't smile now, only shook her head. After I left her that day and thought again about Adolph's remark, it didn't seem so very funny to me either.

Earlier in these pages, I said that we would presently come to the husband I found, or who found me. This is probably the place for it, though it leads me back into my fortune-telling period at the Star Bar in Cleveland, a foolish time I had rather hoped to avoid. Also, looking back now, I find my first encounter with my future husband to be regrettably reminiscent of those familiar Hollywood meet-cutes (she falls down a manhole and there *he* is, or they collide in a revolving door) though, as it turned out, mine wasn't quite that cute or all that accidental either. Anyway, facts are facts, and it seems to me they belong here, starting with Scheidelmann's one-lung advertising agency, because I was married by the time I saw Liz Noah again. Besides, proposals are in general more interesting than propositions.

On the Sunday before the Monday morning I started the new job, I found a room at Mrs. O'Callaghan's boarding-house on Cleveland's East 82nd Street.

Mrs. O'Callaghan was a lean woman in her fifties, a gaunt druid with coal-black hair and bright-red knuckles and a sharp eye on the check-in, check-out times of anyone visiting a female boarder. Though it was a tatty old place, a torn blind here and a mangy rug there, Mrs. O'Callaghan had her standards. A pink crocheted cozy hid the extra roll of toilet paper in our unisex bathroom, and on Sundays she served butter instead of the great lump of bright-orange margarine we'd been working on all week. Moreover, she wouldn't take, as she said with some pride, any transom trade. I finally deduced that she meant transient, but I preferred transom, for the lovely image it gave me of people oozing gently in and out over the doors.

Life was busy, there at Mrs. O'Callaghan's. Presently I was nurse's aiding three nights a week at a nearby hospital, fortunetelling another three at the reasonably nearby Star Bar, shampooing my hair on Monday nights, and sleeping mostly in the daytime, on the job.

It was a love-hate relationship that I had with the agency right from the start; hated to get there in the morning and loved to leave. I am sure Mr. Scheidelmann wanted to fire me quite as much as I wanted to quit, too, but it was undoubtedly hard to find people who would work, or even sleep, for what he considered a living wage.

Besides the low pay, my only complaints were the place itself—a cheap hole in a shabby building—and the accounts the agency handled, plus Mr. Scheidelmann himself, affectionately known to us girls as Old Buzzard-Breath.

Mr. Scheidelmann had, in addition to roving hands, a demented notion that all copy could and should be slanted toward the war effort. Since his two main accounts were a credit dentist and a mortuary, this took some doing.

DR. BAYLEE'S VICTORY DENTAL PLATES FOR BETTER NUTRITION
TO KEEP OUR COUNTRY STRONG! And LET DR. BAYLEE DO <u>ALL</u>
YOUR DENTAL WORK ON THE EASY-VICTORY PAYMENT PLAN! (Actually, Dr. Baylee and his merry men—he had a huge staff—weren't very good at picky work like filling teeth, and they hadn't developed those big bulging biceps by drilling holes. Whatever your dental problem might have been, Victory Plates are what you were virtually guaranteed to emerge with.) And DR. BAYLEE KEEPS WARTIME AMERICA SMILING! But not so happily as he was, I am sure, all the way to the bank.

Mortuaries were harder, or at least ours was. Mr. Purcey, acting head of Purcey & Noble Morticians (they purposely omitted the comma) preferred a more literary approach for their twice-weekly ad, five hundred words of inspirational copy set off by a tasteful floral border.

"Now as never before" . . . I would begin, a little hopelessly. (I often began them that way, though nothing very good ever came of it.) But now as never before what? War or no war, you're supposed to bury people if they're dead, aren't you? Or anyway cremate them or something, because it would be too depressing just leaving them around. And what did Purcey & Noble Morticians' best efforts have to do, precisely, with Victory? "Now as never before" . . . and I'd go back to sleep again.

It is true that our agency wasn't alone in its fondness for the war gimmick and the patriotic tie-in. Everything was Victory: Victory coiffures, casseroles, candles; Victory pedicures and house paints. Forty m.p.h. was the Victory Speed, and my dry cleaner had a Victory Special: AMERICAN FLAGS DRY-CLEANED FREE!! Additional proof that all the atrocities weren't happening overseas was a paragraph from a *Harper's Bazaar* shopping column that I pasted in my journal at the time:

> "... *He'll be tickled to death with bright felt slippers with the army insignia embroidered in bright wools. Or better still, if he's in the air force, the same breed of gay slippers embroidered*

> with a plane flying among pink cherubs and
> white clouds. . . ."

What the Osage Indians were doing was more sensible. Aunt Liz Noah wrote, in one of her infrequent notes, that the tribe on a reservation somewhere west of Ganister had staged a three-day war dance against the Axis. As we know now, it worked, too, although it took a few years.

But to the Star Bar now, the place where, in order to eke out my income, I told fortunes, or, more accurately, analyzed handwriting, or, more accurately still, pretended to, with my new friend Estelle Laderes, who also lived at the boarding-house.

Estelle was a small, dark, pretty art student who went to school four nights a week and worked with me the other three. She could do a quick, recognizable charcoal portrait, and I'd read a book on handwriting once, and so we became partners. She'd sketch while I wrote, and the results, stapled together, we sold for two and a half. Fat Tiny, the waiter, touted for us—he really liked Estelle—and on good nights we'd turn maybe a dozen tricks. I will say here, too, that in those days, thirty dollars was a lot more like thirty dollars.

The Star Bar was a tavern trying without noticeable success to be a night club. It was owned by a friendly couple named Grodske. Karl Grodske was a skinny, pockmarked, black-haired man who tended bar and told bad jokes and laughed a lot, while his wife, Irma, hostessed and sang. Their only employee was Fat Tiny, who didn't know from Shinola, Karl said good-naturedly, but he worked cheap.

Irma Grodske, a brightly blonde former hoofer, had a body that was better than her voice. But Saturday nights when they'd have live music she'd sing anyway, wearing a solid-sequin dress that fit like scales on a goldfish, and you forgave her for whatever she was doing to "I'll Walk Alone" or "Lilli Marlene." (Nobody could ruin those songs then anyway, no matter what they did.) And the Star Bar had a friendly clientele: some neighborhood regulars and some transom trade, mostly blue-collar and white-collar men from the defense plants sprouting like large gray toadstools east of the city.

It was dark at the Star Bar; visibility virtually zero. The deep-blue ceiling was punctured at random intervals so some ten-watt bulbs could twinkle through, and that was it. A coal hole. And while I am sure the Grodskes were neither the first nor the last to discover that the darker you kept it, the dirtier you could let it get, they certainly made full use of the principle. (Once, after the place closed, I was crawling around in the dust and butts under the table, hunting for my fountain pen, and Fat Tiny loaned me a flashlight. When I happened to look up at the underside of that table I was sorry he had. Clearly this was where all Cleveland's old chewing gum went when it died.)

However, though it is difficult to draw or write in total darkness—we used a candle to work by—it had its advantages. If we couldn't see too well, neither could the customers; and so far as my part of it went, this was just as well. I always hoped they'd wait till they got home to read what I had written, because, as I have indicated, my credentials as a graphologist were nil.

Flagrant flattery was the real name of my game. Purse-mouthed people or people who made stingy ending strokes were future millionaires or captains of finance, if they cared to move in that direction; I always hedged some. Any obvious slob was an original thinker with a fine disregard for conformity. People who wrote with fancy flourishes and vulgar capitals had artistic talent. And so on. Then there are certain traits we all like to think we possess, and I'd hand those out like jellybeans: tact, sensitivity, guts, taste, humor. . . .

Prudently, I kept the fortunetelling to a minimum, only occasionally finding intimations of a severe future illness that could, however, be averted—I'd stress this—by proper diet and rest. After all, here they were, losing sleep, soaking up Father Grodske's dubious wartime booze—I was really doing them a favor. I would also dispense romance and babies with a lavish hand to people who looked as though they'd like some.

Thus it was that Estelle and I were sitting in our usual spot one slow Saturday night, doodling and writing letters home, when she said out of the side of her mouth, "That man's here again."

Out of the side of mine I said, "Which man?" Several men, semiregulars at the Star Bar, hung around sometimes, wanting to take us home, mainly Estelle, though, and she was going steady with a boy at art school. We always took cabs.

"Same one that was here last night," she said. "Blond fellow. Don't look now, but he's right across the room, table two. . . . Now you can look."

I looked. A tall, blond, good-looking man. I didn't remember seeing him before. But Estelle had a better memory for faces.

It wasn't long before he came over, put some money on the table, and sat down in our customer chair, saying pleasantly, "Give me the works."

He had a good smile, really stunning teeth. No Dr. Baylee Victory Specials these, no sir. And he had level blue eyes, quite the bluest eyes I'd ever seen, I think, visibly and vividly blue even in the light of the candle.

And so I handed him the pen and asked him to copy off a paragraph from the Preamble to the Constitution. I kept this handy because people seldom know what to write when you ask them to write a hundred words. Tell them to type something and they'll type "Now is the time for all good men" till the cows come home. But handwriting is something else.

Estelle started sketching, and when he finished copying, I studied his firm angular writing with ostensible care, though I'd rather have studied him instead. Then I wrote my usual pageful. Which he started perusing, right there.

" 'A keen mind,' " he read aloud, " 'with marked literary ability.' " He thought about that for a little while. "Yes, well, I doubt if it's really all that keen—my mind, I mean," he said finally, with that engaging smile again. "I suppose I'm smart enough, maybe high average, but . . . no . . . not keen. 'Literary ability' . . . Boy, could I use some."

"What do you do?" I asked.

He was a hydraulics engineer, he said, drafting for a big outfit that made hoists and lift trucks in East Cleveland. He showed me a folded newspaper picture of one he'd worked on, labeled "Somewhere in New Guinea." He was a good engineer, he said, but when it came to writing company reports . . .

He read on. " 'A wanderlust that will take you to far places' . . . I hope not!" he said, with a flash of those good teeth. " 'Wanderlust' . . . No, I wouldn't say so. Don't mind going somewhere if there's some point to it, but just traveling around—no, I don't go for that." And he continued reading. " 'You like people and people like you' . . ."

This was a good dependable jellybean that I often threw in for makeweight. He considered it.

"Well, no," he said finally. "I get along all right, but I think I like people better in the abstract. If I had to choose."

That surprised me, and I couldn't quite understand it. People never stay in the abstract; they always particularize themselves, I wanted to say and didn't, because I didn't want to argue. (But it was thus that our eventual combat zones were being lightly delineated, though we didn't know that at the time.)

He went on. " 'Good sense of humor . . .' " He looked up quickly and said, "Now that's a funny thing—or, no—" he smiled at that—"not exactly a funny thing, but I've thought about this, and I don't think I have much. Sense of humor, that is. I guess I just don't like to laugh as well as some people do. So I don't. Very often."

I couldn't believe it. People will admit to arson and mayhem sooner than no sense of humor. This was astonishing. Not to say embarrassing, for me. Some batting average.

I picked up the sheet of paper in a gingerly way. "Do you want this anyway?" I asked.

"Sure. I paid for it, didn't I?" he said. "Anyway, I think it's good."

"For what?" I said.

"Well, anyway you tried," he said generously. Then we were both laughing. He had a good laugh, and it seemed a shame he didn't enjoy it more.

A bit later he drove us home, Estelle and me, but we left her there and went on to a beer-and-hamburger place, me watching to see if he ate the onion on his before I touched mine. (As I have indicated, in those days it was the good-night kiss you geared up for, not the your-place-or-mine.)

His name was Mike Smith, a forthright name for a forth-right man. He had gone to my college, only six years sooner, and his appearing at the Star Bar hadn't been accidental. A professor we both knew had suggested he look me up, and when he telephoned the boardinghouse, Mrs. O'Callaghan told him where I was.

I asked him why he hadn't come over to our table the night before.

"I thought I'd check you out first," he said.

It made me feel like a defective pump, and I told him so. Besides self-conscious. Nothing makes you feel quite so retro-actively uncomfortable as learning that someone was watch-ing you when you didn't know it.

"But you checked out okay," he offered.

For some reason I thought of my noncommittal father. I was beginning to feel right at home. "You're an honest man, Mike Smith," I said, "and that's a good honest name."

There was a short but remarkably pregnant pause. "You can have it," he said then. "Any time you like . . ."

And, indeed, that is the way it worked out, and surprisingly well, too, all things considered. I took it, not immediately, but eventually, and left the advertising agency, and we moved to a cottage in the country, where I became a Home-Front Soldier. Home-Front Soldiers saved bacon fat and old tin cans and Victory-gardened and smoked bad tobacco. And though the marriage wasn't exactly a rose garden, it was no bramble patch either, and though I was eventually repotted, it lasted quite well for a while.

But this isn't the story of that; it is Liz Noah's chapter, though the marriage belongs in it, too, in a way. For if I hadn't married Mike, who presently decided to heed Horace Greeley and head west, I wouldn't have seen Liz Noah again when I did, for what turned out to be the last time.

As it happened, it was the housekeeping and the food, or the lack of them, that eventually settled her future. More and more, she either couldn't or wouldn't cope; wouldn't dust, sweep, swab out the sink, put the butter away, or change her old erratic pattern of eating whatever was around if she happened to think about it.

Finally, after three months' virtual starvation on toast and tea, she developed an all-over rough red skin rash the doctor called pellagra. He then wrote to Mama, who went over to Ganister immediately but couldn't persuade Liz Noah to come back and live in McKinleyville.

The only solution was The Elms. It was reasonably clean —everyone said that—and they did try to feed their people properly. Homey things like corn pudding and meat loaf, puréed spinach and gentle baked custards.

Aunt Liz Noah had been there almost a year when Mike and I eventually left Ohio for new horizons, with a second-hand car and a calico cat named Minerva. I couldn't have by-passed Ganister, for how did I know if I would ever be back there again? Distance was distance then, and money was money, and credit cards were only a gleam in some banker's eye. Besides all that, I had a profound hunch that I wouldn't be seeing Liz Noah again.

The Elms was a shabby green now instead of shabby mustard, but all in all not greatly changed. The porch had been closed in and they'd added a new wing, but the over-all effect was still one of genteel decay. Better-smelling, perhaps, with a strong lemony scent trying to cloak the pervasive funky mix of vegetable soup and stuffy rooms and bodily secretions. But basically the same: same cute Kate Greenaway pictures on lettuce-green walls, same safety handrails everywhere, and down the brown-linoleumed hall, through half-open doors, the same embarrassingly intimate glimpses of old people in beds and wheelchairs, alike as babies, lost in the anonymity of old old age.

I had asked Mike to fend for himself for a bit, because I wanted him to have a mental picture of the Aunt Liz Noah I'd told him about, not the one who was probably here. When I finally found her room, I was glad I was alone.

She was sitting by a window that overlooked the shabby yard, not reading, only staring, and wearing a jolly blue-and-pink-cotton housedress—Liz Noah, in a housedress! Across from her sat an old lady with thin frizzy white hair, staring out the window, too. Her roommate, apparently.

I hadn't expected that. But it was, after all, a double room. Two beds, dressers, and nightstands, and on one of them a familiar ivory-framed photograph of big John Noah holding Littlepage as a year-old baby.

When Aunt Liz Noah saw me, she stood up, still tall, and took a step forward and hugged me. I hugged her, too, feeling her narrow delicate bones through the crisp cotton, fragile as matchsticks, and I wanted to weep. Lost in that atrocious housedress, she was. No earrings now; I noticed that. And her hair a soiled-looking yellow-gray, wispy and cut in an institutional bob.

"I'm so glad to see you!" I said. Truth, but a lie, too.

"It can't be much of a treat," she said, sounding a lot like Aunt Liz Noah. But she was looking beyond me. "Where is . . . who is . . ." She stopped and looked at me. "My words are all thumbs," she said. "Where is . . ." and she tapped her wedding ring impatiently. She'd remembered I was married but couldn't think of his name.

I told her, and felt clumsy saying I wanted him to meet her (then why hadn't I brought him?), but she dismissed that.

"I'm not dressed for it," she said. "Obviously. How do you like this little number? A Chanel, I think."

"It's awful," I said sincerely. "Do they make you wear that?"

She shrugged. "It makes laundry easier if they can just throw everything in," she said. "It's all right. . . ." For a second her eyes wandered, as though she'd lost the track. "Excuse me, Mrs. Bunty," she said then, to the woman in the other chair, who gave no signs of hearing. "I want you to meet my niece. . . . *Grand*niece," she corrected herself.

I shook the woman's small soft hand. Her eyes looked lost in a face that seemed to have collapsed, I thought, the features somehow run together, the faceness nearly gone, like a candle stump all melted down into itself.

"Poor little thing," Liz Noah said gently, "she couldn't keep on living alone either. She's deaf and she gets all mixed up. They found her standing outside her front door wondering if she was coming in or going out."

"Shucks, half the time I don't know if I'm coming or going either," I said. (Go for the joke.)

Unexpectedly she dropped that eyelid in the old droll wink. "Then do move in and I'll move over," she said cordially. "Be my guest!"

That made me laugh, and Mrs. Bunty laughed, too, seeing it was the thing to do, and, after that, talking was easier. I sat on one of the beds and told Aunt Liz Noah all about the past year, when I'd been too busy to write. (Wrong. Not too busy. Embarrassed. My own life was clicking along now, all systems Go, while hers was—face it—winding down. What do you write to somebody in a rest home? Once, as a small child, I wrote a letter to Grandpa that he often quoted, beginning, 'I would have written you before but I didn't.' That's all I could have said.)

Then presently we were talking about vital, important issues, the way we always had. Like, how come she was my greataunt while I was only her grandniece? And how come they still hadn't changed the dumb THE ELMS' sign outside? A whole new wing but the same dumb apostrophe, and we thought Grandpa was undoubtedly whirling in his sunny grave, out there at Highland.

Yes, and why do little girls skip and little boys run? It was a sex difference I'd noticed only recently, in the preschool across the street from where Mike and I had been living, and I would have written to her about it if I could have written to her at all. And, she contributed, why do old men drool more than old women do? A positive fact, she said. She'd had ample time to notice. Another sex difference . . .

"Someday they'll undoubtedly do one of those big government-funded studies on that," I said. They were doing them even then, and there'd been a hundred-thousand-dollar one I'd just read about, about soldiers in battle, which seemed to suggest strongly that the closer they got to the front lines, the scareder they got.

I mentioned it to her, and she laughed, ruefully, and we talked then about a lot of things. She was sounding much like

herself now, only occasionally vague and sometimes queru-
lous. At one point, she looked at herself in a hand mirror and
then tossed it onto the bed.

"It's indecent, the things that happen to you," she said.
"Did you know that Ninon de Lenclos said if she could have
seen herself old, she'd have hanged herself young? . . . It's
like a mask you can't take off, dammit." And that was something else, she added ruefully: you're not supposed to cuss
when you're an old lady, and just when there's so much more
to cuss about . . .

I thought, If only she'd done better about eating and keeping the place up. "You're not really ready for old-ladyhood
yet," I said.

I don't know if she heard me or not, but I remember wondering then if anyone ever is, and I still wonder. Well, naturally. The closer you get to some new place you're going to
visit, the more you wonder what kind of a place it is; and the
closer I get to old-ladyhood, the more I think they should
quit issuing visas. It has very little going for it, and one of
the worst things must be the sort of input you get. Other people assume you've turned into a nice prudent old white-
haired somebody inside, too, to match the white hair and
wrinkles you're wearing, but chances are very good that you
haven't. Whatever your age is, you don't *feel* different. Everyone knows that. I feel uneasily close, still, to the fourth-
grader who jumped Florence Ashenbrenner in her muddy
front yard. I'm anyway next of kin, you might say, and this is
dismaying.

The fact is, I've always intended to grow up and become
thoroughly mature just as soon as I can work it into my schedule (the way some people are going to write a book the minute they have a minute). But now that I'm in the childhood
of my old age, I can see that there won't be time.

Of course I didn't know all this then, but I must have had
an inkling. I understood what Aunt Liz Noah meant when
she lifted a scanty strand of her hair and said, with scorn,
"This has nothing to do with me; I've got thick dark-brown
hair."

"I know you do," I said. And I did know, and I knew also that she valued my knowing.

She was feeling livelier, and presently we were embarked on one of our more elaborate what-ifs.

Masks. They make such good ones now. What if everyone could choose a new persona before coming into The Elms—Harpo? Rita Hayworth? George Washington? Marie Antoinette?—and wore the mask at all times? Then you could look around comfortably, she said, without seeing all these sorry old crocks that only remind you that you're in the same boat, and you wouldn't be depressing *them*. . . .

And so we were talking and laughing. I chose Mae West, I remember, and Aunt Liz Noah had about decided on F.D.R. because she liked his style and you could do him sitting down, when one of the nurses came in and asked why all the merry ha-ha. We told her, but she didn't find it a bit amusing.

"Why, you look fine, Lizzie, just fine!" she said reprovingly. "What in the world are you talking about?" And that was another thing, Liz Noah confided when the nurse left, the way they act as if you didn't have good sense, and the way they call you by what they imagine your little-girl name was, which is supposed to make you feel all safe and cozy. But she'd never been called Lizzie in her life, she said. Liz or Liza or Liz Noah. But Lizzie? Made her feel like the kitchen help.

And *tests!* Did you know, she asked me, that they give you tests to see if you've got enough brains left to weave those ugly potholders? They ask you, "Who's the President, who's the governor, what day is today, how do you . . ." She stopped.

"What day *is* today?" she said slowly.

We just looked at each other. The tiny busy ticking of a bedside clock was loud in the room, and from down the hall came the distant clattery rattle of dinner carts.

It was past the time I'd told Mike I'd meet him at the gas station a few blocks down. So after I said good-by to Mrs. Bunty, Aunt Liz Noah walked me out to the glassed-in porch, humid, with limp green things dangling from pots. Two old men in bathrobes dozed in rockers.

One of them, sure enough, had a generous rope of spittle attached to his chin. He was trussed into a Chinese lash-up of tubes and cords and jugs, a complex-looking life-support system involving a bottle hanging from the rocker arm and a small portable oxygen tank, but there was a gleam of—was it malice? lust? amusement?—in his watery old eyes and a cocky tilt to his head.

"That's Mr. Kellock," she explained. "Sometimes I sit out here in the late afternoons, and it always tickles Mr. Kellock when he gets the rocker first. That's much the best rocker," she said, "and it's a funny thing, there are always more cars going this way than that way." She pointed toward town.

I looked at her quickly.

"Except when it's the other way around," she added thoughtfully.

Was she joking? I didn't think so, but I couldn't be sure.

Well, so I left. Hugged her again, hard, and she hugged me. Said I'd write, and went down to the street, turned once, looked back, waved. So did she, the other hand shading her eyes from the sun, for she was looking due west. She didn't seem very tall any more, from where I was. I suppose she kept on watching till I turned the corner, but I didn't look again; I felt bad enough anyway.

So I left her, prisoner of her years as I in another way was prisoner of mine, my young husband waiting for me down the block. And walking down the street I know I prayed. "Get her out of there," I prayed, though I knew there was only one way she'd ever leave, but I didn't care. It was no place for Aunt Liz Noah, no place at all.

And so we left Ganister behind us, Mike and I, wanting to cover some distance before nightfall. The low winter sun was bothering our eyes, especially mine, because I was crying.

Mike didn't ask any questions; only patted my knee once in a while and concentrated on the three-lane highway that eventually took us past many a bleak wheatfield and red barn and tall dark mountain, to the far West Coast.

Minerva settled herself lumpily into my lap, and I patted her but had to keep blowing my nose.

And I thought how essentially awkward crying is. How messy, the eyes flooding, the nose filling. In the long evolutionary climb, why couldn't people have evolved something neater? What conceivably constructive role has crying ever played in the business of survival?

And then it occurred to me that Liz Noah and I had once pondered this very same thing, years ago. We had wondered, why not some tidier physiological reaction? I'd suggested, why couldn't your knees turn green for a while, or your elbows itch? Or why—her idea—why couldn't your earlobes grow gently longer and longer till they finally tickled your neck and made you laugh?

But this messy crying, whoever needed it? Drizzle and drip, cough and blow, eyes stinging and filling, nose reddening, nose blowing again and yet again . . .

And so I mourned, for the first, though not the last, time, but in concentrated fashion, for all lovable warm bright people that must grow old and die, and in particular for my aunt Liz Noah. I cried nearly all the way to Salina, I remember, where I had to stop crying so I could eat dinner. It was a good fried chicken dinner that we had, in an old Victorian hotel. And in our room there were big down pillows and a nice old faded calico quilt on a nice old mahogany fourposter bed, and my husband comforted me.

Which would be the logical place to end this, I think, if it hadn't been for the telephone call from my mother, from McKinleyville to Portland, Oregon, about three months later.

Aunt Liz Noah had run away. Just like that. Or, anyhow, walked out. One April afternoon toward sundown she'd packed an overnight bag, put on her old riding pants and shirt and one of her three remaining fine old hats, walked out of The Elms and all the way down Main Street to the Grand Osage Hotel. As she explained to Chip Eddy, the desk clerk she'd known all his life, she was moving in.

Kindly, he accepted her registration and, wisely, he called my mother, who drove over the next day—cars and roads were faster then—to check out the arrangement. The only draw-back Mama could find was that no one had thought of it sooner.

Aunt Liz Noah was happier now; even sketching a little and sometimes holding court in the lobby, sitting tall. Finan-cially it made good sense, too. Even with frequent room serv-ice (courtesy of one of the Coffee Shoppe's big motherly wait-resses) and the occasional attentions of a practical nurse, it cost less than The Elms had. And what happened was that about ten months later she O.D.'d on strawberry shortcake, or so she thought, and went to bed complaining mildly of a stomach ache. It was actually a heart attack, and the next morning she woke up dead.

There is a lovely line that I've always remembered, in something by Camus: "In the midst of winter I finally learned that there was in me an invincible summer." I think of it quite often when I think of my aunt Liz Noah on her own personal independence day, that greening April afternoon. There she goes, the tall frail stork of a lady, hair wispy under the gallant hat, walking purposefully down Main Street. I never heard which hat it was, but I always see her in the red velvet.

A Culinary Afterthought

Back when this new kitchen of ours was still in the conversational stage, when the window was only four straight lines on blueprint paper and the sink lay all anonymous and disconnected in some Honolulu warehouse, I had no idea that the finished product would take me so far afield.

But there is this about a kitchen window: though the eyes may travel and the mind roam, the feet remain firmly planted on the kitchen floor, so that the cook must eventually return to the business at hand, whether that is peeling an apple or stirring the gravy or washing a pot. And despite my frequent complaining, I must grant that there are comforts to be found here. Esthetic comforts, perhaps, in the S curve of the apple peel; and physical comforts, certainly, in the good smell of the gravy; and even some philosophic ones: the charred pot may need scrubbing, but this, too, will pass.

It occurred to me that there may also be a question or

two here about some of the food mentioned in this book. As a reader, I have often felt that when a book mentions a particular food with special enthusiasm, or when that food somehow triggers the action, the writer should explain, if at all possible, how to prepare it or where to get some. Proust should have provided a *madeleine* recipe, and maybe he did —I never quite finished the sixteen volumes, so I don't know —and certainly Louisa May Alcott should have explained those pickled limes in *Little Women,* the ones that got Amy into so much trouble at school. Wondering about them, about what they were and how they tasted, I've wasted a great deal of time that could have been better spent on bigger things.

Accordingly, I want to include here the recipes for anything I mentioned in this book that anyone might want to know more about.

The Good Simple Meringue Cookies on page 17

Grease and flour a cookie sheet, and set the oven at 350°. Then beat 3 egg whites (a half-cupful) till they are stiff, and gradually add a cup each of sugar, chopped dates, and chopped nuts. Drop by the teaspoonful on that cookie sheet and bake for ten minutes.

The Pumpkin Soup on page 28

I suppose this can be made from the pumpkin you've hollowed out for a jack-o'-lantern, but it would not occur to me to do that. Pumpkin to me means canned.

1 large onion, chopped	1½ teaspoon salt
½ teaspoon curry powder	2 cups heavy cream*
¼ cup butter	2½ cups chicken stock
2 cups canned pumpkin	

Sauté the onion and curry powder in the butter till the onion is limp and defeated. Add the pumpkin and salt, stir it

---

* You may interpret this in various ways. If it's all whipping cream, that's the best. Or it may be part whipping cream, part canned milk, and part whole milk—whatever the reefer and the pocketbook afford.

around, then pour the whole thing into the blender and blend for half a minute or so. Pour it into a saucepan, along with the cream and chicken stock. Heat it slowly and serve it steaming hot. A small dollop of sour cream in each bowl is nice, and so is a sprinkle of chopped parsley.

The Brown Bettina on page 67

It still surprises me that such humble ingredients can add up so deliciously. But they do. As my mother wrote in the margin, some chopped nuts make it even better, but they are by no means essential.

> 2 cups sliced apples (3 medium apples)
> 1 cup fresh bread crumbs
> 1/4 cup brown sugar
> 1 teaspoon cinnamon
> 3 tablespoons butter, melted
> 1/2 cup water

Mix the apples, bread crumbs (saving out 2 tablespoons), sugar, and cinnamon. Stir in the butter, then pour it into a middle-sized baking dish. Pour the water over it, sprinkle the crumbs you saved on top, and nuts, if any. Dot with a little more butter and bake 45 minutes at 350°. Makes four modest portions, to serve in rainbow-glass dishes, with cream or hard sauce, but preferably hard sauce.

Basic Hard Sauce

Cream one cube of butter (1/2 cup) with a little over a cupful of sifted confectioners' sugar and a spatter of salt. To make it satiny-smooth, add a tablespoon of coffee cream, but this isn't essential. Flavor it with vanilla, as Mama did, or with Amoretto or Triple Sec, as I do, when I have them.

The Fudge on page 72

3 squares bitter chocolate   1 teaspoon vanilla
3 cups white sugar   3 tablespoons of butter
3/4 cup milk or water   Nuts if you have some

Cook everything except butter and nuts over low heat to the soft-ball stage, or 238° on the candy thermometer, (Lucille and I didn't have a candy thermometer, so we did many tests, dropping a half-teaspoonful of the candy into a saucer of cold water, then trying to shape it into a ball and pick it up. If we could, it was done. In any case, we ate it, blob after blob.)

Add the chunk of butter now, but don't stir it in. Let it cool, and it will do that faster if the fudge pan is set in a larger pan of cold water or ice cubes. Presently, test it with a finger. If you don't scream, it's ready to beat. So beat it, energetically, and when it starts to harden, quickly add the nuts and vanilla, and pour it into a buttered brownie pan.

The Crumpets on page 89

These crumpets take an hour and a half to rise, all told, but some days, don't we all. And you don't need crumpet rings, really. They just result in a neater product. If you haven't any, pretend you're making four-inch flapjacks.

1 tablespoon dry yeast	1 teaspoon salt
¼ cup very warm water	3 tablespoons butter
1 cup milk, scalded	1 egg
2 tablespoons sugar	3 cups all-purpose flour

Sprinkle the yeast into the warm water so they get acquainted while you heat the milk. When it is just hot, pour it into a big bowl and add the sugar, salt, and butter. Stir till the butter melts, then stir up the yeast water, too. Add it to the milk now along with the egg and the flour.

Beat it thoroughly, then cover and let it rise, about half an hour. Beat it again for three or four minutes and let it rise again for another thirty. And do that yet again. This is something of a bore, but if you don't do it, the split crumpets probably won't have that craters-of-the-moon complexion necessary for holding all that eventual butter and jam.

Now grease a griddle, or use an electric skillet at 350°, and put the greased crumpet rings in, if you have some, to fill half full with the batter.

Cook them 8 or 9 minutes per side till they are a nice saddle-leather brown. You can freeze them now if you like. To eat them immediately, split and toast them, then butter and jam them, and pour the tea.

The Rye Drop Cake Chickens on page 149

This is Em's recipe as she wrote it. Em wasn't much on details.

> 1 c rye flour
> ½ c wht flr
> salt
> egg
> 1 c sour milk

Have lard same temp. as for doughnuts, drop batter off spoon. Put in round willoware bowl, make sure it's hot.

My version, which varies only a little, goes like this:

Pour about three inches of vegetable oil (because I seldom have lard around) into a pan, put the deep-fat thermometer in it, and start it heating. Then stir a teaspoonful of baking soda into a cup of sweet milk (because I never seem to have sour milk around either) and let it set, while sifting the two flours with ¼ teaspoon of salt and beating a large egg till it's light.

Add the milk to the egg, mix in the sifted flour, and beat just a bit, till it's all blended. When the thermometer registers 370°, you're in business. Drop half-teaspoons of the batter into it. (If you drop larger dollops in, you won't get chickens; you'll get dolphins and an occasional wart hog and they may not cook properly all the way through.) Don't cook more than three at a time, or it will cool the oil too much. When they're a beautiful golden brown, take them out with a slotted spoon, park them briefly on a paper towel, and serve them hot, to dunk in individual saucers of maple syrup.

Aunt Liz Noah's Kidney Bean Impromptu

This was something that Aunt Liz Noah made often and never the same way twice, though the ingredients themselves were the same, I think, but in different proportions, so we never knew quite what to expect. But it was always very good.

Basically, it was kidney beans soaked overnight, then baked with a chunk of salt pork buried in the middle, and seasoned variously. The closest I have come to duplicating her version was when I added chopped sautéed onions, Worcestershire sauce, a generous sprinkle of salad herbs, some curry powder, some sour cream, and a good bit of lemon pepper—which is odd, because there wasn't any lemon pepper in Liz Noah's day. Perhaps she used plain lemon juice, or lemon rind; I don't know. At any rate, she'd bake it for hours, and then reheat it, day after day, in the top of a double boiler. The last time I made it, it seemed to me to taste almost right, let's say ninety-nine and forty-four one hundredths percent right, but still . . . (See Bracken's Postulate, page 42.)

So that is gone, I suppose, as other things are. Gone with the McKinleyville I knew, which grew up and got swallowed by a large hungry city, and gone with the Ganister that I knew then, too.

The last time I saw McKinleyville, I was visiting my dear friend Emily Lilly. That afternoon we went to the Little Theater, to see a rather extraordinary film (that is what movies are called there now), something of Claude Chabrol's. Then we went straight back to her house to rescue a saucepanful of—no, not fudge—*ghee,* butter she'd been cooking at an invisible simmer nearly all day for her yoga-minded grandson, visiting from his ashram in Florida.

As for Ganister, I have never gone back since that last trip to see my aunt Liz Noah. But I was in Wichita recently, and the two towns aren't far apart. It wasn't a smooth, delectable Orange Ice-cream Soda I was drinking there; it was a crackling dry Boodles with a twist, and I wasn't perched high on a hotel soda-fountain stool but sunk deep in a dark leather armchair at the Petroleum Club, a smashing architectural arrangement in black timber, adobe, and lush greenery, overlooking the town and the long level land. My hosts were barely back from a few days' skiing at Aspen after three weeks at their vacation place in the Seychelles, and I wondered where in the world did Kansas go?

Still, it is a happy thing that a window over the sink can serve as a window on a world now gone. For truly, the loved and long-ago people and places in your memory can be visited only in your imagination; and perhaps the things that you ate and loved then can be tasted again only in your imagination, too.

Afterword

. . . *Finally, I have given myself much private satisfaction in this book. I have mentioned several of my friends, who hardly expected such a thing; I have called up some pleasant memories, and clarified others that were on the point of fading; as the saying goes, I have taken my coffee: humored myself.*

—BRILLAT-SAVARIN